Which Have Received
the Holy Ghost as We

WHICH HAVE *Received the* HOLY GHOST *As We*

CHRISTOPHER MCDONALD

XULON PRESS

Xulon Press
2301 Lucien Way #415
Maitland, FL 32751
407.339.4217
www.xulonpress.com

© 2020 by Christopher McDonald

All rights reserved solely by the author. The author guarantees all contents are original and do not infringe upon the legal rights of any other person or work. No part of this book may be reproduced in any form without the permission of the author. The views expressed in this book are not necessarily those of the publisher.

Unless otherwise indicated, Scripture quotations taken from the New King James Version (NKJV). Copyright © 1982 by Thomas Nelson, Inc. Used by permission. All rights reserved.

Printed in the United States of America.

Paperback ISBN-13: 978-1-6628-0708-4
eBook ISBN-13: 978-1-6628-0709-1

Table of Contents

1. Have You Received the Holy Ghost Since You Believed?....1

2. How to Receive the Baptism in The Holy Ghost Part One 31

3. Receiving the Baptism in the Holy Ghost Part Two 59

4. Hindrances to Receiving the Baptism in The Holy Ghost..83

5. The Initial Evidence One Has Received the Holy Spirit- Part One 107

6. As the Spirit of God Gives the Utterance 147

7. The Benefits of Speaking in Other Tongues 179

8. The Second Work Of Grace After Salvation.............215

9. The Holy Spirit and The Gentiles......................251

10. Questions, Answers About the Holy Ghost.............287

Chapter One

HAVE YOU RECEIVED THE HOLY GHOST SINCE YOU BELIEVED?

TEXT: Acts 19:1-3–And it came to pass, that, while Apollos was at Corinth, Paul having passed through the upper coasts came to Ephesus: and finding certain disciples, [2] He said unto them, Have ye received the Holy Ghost since ye believed? And they said unto him, We have not so much as heard whether there be any Holy Ghost. [3] And he said unto them, Unto what then were ye baptized? And they said, Unto John's baptism.

This book is from a series of journals written over 20 plus years ago from our site "Spirit Journals." The material in this book may seem dated at times but the power behind the messages concerning the baptism in the Holy Ghost remains the same.

It has been said that salvation is the greatest thing that takes place in the life of one who is a sinner and comes to Christ in genuine salvation, while the baptism, or infilling, of the Holy Ghost with the evidence of speaking with other tongues is the greatest thing that happens in the life of the believer AFTER one comes to Christ.

Our text gives us great insight about what SHOULD be the next step after one is saved but sadly, because of unbelief and religious tradition is usually shunned and rejected at a great loss to the believer.

In fact, the WHOLE impression of these verses, along with the entire 19th chapter of Acts, speaks to us that since these disciples claimed to be believers, the Baptism in the Holy Spirit should have been the next step, incidentally a distinct and separate step from the believing.

Let the reader be clear on a fundamental aspect of one's salvation. EVERY Christian who is born again receives the Holy Spirit at SONSHIP and, consequently, has Him when converted. The Holy Ghost is not an "it," or an invisible "force," or some mystical idea, but He is GOD, the THIRD person of a Triune Godhead comprised of God the Father, Jesus Christ, God the Son, and of course God the Holy Ghost, also referred to in Scripture as the Holy Spirit. ALL three are equal and yet distinct persons in the makeup of the Godhead.

When one comes to Christ, the Holy Spirit "baptizes" that individual INTO the Body of Christ through the union and identification of the believing sinner into Christ's DEATH, BURIAL, and RESURRECTION. We become "DEAD" to sin and "ALIVE" in Christ through and ONLY through the work of the Holy Ghost.

> **Romans 8:9**
> **But ye are not in the flesh, but in the Spirit, if so be that the Spirit of God dwell in you. Now if any man have not the Spirit of Christ, he is none of his.**
>
> **Romans 6:11-14**
> **Likewise reckon ye also yourselves to be dead indeed unto sin, but alive unto God through Jesus Christ our Lord. [12] Let not sin therefore reign in your mortal body, that ye should obey it in the lusts thereof. [13] Neither yield ye your members as instruments of unrighteousness unto sin: but yield yourselves unto God, as those that are alive from the dead, and your members as instruments of righteousness unto God. [14] For sin shall not have dominion over you: for ye are not under the law, but under grace.**

> **Romans 8:14-16**
> **For as many as are led by the Spirit of God, they are the sons of God. [15] For ye have not received the spirit of bondage again to fear; but ye have received the Spirit of adoption, whereby we cry, Abba, Father. [16] The Spirit itself beareth witness with our spirit, that we are the children of God:**

However, that is NOT what Paul the Apostle is referring to here in the 19th chapter of Acts when he asked the disciples he met at Ephesus, "Have you Received The Holy Ghost 'SINCE' You Believed?"

There is a vast difference being "BORN" of the Spirit and one being "BAPTIZED" with the Spirit. The term "baptized," I am afraid, is the source of great confusion for many, especially those in the non-Pentecostal and non-Charismatic communities of the Body of Christ.

Many well-meaning non-Pentecostal denominational teachers and theologians argue that there is only "ONE" baptism, referring to the passage in 1 Corinthians 12:3 as their basis for not believing in a second work of grace after one gets saved.

> **1 Corinthians 12:13-15**
> **For <u>by one Spirit are we all baptized into one body</u>, whether we be Jews or Gentiles, whether we be bond or free; and have been all made to drink into one Spirit. [14] For the body is not one member, but many. [15] If the foot shall say, Because I am not the hand, I am not of the body; is it therefore not of the body?**

This "baptism," INTO the body of Christ is NOT the same "baptism" or enduement of power for service AFTER one gets saved. The Holy Spirit baptizes you into the Body of Christ WHEN you get saved; THE LORD JESUS CHRIST baptizes or fills you with His Spirit AFTER you get saved!

That was the testimony and witness of John the Baptist when He spoke of Christ's coming ministry upon the Earth:

> **Matthew 3:11**
> **I indeed baptize you with water unto repentance: but he that cometh after me is mightier than I, whose shoes I am not worthy to bear: HE (JESUS) shall baptize you with the Holy Ghost, and with fire.**

When Paul asked these disciples "have you received the Holy Spirit since ye believed," in the Greek is literally, "**Having believed, DID you receive?**" He was not asking them if they had been born again because these disciples were already saved! These men had already believed in the Lord Jesus Christ, and, because of that believing, they had been saved.

> **John 3:1-5**
> **There was a man of the Pharisees, named Nicodemus, a ruler of the Jews: [2] The same came to Jesus by night, and said unto him, Rabbi, we know that thou art a teacher come from God: for no man can do these miracles that thou doest, except God be with him. [3] Jesus answered and said unto him, Verily, verily, I say unto thee, Except a man be born again, he cannot see the kingdom of God. [4] Nicodemus saith unto him, How can a man be born when he is old? can he enter the second time into his mother's womb, and be born? [5] Jesus answered,**

> Verily, verily, I say unto thee, Except a man be born of water and of the Spirit, he cannot enter into the kingdom of God.
>
> **John 3:16**
> For God so loved the world, that he gave his only begotten Son, that whosoever believeth in him should not perish, but have everlasting life.

However, even though they were now spiritually ready to be baptized with the Holy Spirit, due to having their sins washed away by the Precious Blood of Jesus Christ, they had not gone on and received. Their reason as their answer portrays is that they knew NOTHING about this "baptism" in the Holy Ghost.

That is the state of scores of truly saved, God-fearing, sincere Christians today! Faith comes by hearing and hearing by the Word of God. Yet since little preaching is done on the need for people to be baptized in the Holy Spirit, very few people are aware of this any longer. Whether it is unbelief, ignorance, or just Satan planting doubt in one's mind, all who have believed in Jesus need the Baptism in the Holy Spirit!

> **Luke 24:49**
> And, behold, I send the promise of my Father upon you: but tarry ye in the city of Jerusalem, until ye be endued with power from on high.
>
> **Acts 1:4-8**
> And, being assembled together with them, commanded them that they should not depart from Jerusalem, but wait for the promise of the Father, which, saith he, ye have heard of me. [5] For John truly baptized with water; but ye shall be baptized

with the Holy Ghost not many days hence. [6] When they therefore were come together, they asked of him, saying, Lord, wilt thou at this time restore again the kingdom to Israel? [7] And he said unto them, It is not for you to know the times or the seasons, which the Father hath put in his own power. [8] But ye shall receive power, after that the Holy Ghost is come upon you: and ye shall be witnesses unto me both in Jerusalem, and in all Judaea, and in Samaria, and unto the uttermost part of the earth.

Acts 2:38-39
Then Peter said unto them, Repent, and be baptized every one of you in the name of Jesus Christ for the remission of sins, and ye shall receive the gift of the Holy Ghost. [39] For the promise is unto you, and to your children, and to all that are afar off, even as many as the Lord our God shall call.

Acts 5:32
And we are his witnesses of these things; and so is also the Holy Ghost, whom God hath given to them that obey him.

The question Paul asked those disciples in the upper coasts of Ephesus is the question the HOLY GHOST is asking many at this very second as you read this lesson; "Have you received the Holy Ghost SINCE you believed?"

First, I want to look at why these Ephesus disciples had not received the Holy Spirit. This will give us insight as to why others have not received this mighty infilling as well.

One, this message is NOT for those who are lost and without Christ today!

Jesus said in John that the WORLD cannot receive the things of God through the Holy Spirit. The ONLY requirements for receiving this enduement of service through the baptism of the Holy Ghost are that one be BORN again of the Spirit, and then secondly, one needs to ASK the Lord Jesus to baptize them with His power AFTER they get saved. This "asking," is a step of faith thus "BELIEVING" the Lord can and will fill you after you get saved is a requirement.

Let me interject this thought and it is important, even though it may sound a bit negative.

Some have already read to this point in this journal and have rejected what the Holy Spirit is trying to say through this teaching because of religious teaching, tradition, willful ignorance, or unintentional ignorance. Many pastors and teachers who are reading this have convinced you through their own misguided unbelief and willful ignorance that there is NOT a second work of grace and that these things died with the apostles. Others will be even bold enough and not even nervous about saying that this experience is of Satan and that you should shun it at all costs. These same individuals claim that they are "fundamentalists," who believe the Bible from cover to cover but they will go to great links to discredit the experiences in the book of Acts. Some of the most vicious and dangerous statements concerning the Holy Ghost do not come from the heathen but from so-called preachers who claim they know everything there is to know about God, yet they reject everything under the sun when it deals with the supernatural realm of God's Kingdom.

Some Christians sincerely believe that they received the "gift" of the Holy Ghost at the time they were born again. They do not realize that what we are speaking of here is NOT the gifts spoken of in 1 Corinthians 12, but the ENDUEMENT of power from on high that Jesus spoke of in Luke 24:49 and confirmed to the disciples in Acts 1:8.

Jesus also likened this enduement of power to that of "rivers of living water," flowing out of Himself to the believer who will but ask and BELIEVE the Lord to fill them from head to toe. (John 7:37-39)

The Baptism in the Holy Spirit is for those who believe; it is not for those who doubt and denigrate this glorious experience.

I grew up Southern Baptist and I know every single argument against this experience because I made most of them when I was younger. A lot of my arguments were out of ignorance and from things that I had been taught in churches while growing up.

However, in 1987, all my arguments went flying out the door when on a stormy night in February, on a kitchen floor in my late Aunt Florence's home in Tyrone, Georgia, I received this glorious experience with the evidence of speaking with other tongues that I speak to you of today. My life has never been the same since.

There have been many disappointments, failures, and valleys but those were my fault, not the Lord's fault and certainly not the Holy Ghost's fault. But at this moment, I have never been surer than I have been in my entire life of the surety that the Baptism in the Holy Ghost is so needed by believers!

It is not a cure-all for your spiritual problems, but it is an experience that will empower you to do battle against the devil, his demons, and all that the kingdom of darkness seeks to do to destroy your walk with God. If we as humans walked in the Spirit fully, then our spiritual problems would go away. The Holy Spirit is the POWER God has given us to live this Christian life with.

It still to this day humors me to listen to denominational preachers with their theological "expertise," just blow off this experience " as "redneck theology," "demonic gibberish," and "wrong side of the track thinking." If this is the wrong side of the railroad tracks, I will stay right here, thank you very much, rather than to get on the same track with those controlled by a religious spirit, hard-hearted, stiff-necked, and demonically controlled; to fight against that which God wants to do for His children and church!

We have a little saying, "Preach Acts 2:4 and see the Baptists and all other Holy Ghost deniers hit the door." We either believe and receive or doubt and do without!

Let me put it this way. "IF" and it is not, but "IF" this enduement of power is for the service is of Satan, it is the only thing of Satan that will make you shout! It is the only thing of Satan that will make you want to read your Bible more and more and more! It is the only thing of Satan that will bring a greater and deeper love for Jesus Christ into your heart and soul to the point that everything you see, hear or read you will look for HIM in it! It is the only thing from Satan that causes you to pray more powerfully and intimately with the help of the HOLY GHOST as HE speaks words through you that CANNOT be uttered or articulated in human terms! It is the only thing of Satan that will bring peace and joy within because one's LIFE has been freed from sin!

There are teachers and preachers and pastors and others who proclaim these things are of Satan. I would strongly urge you to watch what you say about God the Holy Spirit!! You may get applause and pats on the back for getting behind your pulpit and declaring tongues and the Spirit's intercessory utterances "of the Devil," and that these things "passed away," and all the other FOOLISHNESS and NONSENSE you spew out of a heart of unbelief.

The church allows homosexuals, lesbians, transgenders, and others to mix and mingle with their fellowship, and some churches even put some of these people in leadership positions. These same churches would be the first to kick someone out if they received the Baptism in the Holy Ghost with the evidence of speaking with other tongues. That is how deep the unbelief and attacks of the enemy are regarding the Holy Spirit.

When That Which Is Perfect Is Come

The Holy Ghost is a gift for the believer for power **after** he has been born again.

> **Acts 1:8**
> **But ye shall receive power, after that the Holy Ghost is come upon you: and ye shall be witnesses unto me both in Jerusalem, and in all Judaea, and in Samaria, and unto the uttermost part of the earth.**

Sadly, many teach that one gets everything at Salvation and this glorious gift that is initially received by speaking in other tongues as the Spirit of God gives the utterance, is not even for today. Even though the Apostles and the early Church possessed this gift then, many feel like God has changed and that this gift no longer exists in modern times. Nothing could be further from the truth.

To justify their unbelief, many quote 1 Corinthians 13:8 to justify that argument.

> **1 Corinthians 13:8**
> **Charity never faileth: but whether there be prophecies, they shall fail; whether there be tongues, they shall cease; whether there be knowledge, it shall vanish away. For we know in part, and we prophesy in part. But when that which is perfect is come, then that which is in part shall be done away.**

In the above scriptures, Paul is trying to explain that above all that we as Christians do, we must operate in the love of God, even when it comes to spiritual gifts. He was not minimizing the Gifts of God to be used in the Church. Notice in verse 8 that he said that prophecies "would fail and 'whether' there be tongues, they shall cease. If these were the only two things that were mentioned in verse 8, it could be possible to believe that this was only for the early Church.

Paul also wrote in that same verse however that "knowledge shall vanish away."

Was Paul telling us that the "knowledge" the early Church had that they wrote down in the Scriptures and that we have enveloped in the Word of God, or the Bible, would vanish away too? He said the same thing about prophecy as well.

Did knowledge and prophecy vanish away with the early Church? Is knowledge not for the Church of today? What about prophetic words?

Paul said "we only know in part" until that which is perfect is to come! What does that mean? Was he telling the Corinthians church that the gifts the Holy Spirit outlined in 1 Corinthians 12 and 14 were merely for just one generation? Of course not.

The Holy Spirit in this passage was not discouraging gifts of the Spirit. He was basically teaching us that the motive in which we should use these gifts was simply love and to edify the church, so that ALL may profit from them spiritually, even today!

How foolish it is to believe that Paul, after writing to the Church to explain how important the gifts were to the Church in 1 Corinthians 12, would then turn around and tell the Church not to use them in the same breath.

When the Holy Spirit mentioned "that which is perfect is to come," He was not speaking of the Written Word of God. The Word of God IS perfect, but the Word without the Spirit will not profit the church! The Word and the Spirit agree and must work in unison in the Body until the Lord comes.

We will never be at a place where "that which is 'PERFECT' is come until we as a Body of Christ experience the glorification of the saints or what we know as the Rapture of the Church. Titus called it a blessed hope. Paul called it a mystery. It is the time when we shall become fully LIKE Jesus!

> **1 Corinthians 15:51-54**
> **Behold, I shew you a mystery; We shall not all sleep, but we shall all be changed, In a moment, in the twinkling of an eye, at the last trump: for the trumpet shall sound, and the dead shall be raised incorruptible, and we shall be changed. For this corruptible must put on incorruption, and this mortal must put on immortality. So when this corruptible shall**

> **have put on incorruption, and this mortal shall have put on immortality, then shall be brought to pass the saying that is written, Death is swallowed up in victory.**

The only time the Church will be "perfect" is when corruption will put on "incorruption" and mortality will put on "immortality." At that point we will no longer need to "know" in part of "prophesy" in part because ALL things will be fulfilled.

Until we meet Jesus at this glorious event when these things take place, the Church will NEED the Holy Spirit to do the purifying! John says in his first epistle that "everyone who has this hope in himself purifies himself;" even as HE (Christ) is pure!

> **1 John 3:1-4**
> **Behold, what manner of love the Father hath bestowed upon us, that we should be called the sons of God: therefore the world knoweth us not, because it knew him not. Beloved, now are we the sons of God, and it doth not yet appear what we shall be: but we know that, when he shall appear, we shall be like him; for we shall see him as he is. And every man that hath this hope in him purifieth himself, even as he is pure.**

> **Luke 11:13**
> **If ye then, being evil, know how to give good gifts unto your children: how much more shall your heavenly Father give the Holy Spirit to them that ask him?**

All we have to do is ask Jesus for the Holy Ghost and He will baptize us with Him. When you do ask Him, believe that you will receive Him and let Him have your tongue. It is like stepping into a stream and being pulled along. This is the reason the Holy Ghost is compared to "being like a river." Let it happen and you will see the greatest moment in your life. One that is equivalent and most of the time more memorable than the day you were born-again. I am praying that God will help you to receive the Gift of the Holy Ghost as soon as possible if you have never received Him.

Does the Believer Receive ALL the Spirit Intends for Him to Receive at Salvation?

Another area of controversy is the discussion of whether the **infilling** of the Spirit automatically comes to a person at conversion. Many teach that there is nothing else to be sought or asked for after salvation. They say, in effect, that once we are born-again, our relationship with God is then "complete." Some do believe in a separate work of grace after one gets saved, but they do not believe this experience is accompanied by speaking in tongues.
I wish I were talking about non-Pentecostal people here, but sadly, even in the Pentecostal and Charismatic movements and realms of Christendom, many have succumbed to this teaching that they really do not need those "tongues."

I had lunch a few months back with a youth pastor of a very large Assembly of God church in Tennessee. We got on this subject and he did not blink an eye when he said to me, "I have realized since I have been to Bible school that we in the Assemblies have missed it; we really do not need to speak in tongues to consider ourselves filled with the Spirit." When I asked him what then would he consider a "sign" then that one was filled with the Spirit and he absolutely had no answer for me. I said, "You mean you cannot think of even one thing that would change in a person's life if they were filled with the Spirit?" He said, "**not according to my Bible teachers at school**." That shows me how far down the road to denying the supernatural of God we have gone in the church, including many in the Pentecostal camp.

It is no wonder that many outside the Charismatic/Pentecostal worlds do not get that enthused about the infilling of the Spirit. They do not see any enthusiasm among those who are supposed to be the root movement of where this glorious experience began, going back to the Azusa Street outpouring, but in reality, going back to the New Covenant Church!

The 12 apostles sent out by the Holy Ghost after the Day of Pentecost were Pentecostal type folks. They spoke in tongues, they prayed in tongues, they sang in tongues, they worshipped in tongues and they preached under the mighty anointing of the HOLY GHOST, not under the auspices of 40 days of Purpose techniques or some teacher's leadership principle concepts and courses.

Acts 2:4 clearly describes the filling of the Holy Spirit with the 120 gathered in Jerusalem at the command of Christ. That is an undisputable fact of Scripture that even the most faithless of evangelicals would have a hard time denying!

Yet it is just as absurd for evangelicals to claim there was ANY evidence that these gathered on the day of Pentecost were not saved and this experience was a one-time never again to be repeated event in the lives of believers. The 120 included eleven of the apostles (and the 12th, who had just been chosen) and Mary, the mother of Jesus. These were the same disciples who, in Luke 10:20, were commanded by Jesus to not rejoice over the fact that the devils were subject to them (within the authority of Jesus), but rather He encouraged them to rejoice because THEIR NAMES WERE WRITTEN IN HEAVEN! These 120 were not sinners waiting in

Jerusalem for salvation; they were waiting for the enduement of power from on high for service; the mighty baptism in the HOLY GHOST with the evidence of speaking with other tongues!

They were not gathering to get MORE saved or be born again "again." They were gathering in Jerusalem for the "promise of the Father," to receive a baptism of POWER that they would need before they went out to build churches, save souls, heal sick bodies and cast out devils.

Before they "started" ministries, the Lord's command was "GET FILLED WITH THE HOLY GHOST!" His command to the 21rst Century modern American church is the same: GET FILLED WITH THE HOLY GHOST; GET FILLED WITH THE HOLY GHOST!

> **Acts 1:4**
> **And, being assembled together with them, commanded them that they should not depart from Jerusalem, but wait for the promise of the Father, which, saith he, ye have heard of me.**

Acts Chapter 8–The Samaritan Revival

We read in Acts chapter 8 that Philip went to Samaria and preached CHRIST to the people there. It says in Acts 8:6 that they "**gave heed to the things Philip preached,**" in other words, THEY WERE BORN AGAIN! It tells of unclean spirits being cast out and of many being healed, along with great "joy" existing among those in the city.

Then in verse 12 it tells of the Samaritans believing what Philip was preaching concerning the kingdom of God and the name of the Lord Jesus, and how they were being baptized both men and women. This is what the Word tells US to do in John 3:16 and in Acts 10:42-43.

These people were saved under the ministry of Philip.

> **Acts 8:6**
> **And the people with one accord gave heed unto those things which Philip spake, hearing and seeing the miracles which he did.**
>
> **Acts 8:12**
> **But when they believed Philip preaching the things concerning the kingdom of God, and the name of Jesus Christ, they were baptized, both men and women.**
>
> **Acts 8:14**
> **Now when the apostles which were at Jerusalem heard that Samaria had received the word of God, they sent unto them Peter and John:**
>
> **Acts 8:16**
> **(For as yet <u>He</u> was fallen upon none of them: only they were baptized in the name of the Lord Jesus.)**

THEN in the 14th verse, the apostles Peter and John heard about the revival. The church in Jerusalem then sent Peter and John to Samaria so that they might receive the Holy Spirit. Now if an individual receives EVERYTHING at conversion, what was happening here? Why were Peter and John there?

What was the point of going down and preaching the Holy Spirit and praying for them if they had automatically received the Holy Spirit at conversion, as is commonly taught today?

The Bible says in the 16th verse that NONE of them had been filled with the Holy Spirit. They had been saved and even baptized in water, but in the 17th verse it says that HANDS WERE LAID ON THEM AND THEY RECEIVED THE HOLY SPIRIT.

> **Acts 8:17**
> **Then laid they their hands on them, and they received the Holy Ghost.**

Acts Chapter 9

The 9th Chapter of Acts describes the conversion of Saul of Tarsus (Paul), and the 12th verse recounts God's command to Ananias to go and pray for Paul and put his hands on him that Paul might receive his sight; Ananias was **not** directed to lay hands on him that he might be saved because Paul had already accepted the Lord Jesus as His Savior because of a great vision that he received and it was recorded in verses 3-7 of Acts 9.

> **Acts 9:3-7**
> **And as he journeyed, he came near Damascus: and suddenly there shined round about him a light from heaven: And he fell to the earth, and heard a voice saying unto him, Saul, Saul, why persecutes thou me? And he said, Who art thou, Lord? And the Lord said, I am Jesus whom thou persecute: it is hard for thee to kick against the pricks. [6] And he trembling and astonished said, Lord, what wilt thou have me to do? And the Lord said unto him, Arise, and go into the city, and it shall**

be told thee what thou must do. And the men that journeyed with him stood speechless, hearing a voice, but seeing no man.

The 17th verse states that when Ananias met Saul, he called him "Brother Saul." He would NOT have done so if Paul had not accepted Jesus. But Paul HAD already accepted Jesus; he WAS saved; his name WAS written in the Lamb's book of Life; he was ALREADY washed in the blood of the Lamb.

Ananias was sent to pray for him that he might receive his sight again AND **that he might be filled with the HOLY GHOST.** If one is baptized in the Holy Ghost at conversion, WHAT was Ananias doing??? WHY was he even bothering to pray for Paul to receive the Holy Spirit?

I can hear the unbelieving say, "I mean come on Ananias, Paul already had all he needs." "He does not need those tongues as many proclaim today."

The answer to that is YES, HE DID! YES, HE DID! AND YOU and I DO TODAY AS WELL!

> **Acts 9:17**
> **And Ananias went his way, and entered into the house; and putting his hands on him said, Brother Saul, the Lord, even Jesus, that appeared unto thee in the way as thou camest, hath sent me, that thou mightest receive thy sight, and be filled with the Holy Ghost.**

Acts Chapter 10

It seems that the outpouring of the Holy Spirit took place immediately after conversion at the home of Cornelius who was saved and baptized in the Holy Ghost at almost the same time. Peter and those with him knew this had happened because "they heard them speak with tongues and glorify God."

> **Acts 10:44-47**
> **While Peter yet spake these words, the Holy Ghost fell on all them which heard the word. [45] And they of the circumcision which believed were astonished, as many as came with Peter, because that on the Gentiles also was poured out the gift of the Holy Ghost. [46] For they heard them speak with tongues, and magnify God. Then answered Peter, [47] Can any man forbid water, that these should not be baptized, which have received the Holy Ghost as well as we?**

Acts Chapter 19

The 19th chapter of Acts describes the Apostle Paul as speaking to the disciples of John at Ephesus. He asked them "have you received the Holy Spirit SINCE you believed?" And they replied that they did not even know what Paul was talking about. He then explained to them, and in the 6th verse it says he laid hands on them, and "the Holy Ghost came on them."

> **Acts 19:6**
> **And when Paul had laid his hands upon them, the Holy Ghost came on them; and they spake with tongues, and prophesied.**

Every Christian receives the HOLY SPIRIT of adoption into sonship with God at the time of salvation (Romans 8:9 with Romans 8:14-16).

This was NOT what Paul was addressing here. He was asking them about the Spirit baptism that John had preached, and he was describing how Jesus would baptize them with the Holy Spirit and fire.

Paul's remarks to the Ephesus disciples had nothing to do with NEW BIRTH by the SPIRIT. It was for the endowment of power for service. It still is today!

> **John 1:31-34**
> **And I knew him not: but that he should be made manifest to Israel, therefore am I come baptizing with water. [32] And John bare record, saying, I saw the Spirit descending from heaven like a dove, and it abode upon him. [33] And I knew him not: but he that sent me to baptize with water, the same said unto me, Upon whom thou shall see the Spirit descending, and remaining on him, the same is he which baptizes with the Holy Ghost. [34] And I saw, and bare record that this is the Son of God.**

> **Acts 1:4-5**
> **And, being assembled together with them, commanded them that they should not depart from Jerusalem, but wait for the promise of the Father, which, saith he, ye have heard of me. [5] For John truly baptized with water; but ye shall be baptized with the Holy Ghost not many days hence.**

Romans 8:9
But ye are not in the flesh, but in the Spirit, if so be that the Spirit of God dwell in you. Now if any men have not the Spirit of Christ, he is none of his.

Romans 8:14-16
For as many as are led by the Spirit of God, they are the sons of God. [15] For ye have not received the spirit of bondage again to fear; but ye have received the Spirit of adoption, whereby we cry, Abba, Father. [16] The Spirit itself beareth witness with our spirit, that we are the children of God:

When one reads this, one must be able to see that a person can be saved by the blood of Jesus and have believed God for salvation yet be in ignorance of the baptism in the Holy Spirit. This was what happened at Ephesus and that is what has happened to millions today.

Let the reader be clear; a sinner cannot receive this experience for obvious reasons. The sinful heart cannot receive the things of God and as a result, as a sinner without Jesus in one's heart, NONE can be "filled" with the Holy Spirit. The sinner must be "born again" to become a candidate for the Holy Ghost baptism and to be FILLED with the power of God.

How is that possible one may ask? Simply put, it is because the blood of Jesus Christ has paid the price for man to be filled with the Spirit! Jesus did not come to just die for your salvation, He died so that you may be filled and baptized in the Spirit as the Spirit of God gives the utterance! Yes, the Spirit dwells the believer at Salvation because He "dwells" with the believer and "in the believer."

> **John 14:17**
> **Even the Spirit of truth; whom the world cannot receive, because it seeth him not, neither knoweth him: but ye know him; for he dwelleth with you, and shall be in you.**

But there is a HUGE difference in being "born" of the Spirit and "baptized" IN the Holy Ghost! Being born of the Spirit brings one INTO the body of Christ; the baptism IN the HOLY GHOST brings the believer OUT of cold, dead religion INTO a vital, vibrant, powerful, intercessory, relationship a Crucified and Glorified Christ! Salvation brings you into the Body of Christ. The Baptism in the Holy Ghost brings you OUT of lifeless religion and reveals CHRIST to you like never before!

One Must Ask to Receive This Experience

> **Luke 11:13**
> **If ye then, being evil, know how to give good gifts unto your children: how much more shall your heavenly Father give the Holy Spirit to <u>them that ask him?</u>**

The reader may ask, "well how does one 'receive' the enduement of power from the Holy Ghost?

Very simply, it is a matter of faith, just as faith was required when we were born again! When we came to Christ for salvation, we came confessing, believing, repenting, and ASKING. When one is baptized in the HOLY GHOST, one must STILL come confessing, repenting, asking, and BELIEVING!

Jesus made it clear through His words, as recorded by Luke, that one must **ASK** to receive this experience; it is not an automatic gift from the Heavenly Father. But without question and compromise, let this writer make it crystal clear to the believer that THE BAPTISM IN THE HOLY GHOST IS SOMETHING THAT EVERY SINGLE CHRISTIAN, BORN AGAIN CHILD OF GOD SHOULD SEEK AFTER ONE IS SAVED!

There are some who read that and say, "I just don't feel worthy to ask" the Lord to fill me with the Spirit. I have issues in my life. I have a bad temper. I cuss. I smoke. I do things I know that are not pleasing to the Lord in my Christian walk. Well let me be of encouragement to you.

YOU are exactly the one who NEEDS the baptism in the Holy Ghost to help you overcome these sins of the flesh. Jesus died that we may be free of the sin nature! The power in which He does that is through faith in His death, burial, and resurrection THROUGH the power of the Holy Spirit!!

Let me declare this to the reader. There are two trains of thought in the Body of Christ which are both extremely dangerous.

The camp that teaches that once you get saved, you have everything from God that you will ever need is short-changing their people. The camp that teaches once you receive this enduement with power you have received everything you will ever need from God is also extremely dangerous.

THERE WILL NEVER BE A TIME WHEN YOU CAN SAY I DO NOT NEED THE HELP OF THE HOLY GHOST in my walk with God!!! NEVER!

But seeking more of God MUST be sought after. It will not come to any of us automatically, and in our own strength it is NEVER accomplished!!!!

ONLY THE HOLY GHOST CAN PRODUCE MORE OF GOD'S SOVEREIGN NATURE AND CHARACTER INSIDE ANY OF US and in a corporate view, the BODY OF CHRIST in general.

One may ask, well "is tongues the only sign one is Spirit-filled?"

Absolutely NOT, but without compromising or backing away in any fashion, this writer believes the WORD OF GOD teaches and states without debate that the **initial physical evidence that one has been baptized in the Holy Ghost is speaking with other tongues as the SPIRIT OF GOD gives the utterance.**

Once that occurs then there is a wide-open door of greater Holy Spirit ministry that is open to ALL who will walk in the leading, guidance, prompting, and unction of the Spirit! There will be greater graces that the Lord will bestow upon the Spirit filled Christian as they see their walk with God become more intimate and vibrant. Many who have been Spirit filled and walk in this glorious experience daily, see themselves often used in the gifts of the Spirit in ministry to the church.

Here is a warning though for ALL who are seeking this glorious experience. If you are merely seeking tongues, then you are headed for trouble friend! We are not seeking "tongues," or an "experience." We are seeking MORE OF JESUS through the ministry of the HOLY GHOST!

As a result of the sincere seeker and the believing heart, the Lord Jesus will more than willingly baptize us IN HIS SPIRIT with the evidence of speaking with other tongues!

There have been those who have discontinued friendships over the years because of this subject. Sadly, while some disagreements over the glorious infilling of the Holy Spirit is ignorance, MOST of the resistance, if not ALL, is rooted in sinful, wicked UNBELIEF!

The reason I write with such a passion is that I know without blinking or pause, that the church in America has become very adept at "accomplishing" a great deal without the power of God being involved!

The CHURCH OF THE LORD JESUS WILL NEVER SEE THE FULFILLMENT OF THE HARVEST in these last days in the strength of our own humanistic efforts in the church.

ONLY THE HOLY GHOST can do those things!

> **Zechariah 4:6**
> **Then he answered and spoke unto me, saying, This is the word of the Lord unto Zerubbabel, saying, Not by might, nor by power, but by my spirit, saith the Lord of hosts.**

You and I need this endowment of power. I cannot say that enough. We ALL need the baptism in the Holy Spirit with the evidence of speaking in other tongues! We will look at why tongues are so important in a future message coming soon.

I found a beautiful song to sum everything up this writer has stumbling and humbly tried to allow the Holy Spirit to write through him: YOU AND I NEED THE BAPTISM OF THE HOLY GHOST TODAY! And as this song written over 100 years ago says,

> *Ye are the temples, Jesus hath spoken,*
> *Temples of God's holy Spirit divine;*
> *Have ye received Him, bidden Him enter,*
> *Make His abode in that poor heart of thine?*
> *Refrain:*
> *Have ye received, since ye believed,*
> *The blessed Holy Ghost?*
> *He who has promised, gift of the Father,*
> *Have ye received the Holy Ghost?*
> *He who has pardoned surely will cleanse thee,*
> *All of the dross of thy nature refine;*
> *Cleansed from all sin, His power will enter,*
> *Fill you and thrill you with power divine.*
> *Showers of mercy, fullness of blessing,*
> *Ever the Spirit's indwelling attend;*
> *'Tis this enduement, power of service,*
> *Fruits for your labor He surely will send.*
> *Weary of wand'ring, come into Canaan,*
> *Feast on the fullness and fat of the land;*
> *Feed on the manna, dwell in the sunshine,*
> *Led by His Spirit and kept by His hand.*

I ask you today, "Have you received the HOLY GHOST SINCE YOU BELIEVED?

For now, let me pray with you. Some of you are former Pentecostals who once experienced this mighty, glorious infilling but because of whatever reasons, be they unbelief, pressure from church systems, and just the utter foolish babblings of backslidden preachers who know NOTHING of the ways of God or of the Spirit, have allowed this experience to dry up and be of no value to your Christian walk. When we place our faith in the Cross and what Jesus did for us ALL there, then He will gladly do just that! Pray with me today:

Chapter Two

HOW TO RECEIVE THE BAPTISM IN THE HOLY GHOST PART ONE

TEXT: Acts 1:4-5–And, being assembled together with them, commanded them that they should not depart from Jerusalem, but wait for the promise of the Father, which, saith he, ye have heard of me. [5] For John truly baptized with water; but ye shall be baptized with the Holy Ghost not many days hence.

The Holy Spirit is not a denomination, a movement, or a church. Thus, when one is baptized in the Holy Ghost there are requirements for one to part of a certain group to receive this glorious infilling!

The Baptism in the Holy Spirit is a life-transforming experience that is meant to be received by every individual who has turned his life over the Lord and accepted Jesus' sacrifice for his or her sins. Salvation gets one ready for heaven, the Baptism in the Holy Ghost gives one power and anointing for service in their Christian walk with God. This great experience is not an optional experience for a select few or just those who belong to a "Pentecostal" denomination, but it is intended for EVERY CHRISTIAN who will but ask and believe the Lord Jesus.

The baptism in the Holy Ghost is NOT a voluntary or "Christian elective," as I heard one preacher proclaim recently, on the part of the Christian. The baptism in the Holy Spirit is an OBLIGATION within God's plan for His Children once they are born again.

I have stated the following many times before, but I will state it again, Christians who neglect or refuse to seek the baptism in the Holy Spirit after salvation will not lose their soul. In other words, one does not have to speak in tongues to be saved. In our text it's clear the Lord commanded the disciples, not asked, but commanded them to not depart from Jerusalem until they had been "endued with power" from on high by the "promise of the Father," which they had heard of Him.

There is no other source of power whereby souls are saved, bondages broken, marriages restored, deliverances realized, and sick bodies healed outside the mighty work of the Holy Spirit, who can do these things because of the price Jesus paid with His blood on the Cross.

Without the moving and operation of the Holy Ghost, any church or church system will be a failure no matter how big it is or how many human activities it places on its weekly bulletin boards or outside marquees. Human effort has replaced the moving of the power of God and because of it, souls have perished without God. Only God the Holy Spirit can convict souls and bring people to Jesus in the way God wants.

A church may consist of a beautiful building, an ambitious program, and a paper organization that makes it appear to be perfection itself, but without the power of the Holy Ghost, it will have little impact on the lives of the individuals with which it comes into contact. A church that denies and rejects the baptism in the Holy Ghost would be better off to place gasoline tanks outside and pump gas to its members, than put the name "church" outside its walls; it would serve the community better.

The Lord Jesus is the HEAD of the true church and we as His children are part of HIS Body. Membership in this body does not depend ONE IOTA on what denomination one belongs to, but instead it depends FULLY on whether one has been Born Again, washed in the Blood of the Lamb, filled with the Holy Ghost, and delivered from the kingdom of darkness! Regardless of which "church" system one belongs to, EVERYONE who is in CHRIST is a member of HIS BODY!

As MEMBERS of His Body, the Lord has "SET," ordained, and established various ministries AND gifts in His Body to carry out the work of the ministry of His Body on this earth. These gifts and ministries are Holy Ghost birthed, and nothing more or nothing less. You cannot have these ministries in the church based upon man's declarations or approval. These are God-ordained, Jesus driven, and birthed MINISTRIES of the Holy Ghost!

> **1 Corinthians 12:28**
> **And God hath set some in the church, first apostles, secondarily prophets, thirdly teachers, after that miracles, then gifts of healings, helps, governments, diversities of tongues…**

Jesus COMMANDED His disciples to remain in Jerusalem until they should receive the PROMISE of the FATHER and be baptized in the Holy Ghost. The specific word used is "commanded." That is strong language with NO suggestion of option or decision here, quoting directly from the Word of God.

> **Acts 1:4**
> **And, being assembled together with them, commanded them that they should not depart from Jerusalem, <u>but wait for the promise of the Father, which, saith he, ye have heard of me.</u>**

The Baptism in the Holy Spirit with the evidence of speaking with other tongues is a MUST, an IMPERATIVE, a circumstance, and condition COMMANDED by the HEAD of the Church, our Lord Jesus Christ. The question today is simple. Do you listen to men behind pulpits preaching unbelief and mockery of the Holy Ghost, or are you going to listen to the HEAD of the CHURCH!?

I ask that in the strongest of terms. I ask that with the strongest of passion to stir your heart today and get you to understand that there has NEVER been anyone who has received this glorious experience that found the Baptism in the Holy Ghost to be unreal or unnecessary for today.

There are two main doctrines that are attacked the most in the Body of Christ. One is the Rapture of the Church and a close second if not first, is the Baptism in the Holy Ghost with the evidence of speaking with other tongues!

Since the outpouring of the Holy Ghost in Los Angeles, California, on Azusa Street in the early 1900s, the mighty Pentecostal experience of speaking with other tongues has come under attack, not so much from the world, but from evangelical circles and even mainline Pentecostal denominations. These so-called Pentecostal denominations have insanely believed that for there to be "unity" in the Body of Christ, we must believe the "unbelief" of the evangelical and denominational world.

That is a false unity and one that produces death not life. I am not interested in shaking hands with those who denigrate and mock the Holy Ghost, and neither should you!

Those who have been baptized in the Holy Ghost have found out firsthand how glorious this experience is. None who have received the Baptism have ever went back and said, "this is not for today," or "this is of the devil," or "you don't need this for your Christian walk." No! Those who have received the "rest" and "refreshing" the Holy Ghost brings have had their lives changed forever!

I sat down and talked with a former presbyter of the Assemblies of God many years ago and was shocked to hear what he told me. He said that for a denomination to be considered "Pentecostal," that at least 51% of their members should speak in tongues and believe in the Pentecostal experience of Acts 2:1-4.

In the case of the Assemblies of God, one of America's oldest Pentecostal denominations, that figure was less than 30% which basically meant the AOG was no longer even considered "Pentecostal." That could also be said about the church of God, the Pentecostal Holiness, and the Foursquare movements as well.

I hear from those who reject the Baptism in the Holy Spirit that one of the reasons they are turned off by the Pentecostal experience is that "Pentecostals" tend to "shove" it down people's throats. Well evidently, that is not a problem anymore because even the Assemblies of God deny the validity of this glorious experience.

Neighbor, I do not want to be ugly about what I am going to say but say this I must.

I do not care if the Assemblies of God, the Baptists, the Methodists, the Presbyterians, the Church of God, the Foursquare, the Pentecostal Holiness, the Lutherans, the Catholics, the Independent Baptists (many of who need to just get saved to begin with), or whatever else the denominational leaders say about the baptism in the Holy Ghost. Jesus has told us to receive the PROMISE of the FATHER!

Many who speak in tongues today are labeled as fanatics, unlearned and ignorant, while others are even accused of being of Satan. This writer is not ashamed that he speaks in tongues. On a glorious night in February 1987, I was gloriously baptized in the Holy Ghost, filled with enduement of power, filled, filled, filled with the power of Almighty God.

In the book of Acts chapter 4 we see that When Peter and John were brought to the Sanhedrin to explain the power by which the crippled man they laid hands on was healed, they were labeled by the religious leader s of Israel as "ignorant" and "uneducated" but these leaders could not deny "that they had been with Jesus."

> **Acts 4:13**
> **Now when they saw the boldness of Peter and John, and perceived that they were unlearned and ignorant men, they marveled; and they took knowledge of them, that they had been with Jesus.**

I humbly ask the reader with all due respect, "what is more important?" Being with Jesus and being labeled ignorant and unlearned, or accepted by those who feel their so-called education and riches are more important than feeling shame over our churches being void of all power and the presence of the Lord Jesus Christ in our services?

Jesus stands at the door of our churches and KNOCKS outside wanting to get inside because we have rejected the power of the Holy Ghost!

> **Revelation 3:20-21**
> **Behold, I stand at the door, and knock: if any man hear my voice, and open the door, I will come in to him, and will sup with him, and he with me. [21] To him that overcomes will I grant to sit with me in my throne, even as I also overcame, and am set down with my Father in his throne.**

The modern church brags about its "education" and "knowledge of the scriptures," but we are never accused of "being with Jesus" anymore. We have become more sophisticated in our ministry efforts, yet little is being done to deliver a world steeped in idolatry, sin, and demonic bondage. The bondages we fight today will not go away with a three-point sermon, a cute prayer, and an offertory hymn.

We are engaged in a spiritual battle beyond comprehension and knowing we are on the front lines of this battle against Satan's power as the Body of Christ our HEAD, the Lord Jesus Christ, prescribed a procedure which would prepare us to adequately stand against the powers of darkness.

THIS BATTLE WILL NOT BE WON ON AN EDUCATIONAL, SOCIAL OR PSYCHOLOGICAL PLAIN! It will be won in the SPIRIT realm and through the power of the HOLY GHOST!

The power that the Church world fights (the baptism in the Holy Ghost) is the power that will set men free, deliver the alcoholic from alcohol, deliver the drug addict from drugs, and deliver the pornographer and the one hooked on pornography. The Blood of Jesus through the power of the Holy Ghost will cause the thief to stop stealing, the liar to stop lying, the cheater to stop cheating, the drunk to stop drinking, and the drug addict to stop drugging.

Jesus Christ can set the sinner free of the worst bondage and do it without 12-step programs, psychology tables, and confessional booths in a cathedral.

The Holy Spirit preacher will chase away that religious ODOR that stinks up your church every Sunday and causes people to leave vomiting and retching from the sickness they feel because of the cold, dead atmosphere they sit in for an hour or less in what we call "church." That is not church that is a MORGUE. Sitting on our pews and listening to a sermon that puts us to sleep instead of hanging the sinner over hell on a broken stick does NOTHING to help one spiritually!

To those who claim the Baptism in the Holy Ghost with the evidence of speaking with other tongues is of the Devil I say to you, "well it is the only thing then of Satan that will make one know Jesus more intimately and in real truth and grace!"

It is the only thing of Satan that will cause one to love the Word of God more and more and develop and hunger and thirst for righteousness unlike they have ever experienced. It is the only thing of Satan that puts LIFE in our dead Sunday services that do more to hurt the cause of Christ than help." Jesus, through the Holy Spirit will set us free!

While we try and cultivate the "minds" of our people and stroke the seared conscience of sinners in our midst with an apostate gospel and false pretense of the true faith, the world slips off into hell in a hand basket bound by the powers of darkness.

Our education may have a small place in our Christian experience but in MOST cases, the pride that develops from our education keeps us from **BEING WITH JESUS**. Holy boldness from a fire-breathed revival is needed to confront and love a sinful society that mocks and laughs at God and lampoons everything that is holy and just. God's not looking for just angry preachers; He is looking for someone with His heart and is so ablaze with His love and power that not one ounce of self-righteous judgment falls from their lips. But when they do speak, demonic **powers of darkness flee in their presence because they have BEEN WITH JESUS!**

The ONLY POWER THAT CAN PRODUCE SUCH AN ANOINTING IS THE POWER OF THE HOLY GHOST, THE POWER OF ALMIGHTY GOD, THE POWER OF THE HOLY SPIRIT, THE POWER OF THE HOLY GHOST!

The greatest threat to the power of God that will change society is not society. It is backslidden, mossy-backed, pharisaic, religion that stands in the way of God and what He wants to do in this last hour. Statements like the recent ones made the Southern Baptist Convention underscore a greater problem in the church that is pushing us closer to all out apostasy and delusion and the advent of the rapture of the Church. The Spirit of Antichrist is IN the church right now preparing both the world AND the apostate church for the advent of the man of sin.

> Acts 4:1-2
> And as they spoke unto the people, the priests, and the captain of the temple, and the Sadducees, came upon them, [2] Being grieved that they taught the people, and preached through Jesus the resurrection from the dead.

Most of the church is like this council in Acts 4. They could not argue over the miracle that had taken place; the man lame from birth stood healed in front of them. Yet, instead of praising God, they had to "confer among themselves" about it and then threaten Peter and John to stop preaching in the name of Jesus.

> Acts 4:3-10
> **And they laid hands on them, and put them in hold unto the next day: for it was now eventide. [4] Howbeit many of them which heard the word believed; and the number of the men was about five thousand. [5] And it came to pass on the morrow, that their rulers, and elders, and scribes, [6] And Annas the high priest, and Caiaphas, and John, and Alexander, and as many as were of the kindred of the high priest, were gathered together at Jerusalem. [7] And when they had set them in the midst, they asked, By what power, or by what name, have ye done this? [8] Then Peter, filled with the Holy Ghost, said unto them, Ye rulers of the people, and elders of Israel, [9] If we this day be examined of the good deed done to the impotent man, by what means he is made whole; [10] Be it known unto you all, and to all the people of Israel, that by the name of Jesus Christ of Nazareth, whom ye crucified, whom God raised from the dead, even by him doth this man stand here before you whole.**

Peter and John said, "whether it be right in the sight of God to hearken unto you more unto God, you be the judge." Then they say something that is very key to that which I hope rings in your heart reader: **"WE CANNOT BUT SPEAK THE THINGS WHICH WE HAVE SEEN AND HEARD."**

The church has a hard time arguing away that millions and millions and millions of people who love Jesus, have been born again, and have received this glorious experience of being baptized in the Holy Ghost with the evidence of speaking with other tongues.

Despite the scriptural experience of millions, the church world, both the denominational and a growing number in the Pentecostal denominational world, claim that speaking in other tongues is not scriptural or a valid experience today, and in some extreme cases, they come close to blaspheming the Holy Spirit by attributing the experience to Satan.

I was at a church not too long ago in Central Tennessee whose doctrinal pamphlets stated, "we cannot believe this (the baptism in the Holy Spirit) is real just because so many people have experienced it. We don't believe in experience; we believe in the Bible." Well, I ask you a question a ten-year-old can understand, even though preachers with degrees from Georgia to Texas cannot. Is not the Bible full of stories of "EXPERIENCES" with men and women of faith from Abel to the Apostles? Was Paul being struck by blindness on the Road to Damascus an experience? Was what happened on the Day of Pentecost in Acts 2:1-4 an "experience?" Was not Jesus raising Lazarus from the dead an experience?? Were people getting healed by Peter's shadow an "experience?"

If we do not believe in experience, then we do not believe in salvation. **Salvation is an experience**. If we do not believe in experience, then we do not believe in people rededicating their lives to the Lord. When people come down and rededicate their lives to the Lord weeping, repenting, and crying out for mercy that is an experience!

If we do not believe in experience, then we do not believe in healing (many do not). What would many evangelicals tell the lame man that got healed in Acts 3 if he were here today? "Your experience is not valid because we do not believe in experiences, and we believe these things went away 2,000 years ago with the apostles."

Do you think that lame man would really care what you believed? HE WAS HEALED!

Reject and resist His power if you will to your own peril preacher, but as Paul said, "if you want to be ignorant of these things then be ignorant." If your "bible" has become the Purpose Driven Life or any other self-help new age pamphlet and outline, you need to get shaken to your core and filled with an enduement of power from on HIGH!

Paul said he did not come preaching with the "excellency of speech," or of "wisdom," of men's words, but by the demonstration and POWER of the HOLY GHOST!

The Night My Life Changed- February 4, 1987

Without the indwelling presence of God's Holy Spirit to augment our poor worldly powers, we are going to be ineffectual at best, and perhaps soundly defeated at worst. The life of the Christian, even those who ARE Spirit-filled, is not easy.

I have been baptized in the Holy Ghost for nearly 20 years now, and I can tell you from firsthand experience that NO experience zaps us into Christian perfection, not even the Baptism in the Holy Ghost.

Because we are but earthen vessels through which this glory resides and operates the Holy Spirit is hindered many times. But just because we are still subject to failure, HE IS NEVER SUBJECT TO FAILURE, and if there is any defeat in our lives it is because of US, not Him.

That is the purpose of this writer literally screaming through the words of this journal that the reader needs the baptism in the Holy Ghost; that as hard as this Christian walk can be at times, WITH the Baptism of the Holy Ghost you can make this walk and it is almost impossible without the Baptism in the Holy Ghost! I know some would disagree and say, "well you're saying that those who are baptized in the Holy Ghost and speak in tongues are better than those Christians who are not."

That is NOT what this writer is even remotely hinting at. What I AM saying is that without the believer wanting and embracing the FULLNESS of the power of the Holy Ghost, that believer is going to have tremendous difficulties.

February 4, 1987, which seems like yesterday in my mind, was a night I will never forget as it relates to what I just spoke to you.

I remember calling my late Aunt Florence in the fall of 1986 right after I got truly born again that summer. I was wanting to know more about the Holy Ghost.

I had met a young lady who belonged to a Pentecostal church and in pursuing her (yes, I was young), I found myself sitting every Sunday night in an atmosphere of people who were doing things I had never experienced before in my life in the Southern Baptist churches that I had attended and my dad had pastored.

Some of the things I saw I had been exposed to in some degree during the times I had visited my mother's family. Mom's sisters were all Pentecostal; they spoke in tongues; they laid hands on people to be healed; they shouted and were not ashamed of who they were in Christ.

I remember the first time I ever heard anyone speak in tongues I thought I would run like a rabbit out of the church. It scared me to death, to be frank. But even as a young child not understanding what he was witnessing and hearing, I was fascinated with the experiences of those who spoke in tongues because, despite what I was being told by Baptist preachers, I knew in my heart that it was supernatural in scope and beyond my own understanding.

I remember the first time that I heard my Aunt Florence speak in tongues was when she kept us as children. She would put us down for our naps in the early afternoon before she would go downstairs to her prayer closet and call our names to God. My brother Todd and I would listen to her call and cry our names out before the Lord in English, pleading the blood of the Lord Jesus over us, and asking God to touch our lives, protect us, call us into the ministry, and FILL us with the HOLY GHOST. My brother and I would then, all of sudden, feel the hairs on our arms began to tingle as the power of God began to fall on our Aunt as she started to pray not just in English, but she also prayed in other tongues as the Spirit of God would give her the utterances that neither her nor us knew but HEAVEN knew. My Lord, I am having a hard time writing this right now because of the tears. This went on daily and it left an eternal impression upon this writer.

When I got saved and the Lord gave me the hunger to know more about the Holy Ghost, there was no other person in the world that

I knew would have the answer but my. Aunt Florence. I had started attending a small Pentecostal church and a couple of times, I had gone down to the altar to receive the baptism in the Holy Ghost, but to be frank, I was scared and I had tons of fear and doubt that would not be easily overcome with hundreds of eyes looking and staring at me seeking to receive the Holy Spirit.

The Lord knew I have always been a private person and He opened the door for me to visit my Aunt on a cold, rainy and stormy night in February As I sat in my aunt's kitchen, I shot question after question at her about the experience of speaking with other tongues. I told her my fears, my opinions, my concerns, my "doctrinal stance," and my curiosity. But above all, I told her the Lord had dealt with me, that the Baptism in the Holy Ghost was real, and I needed to receive the experience for my Christian walk.

I also told Aunt Florence that I had felt a tug at my heart at times in 1985 and 1986 that. the Lord was calling me to preach and I wanted to obey that call, but that I did not know how or where to start. After all the talk, my aunt just smiled and said, "Chris we can talk all weekend but the Lord did not send you up here to Atlanta to just talk; He sent you up here to be filled with the Spirit." I felt tears well up in my eyes and my heart enlarged as I asked her if she would pray for me to receive the Holy Ghost.

That friend is VERY scriptural; just ask the Apostle Paul when he was told by Ananias that the Lord had commanded him to lay his hands on Paul "that he might receive his sight and be filled with the Holy Ghost."

As my aunt began to pray at first in English, I heard her suddenly begin to pray in another language. It was the same beautiful language I remembered her praying in when as a child, during the years she kept me and my brother Todd, I laid upstairs in my bed listening as she wept and moaned in utterances known only to God and the angels perhaps. Those moments when we heard Aunt Florence pray, she was touching another world and the power of God from another world was touching her.

I had that same feeling on this night in the kitchen in February 1987. It was a time that while I was older than when she kept my brother and me, I had become so "churched" as to believe the Southern Baptist line that speaking in tongues was not of God and even demonic which was what some extreme viewpoints believed.

As I sat there in her kitchen, I did not have the same innocent heart that I did when she had kept me years earlier. It is a fact that children tend to accept this experience quicker than adults many times, because as children our hearts are still tender to God and the Holy Spirit. I believe that is why Jesus taught His disciples that only those who accepted the Kingdom of God "as a little child," would receive true salvation and eternal life.

We adults tend to be hardened by religious tradition, pride and arrogance and we set ourselves in agreement with our traditions instead of setting our hearts, minds, and souls in agreement with the Word of God. Some of us are so set in our ways that even if someone came back from the grave itself and told us something other than our own religious traditions, we would not believe them. How tragic is it that much of what God wants to do in our lives is not stopped by Satan, but it is stopped by our own ignorance and arrogant religious attitudes.

As my aunt laid hands on me that night as I began to weep and pray with her and before I knew what had happened, the power of God hit me and I was on the floor with both my hands raised in the air. As my aunt knelt on the floor with me and she just continually interceded for me in tongues. She wept and wept and wept as she began to prophesy over me things only the Holy Spirit knew, for He was the one doing the speaking in another language through my Aunt.

One would say, "well how did you know what she was saying was from God?" Very simply put, I knew because whenever she prophesied in another language she would interpret in English the utterances which were things that, even though I was close to my aunt, she was saying things that even she would not have known in the natural! She warned me that the enemy had planned a hurtful end to my life. She revealed to me that Satan had decreed suicide over the hidden hurt in my heart towards my parents for their divorce that had taken place in 1983. She encouraged me to ask the Lord to remove all the unforgiveness in my heart and that if it were not dealt with, it would hinder the flow of the Holy Ghost.

All I remember from that point on was speaking the words, "Lord, forgive me for my unforgiveness," and when I did, I felt a rush of power go through my soul and as John writes in his gospel, the of words my mouth became "rivers of living water" from within my "belly."

> **John 7:37-39**
> **In the last day, that great day of the feast, Jesus stood and cried, saying, If any man thirst, let him come unto me, and drink. [38] He that believeth on me, as the scripture hath said, out of his belly shall flow rivers of living water. [39] (But this**

spake he of the Spirit, which they that believe on him should receive: for the Holy Ghost was not yet given; because that Jesus was not yet glorified.)

The words I began to speak were no longer English, but another language I spoke in tongues nearly all night long. I remember it was at least 4 a.m. before we even got off the floor. My aunt just laid beside me and wept and prayed in tongues with me. I have never felt so clean in my innermost being as I did that night. I was doing more than just speaking gibberish. **The Lord Jesus had baptized me with the Holy Spirit and the** tongues were just the evidence that this had happened.

As we drove home the following day, I could not stop crying. Every song I heard was more powerful. Every message I heard became clearer. Everything that was of God became more powerful. I felt so "clean" in my spirit man I cannot describe it to you by written words in this lesson. I could literally "hear" the river John spoke of flowing through my heart. That is how real this experience was to me. What Jesus promised; what the prophets declared would come; what the 120 at the Day of Pentecost experienced; what the disciples at Ephesus experienced in Acts 19; what the Samaritan believers experienced after Philip's revival in Acts 8; what Paul experienced in Act 9; what Cornelius experienced in Acts 10; what millions of believers with open hearts and minds have received since Pentecost have experienced; Chris McDonald experienced for himself, and his life has never been the same since.

As I stated, the entire day after this happened, I could not quit crying. Part of the tears were tears of joy and part of the tears were just a cleansing of my heart and soul of all the unbelief that had kept me from this glorious experience for most of my teen life while in the church. The first person I told when I got home was my pastor, the late Rev. Joseph, and Ruby Price. They had been praying for over two months for me to receive the baptism in the Holy Ghost. When I told them what happened, Joe and Ruby, who were in their 80s, rejoiced with me as if they were in their 30s.

After I told the Prices, I told my dad and then I told my mom shortly after. My life never has been the same again and yours will not either friend, when you receive the Baptism in the Holy Ghost!

Hungering and Thirsting Are Two Requirements to Receive This Infilling

To hunger and thirst after the Lord and to want more of Him is not something one can teach. This thirst and hunger for what I speak of, must start in our innermost being. This writer believes that God is going to hold America so accountable for our lack of hunger and desire for Him. In a country where we have been given so much, and God is reverenced so little, and He is blasphemed almost daily by godless politicians, performers, entertainers, and sadly, even so-called preachers of the gospel, we are headed for a confrontation with a Holy, Jealous God.

Neighbor hear this writer. It will be more tolerable for Sodom and Gomorra than for America in the Day of Judgment. As I write this, I think about the events that took place at the house of Cornelius in Acts 10, prior to his house being saved and filled with the Holy Ghost almost simultaneously.

When Peter arrived at his house, Cornelius was not even saved, yet he was seeing visions, doing alms before God, and was so sensitive to God that he asked the Lord what was he supposed to do when he saw the vision.

> **Acts 10:1-5**
> **There was a certain man in Caesarea called Cornelius, a centurion of the band called the Italian band, [2] A devout man, and one that feared God with all his house, which gave much alms to the people, and prayed to God always. [3] He saw in a vision evidently about the ninth hour of the day an angel of God coming in to him, and saying unto him, Cornelius. [4] And when he looked on him, he was afraid, and said, What is it, Lord? And he said unto him, Thy prayers and thine alms are come up for a memorial before God. [5] And now send men to Joppa, and call for one Simon, whose surname is Peter: [6] He lodges with one Simon a tanner, whose house is by the sea side: he shall tell thee what thou ought to do.**

That is hunger for God! He was so dedicated to serving God without even knowing the real truth about God. Does that not send a loud rebuke to this modern church atmosphere today where millions supposedly **know** the truth about God, but have very little desire to truly serve Him or press in and receive all that He has offered to His Church through His Son and Holy Spirit?

We are going to be held SO accountable for the unbelief of our hearts and churches. God is a rewarder of those who DILIGENTLY seek him, and the type hunger seen in Cornelius' actions is the only hunger and thirst God honors and blesses. **The casual seeker of God will not find much**. The faithless will not find God. Doubt and do without; believe and receive; as my good friend the late Rev. Neal Baggett of Cairo, Ga. used to always tell me.

It is when we seek Him with ALL our heart and all our soul that He is so willingly and excited to REVEAL HIMSELF TO US.

> **Hebrews 11:6**
> **But without faith it is impossible to please him: for he that cometh to God must believe that he is, and that he is a <u>rewarder of them that diligently seek him</u>.**

> **Jeremiah 29:13-14**
> **And ye shall seek me, and find me, when ye shall search for me with all your heart. And I will be found of you, saith the LORD: and I will turn away your captivity, and I will gather you from all the nations, and from all the places whither I have driven you, saith the LORD; and I will bring you again into the place whence I caused you to be carried away captive.**

It is impossible for a child of God to receive anything from God unless the Holy Spirit is a co-participant in that which is received. While one receives the Holy Spirit at conversion (that is theologically and scripturally correct for those who argue that point), there is a very real and definite difference in being BORN of the Spirit and being baptized in the Spirit.

A person is NOT baptized in the Holy Spirit when they are saved. The believer is baptized into the Body of Christ when he is saved. The Baptism in the Holy Spirit is an experience complete and separate from salvation; it can only come AFTER salvation and must be consciously sought after by the thirsty and hungry believer for more of God. Jesus Himself declared that our Heavenly Father would GIVE the Holy Spirit to them "THAT ASK HIM!"

Luke 11:13
If ye then, being evil, know how to give good gifts unto your children: how much more shall your heavenly Father give the Holy Spirit to them that ask him?

As we end this second lesson in this study, let me ask you a serious question. Why is the modern church in America so lethargic, weary, and steeped in so much dead and lifeless religious exercise?

Could it be that most Christians have been taught (and many of those have bought into this) that conversion is an experience complete within itself and, once experienced, leaves nothing further to be received or sought after. Could it be, sadly, even when one is Baptized in the Spirit, he is taught the same thing. "You got it, praise God, that's all" as many are falsely told.

No experience with God can produce Christ-like character and faith. Character and faith are processes that take place throughout one's Christian walk with God. There are no "zaps" to make you an instant saint. To be like Jesus one must walk in faith and "ENDURE" to the end, so that same one "shall be saved."

The key person in this walk is the HOLY GHOST! He was sent back from the Son to be the comforter and POWER through which we fulfil the righteous demands of God on all mankind. It is not a simple list of things we should or should not do. It is a faith walk that will be tested at every turn, every moment, and every chance the enemy feels he as the permission to do it.

The ones who endure these tests are the ones who have the HOLY GHOST living strongly inside them!!! To be frank, even those individuals face tremendous warfare due to the arena they have entered in the realm of the Spirit!

There is a great difference between all the humanistic activity and programs we call "accomplishment" in the church world today and accomplishments for the Kingdom of God.

The Holy Ghost is interested in souls being saved, bodies being healed, believers being baptized in the Holy Ghost, bondages being broken, marriages restored, lives being changed for eternity by the power of almighty God and the captives of the enemy being set free from the forces of darkness.

Notice as you read your Bible, how many times the words "fire," and "power," are used in conjunction with the Holy Spirit! That is because God's Holy Spirit is the FIRE POWER factor in the life of a Christian.

Without the Holy Spirit dwelling within us, we are shells with little substance, cannons with no ammunition, engines with no fuel, and CHURCHES with no presence of God! We may go through the MOTIONS of Christianity that usually include having all the fine-tuned and wrapped up machinery in nice religious wrappers for the world. The results, however, of Christianity without the Holy Ghost are DEATH!

Those who are baptized in the Holy Ghost may be lampooned, laughed at, snickered at, rejected, shunned, and mocked. These same ones are usually the ones who are standing in the breach against the powers of Satan and they defy the powers of darkness that come against the Lord's Church. Tongue-talking Christians may be labeled as "unlearned," and "ignorant," but they have been with Jesus and they have the power to set captives free and to see things happen in the Spirit realm for the Kingdom of God.

They may not be called to be interviewed on CBN, TBN, Fox News, or be asked to preach at 99% of most churches in America, but they ARE known in the halls of heaven. What is rejected on earth is always embraced by heaven and what is loved by most of the world and church today is loathed by heaven.

It is through FAITH one receives the baptism in the Holy Ghost, not doubt and unbelief. It's the same faith that the Holy Ghost wrote about through Paul in Hebrews 11, in which He says, "quenched the violence of fire," "stopped the mouths of lions," "obtained promises," "wrought righteousness," "escaped the edge of the sword," and "out of weakness were made strong!"

THAT IS WHAT THE HOLY GHOST CAN DO FOR YOU CHILD OF GOD! That is what the power of Almighty God can do for you man of God, pastor, teacher, prophet, apostle, evangelist. You say your ministry is drying up and dying; GET FILLED WITH THE HOLY GHOST with the evidence of speaking with other tongues and you will be surprised at just how much life begins to flow in and through your ministry!

> **Hebrews 11:33–38**
> **Who through faith subdued kingdoms, wrought righteousness, obtained promises, stopped the mouths of lions, [34] Quenched the violence of fire, escaped the edge of the sword, out of weakness were made strong, waxed valiant in fight, turned to flight the armies of the aliens. [35] Women received their dead raised to life again: and others were tortured, not accepting deliverance; that they might obtain a**

> **better resurrection: [36] And others had trial of cruel mockings and scourgings, yea, moreover of bonds and imprisonment: [37] They were stoned, they were sawn asunder, were tempted, were slain with the sword: they wandered about in sheepskins and goatskins; being destitute, afflicted, tormented; [38] (Of whom the world was not worthy:) they wandered in deserts, and in mountains, and in dens and caves of the earth. [39] And these all, having obtained a good report through faith, received not the promise: [40] God having provided some better thing for us, that they without us should not be made perfect.**

We must come forward in FAITH and ask our Heavenly Father to GIVE us the Holy Spirit! Yes, when we are saved, we receive Him in measure. There is-no argument on that, but just as salvation is the greatest thing that takes place in the life of the sinner, the baptism in the Holy Ghost is the greatest thing that takes place in the life of the believer AFTER he gets saved.

I pray you are saved today. I pray you have been filled with the Spirit according to Acts 2:4 today. I pray you speak in tongues as the Spirit of God gives you the utterance every day.

I am not ashamed to tell you that I have been born again and I have been gloriously baptized in the Holy Ghost. I speak in tongues every day in prayer and I hope the Spirit of God takes this writer into a greater intimacy with Jesus than I have ever known before in this current year and beyond. His work in us all is never temporal but eternal, which is why we cannot get discouraged when failure comes.

Failure is never final with the Holy Ghost! Failure just makes the Holy Ghost come in stronger and "like a flood," raise up a standard against the enemy. He is yours for the asking child of God. Receive the mighty Baptism in the Holy Spirit today and be filled with the Spirit!

Chapter Three

Receiving the Baptism in the Holy Ghost Part Two

TEXT: Acts 1:4-5–And, being assembled together with them, commanded them that they should not depart from Jerusalem, but wait for the promise of the Father, which, saith he, ye have heard of me. [5] For John truly baptized with water; but ye shall be baptized with the Holy Ghost not many days hence.

This writer wants to make it clear that there are no "formulas" for one to receive other than one being born again, having simple childlike faith, and ASKING the Lord Jesus to baptize one in the Holy Ghost.

Let the sincere seeker know that it is the Lord's will that ALL believers be filled with the Holy Ghost after salvation.

There are some who call themselves "fundamentalists," that claim they believe the whole Bible yet deny miracles are for today. They deny that divine healing is for today. They deny the gifts of the Spirit are for today, and they deny the Lord still baptizes folks in the Holy Ghost with the evidence in speaking in other tongues. They believe tongues are not for the modern church any longer, they deny tongues are a benefit to the believer, deny that tongues have any merit or validity in the life of the church and the list goes on. That is not fundamentalism neighbor, that is rank demonic unbelief. As I heard one evangelist put it recently, these men are not fundamentalists; they are "mentalists!"

I humbly ask those with this type theology, "JUST WHAT **DO** YOU BELIEVE????" I can hear them say, "we believe the Bible from cover to cover and the Bible alone."

My question then becomes, "If you believe the Bible from cover to cover, then how can you not believe in the supernatural ministry of the Holy Ghost which is on every page of the Bible from Genesis to Revelation?"

The Holy Spirit is mentioned in the SECOND verse of Genesis and He is also seen in the last verses of Revelation "crying" for the soon return of the Lord Jesus, "and the SPIRIT and the Bride say 'Come.'"

> **Genesis 1:2**
> And the earth was without form, and void; and darkness was upon the face of the deep. <u>And the Spirit of God moved</u> upon the face of the waters.

> **Revelation 22:17**
> And the Spirit and the bride say, Come. And let him that heareth say, Come. And let him that is athirst come. And whosoever will, let him take the water of life freely.

Statements made at times among various denominational camps, especially the Independent and Southern Baptists, come dangerously close to blaspheming the HOLY GHOST, and they are no different than those made by the Pharisees and Sadducees in Jesus' day.

There is no greater danger facing any New Testament church or movement than those steeped in self-righteousness, trying to establish righteousness outside of the Cross of Christ and the power of the Holy Spirit by exchanging true faith for New Age humanism wrapped up in religious wrappers.

Any righteousness established outside the confines of the Cross of Christ is SELF RIGHTEOUSNESS, which is what most churches preach and proclaim. If the Holy Ghost is not producing the righteousness, it is SELF righteousness!!!

> Romans 10:1-3
> **Brethren, my heart's desire and prayer to God for Israel is, that they might be saved. [2] For I bear them record that they have a zeal of God, but not according to knowledge. [3] For they being ignorant of God's righteousness, and going about to establish their own righteousness, have not submitted themselves unto the righteousness of God.**

> Romans 3:21-24
> **But now the righteousness of God without the law is manifested, being witnessed by the law and the prophets; [22] <u>Even the righteousness of God which is by faith of Jesus Christ unto all and upon all them that believe</u>: for there is no difference: [23] For all have sinned, and come short of the glory of God; [24] Being justified freely by his grace through the redemption that is in Christ Jesus:**

ANY DOCTRINE OR MOVEMENT THAT DENIES THE POWER OF THE HOLY GHOST IS IN EFFECT DENYING THE POWER OF THE CROSS!

You cannot have true faith in the Cross without believing in the power through which the Finished Work of Christ becomes a reality and works in our lives, the power of the Holy Ghost!

The Holy Ghost in turn only works within the parameters of the Cross of Christ.

One of my favorite sayings is from a ministry that feeds this writer often, and I cannot say that there are many out there who do; "Jesus is the Source, the Cross is the means," and because of Jesus and what He did for us at the Cross, the Holy Ghost then becomes the POWER, the FIRE, the UNCTION, the SEAL, the LEADING, the LIGHT, the DYNAMITE, the DUNAMIS, and the POWER, of the Cross in our hearts and lives!

Man's ONLY hope for righteousness is by placing his faith in what Christ did at the Cross through faith and repentance. Man's only hope for deliverance is to then allow the Holy Ghost to take control of his walk with Christ and make the Cross a reality, not just a necklace that he wears around his neck.

Man does not have righteousness with God because man has the right "purpose" or the right "destiny" or the right anything else. Man does not have righteousness with God because he has the right education, the right financial standing, the right church membership, the right amount of self-esteem or the right psychological profile. Man can "find the champion inside," and be lost and on his way to hell a "champion."

Man is righteous because of CHRIST and CHRIST ALONE. It is the Cross, it is the Cross, it is the Cross, it is the Cross, it is the Cross, it is the Cross!

And the HOLY SPIRIT's work in our lives MAKES us righteous as Christ is righteous. True salvation is not a sinning salvation, it is a change holiness, from bondage to freedom, from sickness to health.

The only way one can experience such is by keeping one's faith anchored in what Christ did for them at the Cross. There are no formulas for sainthood, neighbor.

As stated in part one of this journal, it is impossible for the child of God, no exceptions, to receive **anything** from God unless the Holy Spirit be a co-participant in that which is received.

While one receives the Holy Spirit at conversion (that is theologically and scripturally correct for those who argue that point), there is a very real and definite difference in being BORN of the Spirit and being BAPTIZED in the Spirit. Simply put, a person is NOT baptized in the Holy Spirit and now he is saved. He is baptized into the Body of Christ, but he is not baptized in the Spirit. There is a great difference in the Born-Again experience and the experience of Jesus literally immersing that same individual FULLY in the power of the Third Person of the Godhead.

So, when people say we receive the Holy Spirit at salvation, actually, they are right, but wrong in their thinking. The Baptism in the Holy Spirit is an experience separate from salvation; it can only come AFTER salvation; it must be consciously sought by the thirsty and hungry believer for more of God.

> **Luke 11:13**
> **If ye then, being evil, know how to give good gifts unto your children: how much more shall your heavenly Father give the Holy Spirit to them that ask him?**

Let us look at a few powerful points as to how to receive the Baptism in the Holy Spirit.

1. It Is Our Belief That the Word of God Teaches that EVERY Recipient of The Holy Ghost Speaks in Other Tongues at The Time of Receiving The Holy Spirit; There are No Exceptions.

Everywhere in the book of Acts where the baptism in the Holy Spirit is mentioned, the recipients spoke with tongues.

Acts 2:4 says that, "and they began to speak with other tongues as the Spirit gave them the utterance."

Acts 10 says that Cornelius and his household "spoke with tongues" and prophesied.

In Acts 19 it says that the Apostles of John (when the Apostle Paul prayed for them to receive the Holy Spirit), "spoke with tongues" and prophesied as they were filled.

It is clear from scripture then that if that was the pattern in the Book of Acts, it is the pattern today. Every single recipient of the baptism in the Holy Ghost speaks with other tongues (as the Spirit gives the utterance) when they are filled with the Holy Spirit according to Acts 2:4.

This what we will refer to as the initial baptismal filling, not the same "spiritual gift" spoken of in 1 Corinthians 12:8-10. These two things are basically the same but their use in the church are two totally different things altogether.

The bottom line is that tongues are part of the New Testament experience of salvation. You get saved, then you get filled with the Spirit of God! And those who denigrate tongues need to stop and realize the following. Paul spoke with tongues, John spoke with tongues, Timothy spoke with tongues, Matthew spoke with tongues, Mark spoke with tongues, Luke spoke with tongues, Peter spoke with tongues, MARY THE MOTHER of Jesus spoke with tongues, Andrew spoke with tongues, and all who were there on the Day of Pentecost spoke with tongues!

We will deal with tongues in extensive detail in the next lesson in this series but there is NOTHING to fear when it comes to speaking in tongues. The only people scared of speaking in tongues are scared because of false teaching or outright lies concerning this grand experience.

Tongues are for today, for the believer, and extremely relevant to the victorious life of the Christian. And furthermore, tongues are available for ALL believers who will be believe and ask.

2. There is ONE, and ONLY ONE, Prerequisite to Receiving the Baptism or Infilling of the Holy Spirit and That Is Salvation

Many individuals and many Pentecostal denominations sadly have tried to conjure up and list a great number of requirements which must be met before a saved person can aspire to the baptism.

In all honesty, there is only one and one requirement ONLY according to Scripture and that is the seeking individual must be saved.

The sinner cannot receive the things of God, only the believer can receive. The sinner can only aspire to salvation through the conviction and drawing of the Holy Spirit while one is lost and without God.

> **1 Corinthians 2:14**
> **But the natural man (THE LOST MAN WHO HAS NOT BEEN BORN AGAIN) receives not the things of the Spirit of God: for they are foolishness unto him: neither can he know them, because they are spiritually discerned.**

The incidents of Acts 19:2 and Acts 8:14-17 describe the condition of BELIEVERS who had not yet received the baptism in the Holy Ghost.

> **Acts 19:2**
> **He said unto them, Have ye received the Holy Ghost since ye believed? And they said unto him, We have not so much as heard whether there be any Holy Ghost.**

> **Acts 8:14-17**
> **Now when the apostles which were at Jerusalem heard that Samaria had received the word of God, they sent unto them Peter and John: [15] Who, when they were come down, prayed for them, that they might receive the Holy Ghost: [16] (For as yet he was fallen upon none of them: only they were baptized in the name of the Lord Jesus.) [17] Then laid they their hands on them, and they received the Holy Ghost.**

These who received the infilling or baptism in the Holy Ghost were **saved** believers. They had not gone through any rituals or met any list of "pre" conditions. They were born again. Knowing this, the apostles prayed for them for the reception of the Holy Ghost and they received just that!

These passages are confirmation in God's Word that salvation is the only prior condition which MUST be met before the individual can become a candidate for the baptism in the Holy Ghost.

One may ask then and rightly so, "where then do all the lists of prerequisites come from?" Sadly, all too often they come, directly or indirectly, via the intervention of Satan.

Satan, more than most Christians, sadly, is well aware that the Holy Ghost is the SOURCE of ALL Godly Christian living and victory over the flesh, the world and himself. He knows that "greater is HE that is in you, than He that is in this world!"

Truly Spirit-filled Christians top the list of things Satan does not want anything to do with!!

We as believers in our own natural flesh and abilities are no match for the powers of darkness or the enemy–no matter how religious we think we are.

Ask the seven sons of Sceva!

> **Acts 19:14**
> **And there were seven sons of one Sceva, a Jew, and chief of the priests, which did so. [15] And the evil spirit answered and said, Jesus I know, and Paul I know; but who are ye? [16] And the man in whom the evil spirit was leaped on them, and overcame them, and prevailed against them, so that they fled out of that house naked and wounded. [17] And this was known to all the Jews and Greeks also dwelling at Ephesus; and fear fell on them all, and the name of the Lord Jesus was magnified. [18] And many that believed came, and confessed,**

> and showed their deeds. [19] Many of them also which used curious arts brought their books together, and burned them before all men: and they counted the price of them, and found it fifty thousand pieces of silver. [20] So mightily grew the word of God and prevailed.

When religious men tried to come against the enemy in their own strength, the demonic powers leaped on them, overcame, and prevailed against them.

That is the state of the modern church world in most cases.

We try and come against the powers of the devil with our programs, softball teams and other such foolishness and we find out quick just how powerful the enemy is.

For those who even believe in doing such, we think that somehow, we can just rebuke the powers of darkness and those powers will leave.

That is why Satan loves to send schemes and gimmicks into the Body of Christ to embrace. We spent nearly 10 years in the late 2000s trying to find our "purpose" through the Rick Warren models. When that did not work, we tried the mega-church leadership models by Joel Osteen. When that scheme did not work then another popped up and another popped up there.

Finding one's purpose does not mean one is walking in Christian victory! The powers of darkness could care less how much purpose you have, neighbor. If you are not baptized in the Spirit and filled with the Holy Ghost, then all the "purpose in the world," will not keep you or your children from being bound, strung out on drugs, alcohol, lust, false doctrine, and darkness.

Satan will put any stumbling block in the path of the Christian and do anything in his power, including inspiring preachers and teachers to speak against it, seeking to get people to reject the doctrine of the baptism in the Holy Ghost.

Satan's other weapon is telling those who are seeking with sincerity that they are "unworthy," or that one must work out their own solutions in the areas in which they are not yet victorious. Satan is a master deceiver pointing out our faults claiming that the Lord Jesus will not baptize us in the Spirit if we still have a "temper," or "lust," or whatever bondage we have.

The enemy brings problem after problem, failing after failing, up into our mind when we start seeking more of God. But the TRUTH of the matter is that nowhere in God's Word are we cautioned to "do" certain things BEFORE we go before God and ask Him for the infilling with His mighty Holy Ghost. All these false pretenses are manufactured by Satan, not God.

Let the reader hear this writer. If you are struggling with a weakness in your Christian life, you are the greatest candidate for the Spirit's power and help!!

You need Him to help you overcome those weaknesses and He is more than willing and ABLE to do so!

> **Romans 8:26-28**
> **Likewise the Spirit also helpeth our infirmities: for we know not what we should pray for as we ought: but the Spirit itself**

> makes intercession for us with groanings which cannot be uttered. [27] And he that searches the hearts knoweth what is the mind of the Spirit, because he makes intercession for the saints according to the will of God. [28] And we know that all things work together for good to them that love God, to them who are the called according to his purpose.

Many who have been baptized in the Spirit were STILL smoking cigarettes, still battling bad tempers, still battling lust, etc. WHEN they were baptized in the Holy Ghost but AFTER they were baptized in the Spirit, they were able to OVERCOME these wayward impulses through the help of the HOLY SPIRIT.

How like God it is, recognizing our earthly weakness, to send us the COMFORTER and the STRENGTHENER while we are still imperfect, rather than demanding that we clean up our abode all by ourselves.

> **John 14:16**
> And I will pray the Father, and he shall give you another Comforter, that he may abide with you for ever

Satan on the other hand does everything at his command to prevent us from seeking and receiving God's help. I am sure Satan knows Greek and he surely knows that the name of the Holy Spirit in the original Greek is *"Paraclete,"* which is translated as "one called alongside to help."

What a beautiful way of expressing the role of the Holy Ghost. NONE of us is capable of completely living this Christian life on our own. Honestly, there is NOTHING we can do on our own that usually works out right.

One thing is for sure. None can clean up their own life without the help of the third person of the Godhead! The struggles of the Christian faith are nothing to laugh at; this is not "play church," or "let us come and have a picnic for Jesus," friend.

This is eternity.

Scores of well-meaning Christians have fallen by the wayside and are littered on the shores of eternal time because they just "gave up" in this struggle saying, "I cannot live this Christian life so I would rather quit than be a hypocrite."

This writer went through that very same experience many years back and it almost cost me not just my spiritual life, but my physical one.

These same struggling Christians come to the church and seek help with their struggle and are given NOTHING to help them because of the church's UNBELIEF in the HOLY GHOST. Then these same church establishments stand in self-righteous judgment when Christians reach a point where some start committing suicide only to have the same self-righteous judges say "aww, that's so terrible." God help us.

I feel in my heart as I write this, I may be writing to a struggling Christian right now.

You know EXACTLY what I am talking about and the thought of giving up has crept in many times recently and the enemy has done nothing to help stop that voice from screaming at you "give up." this struggle is too great, you cannot live this Christian life," "turn your back on God," and a myriad of other lies the enemy spreads.

Listen neighbor and listen well. None of us can have a Christian life in the confines and resources of our own flesh and strength.

Our only hope is the HELP of our Heavenly Father through what Christ accomplished for us at the Cross through the ministry of God's power source, the HOLY GHOST. This is why the father of lies sets up every obstacle to PREVENT us from seeking GOD'S help and I emphasize GOD'S help in our lives.

Satan does not set up obstacles when we are seeking man's help i.e. rehab centers, AA meetings, 12-step programs and all the other stupid things the church holds up to those bound by sin as ways to get free. It is shameful that we have "celebrate recovery," in our churches which is nothing more than a wrapped up 12-step program that has no life in it, no power in it, no way for men to be free, no HELP in time of need, NOTHING. It does not take Jesus 12 steps to set you free. HE THAT THE SON HAS SET FREE IS FREE INDEED! Jesus has a ONE STEP program and that one step is the power of the HOLY GHOST.

It is shameful when the Assemblies of God publication tells its pastors that the best thing to do for those in their congregations bound by any addiction is to suggest finding a human based program. It is even more shameful that this thinking from one of the largest "PENTECOSTAL" and I put the term Pentecostal in BIG parenthesis, denominations that is supposed to know the power of God and the baptism in the Holy Ghost, only has less than 30% of their membership even believing anymore in the baptism in the Spirit!

If we go by a standard that for a denomination to considered Pentecostal, they will need 51% to believe in tongues, then the

Assemblies (and the Church of God is not far behind right now) falls WAY short!

When a denomination or a church or an individual believer rejects the working of the Holy Ghost, they are then open game for every scheme of Satan, no matter how religious it may look and how popular it may be. Many get angry and offended when someone speaks the truth in love and touches their golden calf of humanism by telling the believer that their answer is the CROSS OF CHRIST and the power of the HOLY GHOST! At the same time, those same people WILL NOT get angry when demonic forces come in, seeking to control the church and promote everything ungodly and wicked under the sun. Let me make that point a little clearer.

If someone gets up and suggests their people read the Purpose Driven Life book, you cannot get enough books into the hands of the people. Get up and say, "let us do a Bible study and let the Bible be our textbook and textbook alone," you cannot get enough hands to take the Book!

Hire ungodly entertainers to come in and "thrill" our young people with their wicked, worldly-based music and the lines will reach ten blocks. Call a prayer meeting for people to come together and seek God's face you cannot fill a front row.

The new golden calves of the church are "SELF" and "Entertainment," and we do all we can today in the modern church world to protect both of these idols! When our self-help schemes fail to deliver people from the powers of darkness, we then call on the entertainers to keep them coming to keep them from dying of boredom.

When the smoke clears, sadly, men remain bound by sin and the powers of darkness while hearts seeking for God remain thirsty and parched in a dry dessert wasteland we call "church."

If you are in that dry place today, listen up to this writer. I have good news for you. 2,000 years ago Jesus Christ came and died on the cross not only for our sins but that we might be filled with the Holy Spirit and that same Spirit, who is called "living waters," by Jesus Himself, can quench any thirst, fill any hungry heart, and wash away all the sin, guilt and doubt the enemy can bring.

It is not about "doing" neighbor, it is about "BELIEVING."

The more things we must do "before" we seek God's help; the more time Satan has to work his devilment in our lives and in the lives of those we might have influenced. Is it not logical to realize that ANY prerequisites work for the benefit of Satan and NOT for the good of the besieged Christian? Any Christian, no matter how well motivated and no matter the degree of commitment, is NOT helping his Christian brother when he complies or condones a LIST OF MUSTS which have to be met before the assailed member can hope to receive the help of the Comforter!

The Baptism in the Holy Ghost is truly a "come as you are" invitation. Recognize the methods of the enemy and refuse to accept his lies. It is God's Word, NOT Satan's WORD, that we should trust.

The Lord will baptize you in the Holy Spirit even though you have weaknesses and flaws within your character and life. If you are sincere before the Lord and you recognize and reject these shortcomings, He will account to you YOUR recognition of them and baptize you in the HOLY GHOST!

Once you have God's Spirit working within your life, once you are plugged into God's great power source and not man's, how much more favorable is the prognosis for overcoming these faults? On your own, you will NEVER overcome sin and live victoriously in your Christian walk. WITH God's Comforter, it might still be a battle, but how much better are the chances of victory and how much easier the contest.

Satan knows this and therefore, he promotes all the false requirements and false doctrines that hinder MILLIONS from aspiring to God's next great step for the believer AFTER salvation! When he or a fellow Christian tell you that you must do this, or you must do that, or this is not for you, or this is not for today, or I hear that this is evil and I hear that those who do such are of Satan, or I hear you need an interpreter before you are supposed to speak in tongues.

IGNORE THE VOICE OF SATAN! REJECT THE WORDS OF MEN AND EMBRACE THE WORD OF ALMIGHTY GOD AND BE FILLED WITH THE HOLY GHOST. The ONLY one prerequisite is that you are saved.

3. One Does Not Have to Tarry to Receive the Baptism in The Holy Ghost!

Another myth connected with the Baptism in the Holy Spirit is that we must "tarry" before God for some indeterminate period before we can expect to be filled. This is not true.

No doubt, the basis for this is that the disciples were commanded to WAIT in Jerusalem before departing to spread the gospel. The point missed here is that they were told to wait for the Promise of the Father BEFORE departing.

This was to be the beginning of a completely new phase of God's relationship to man. Tremendously important accomplishments were to be required of the disciples. Unimaginable persecutions awaited them and there was a whole world of unsaved waiting to hear the Word of God which only they could deliver. Jesus knew, human nature being what it is, that it would be only natural for the disciples to strike out immediately on their missions. Instead, He cautioned them that they were NOT to attempt their ministries before they had received the irreplaceable help of the Comforter.

Unfortunately, this has been twisted to mean that there is a "waiting" period as part and parcel of the Holy Spirit baptism. This simply is NOT true. Although Acts 1:4 and Luke 24:49 recount this admonition from the Lord to the disciples, other Scriptures clearly indicate there is NO tarrying period involved.

In the eighth chapter of Acts, the incident is recounted where Peter and John came from Jerusalem and prayed for the believers in Samaria. These were saved Christians who had NOT yet received the Baptism in the Holy Ghost. And what happened? They were IMMEDIATELY filled when John and Peter prayed for them and laid hands on them.

Again, in Acts 9 when Ananias came to Paul and laid on hands and prayed for him, Paul was FILLED ON THE SPOT with the HOLY GHOST.

Later, in Acts 10, while Peter was preaching a great salvation message to the kinsman and friends of Cornelius, "while Peter YET SPAKE THESE WORDS, the Holy Ghost fell on them all which heard the word." (Acts 10:44)

Acts 10:44
While Peter yet spake these words, the Holy Ghost fell on all them which heard the word.

In Acts 19:1-6, an incident is recounted where Paul came across a group of Christians who were baptized believers (by John) but they had not heard of the baptism in the Holy Ghost. Paul explained the Spirit baptism to them, and immediately they were filled with the Holy Ghost. Each of these incidents involves INSTANT baptism with absolutely no suggestion of tarrying.

All the above-mentioned scriptures show those who received the Holy Ghost received the Holy Ghost immediately. This does not mean that everyone who seeks the Baptism in the Spirit will receive it right off the bat. I have seen people filled instantly and I have also seen it take many attempts before one is filled. It took me about 5 months before I received the Baptism after initially starting to seek more of God.

Let the reader be clear. God does not run a "redemption" center where we come to pick up trinkets once we have saved enough 'brownie' points.

Acts 2:38 clearly describes an occasion when Peter points out that the assembled would receive the GIFT of the Holy Ghost. A gift is something entirely different from wages. We earn wages but we RECEIVE gifts without expending labor for them. Every Christian understands that salvation is a gift, unmerited and freely given to the undeserving through the generosity of God.

Yet knowing this, some try to make the Baptism in the Holy Ghost (also defined scripturally as a gift) as something to be earned. The only major difference between the gift of salvation and the gift of the Holy Ghost is that salvation is God's gift to the world, while the Holy Spirit is God's gift to His children.

The sinner may receive God's gift of salvation no matter the depth of his sins. This great salvation is received freely and without prerequisites for all who will but BELIEVE.

> **Hebrews 2:1-3**
> **Therefore we ought to give the more earnest heed to the things which we have heard, lest at any time we should let them slip. [2] For if the word spoken by angels was stedfast, and every transgression and disobedience received a just recompence of reward; [3] How shall we escape, if we neglect so great salvation; which at the first began to be spoken by the Lord, and was confirmed unto us by them that heard him;**

God's gift of the Holy Spirit is reserved for His own children, those who have COME OUT of this world through accepting salvation. ONLY THEN does one become eligible to receive the Holy Ghost. Beyond this however, there are NO prior conditions, which must be met before we can aspire to receiving the Holy Ghost.

As Paul said in Ephesians 2:9, "Not of works, lest any man should boast." The conclusions are the same when it pertains to the baptism in the Holy Ghost! We are saved by faith not of works, and we receive the baptism in the Holy Ghost by faith not of works, and as such it may be received instantly for those who seek this glorious experience.

As we close, let the writer make a few especially important points.

When we speak of "tongues," we are not glorifying tongues in themselves. Some well-meaning Pentecostals have made tongues an idol of worship as well, which does not do them or anyone else any good. What we ARE saying is this. **We are pointing the believer to the POWER OF THE HOLY GHOST**, which works because of the **Finished Work of Christ.**

Tongues are but the **INITIAL** physical evidence the believer has received in infilling or baptism in the Holy Ghost.

Not to be redundant but many Pentecostals get caught up in the "phenomena" of tongues and miss out on the more important ministry of the Holy Spirit in our Christian walk and lives.

The Holy Ghost is given for us to become WITNESSES of the power of the Cross to a lost and dying world without Christ! This is not about going door to door and telling others of Jesus. What it means is that the world is going to see the WITNESS of Jesus in our hearts and lives by the anointing of the Spirit that rests upon those who are baptized in the Spirit!! The same fisherman who cowered down in an upper room scared for their lives changed the world of their day after the Baptism in the Holy Ghost!

He can do the same for you today as well.

Reader, you need the baptism in the Holy Ghost! You need the power of God in your life to walk victoriously in this earthly sojourn.

The believer, once they have come to Christ, needs to know in detail the MINISTRY of the Holy Spirit in one's life. If we will remember this simple fact; that the Holy Spirit works in our lives because of the Cross and the Cross means nothing without the power of the Holy Spirit, we will be very wise in our Christian walk and if we will not faint and grow weary in faith, we will see victory through JESUS CHRIST OUR LORD!

Your battle neighbor is not against sin, your battle is your faith! Place your faith in Christ and Him alone today; place it in the nail-scarred hands of Jesus where the blood flowed down 2,000 years ago for man's deliverance and salvation. The blood flowed so we could be filled with the Holy Ghost and neighbor, He wants to fill you today if you will but BELIEVE. Praise God.

Which Have Received the Holy Ghost as We?

Chapter Four

HINDRANCES TO RECEIVING THE BAPTISM IN THE HOLY GHOST

The Baptism in The Holy Spirit

> TEXT: Acts 2:4– And they were all filled with the Holy Ghost, and began to speak with other tongues, as the Spirit gave them utterance.

> Acts 7:51
> Ye stiffnecked and uncircumcised in heart and ears, ye do always resist the Holy Ghost: as your fathers did, so do ye.

> Acts 1:4-5
> And, being assembled together with them, commanded them that they should not depart from Jerusalem, but wait for the promise of the Father, which, saith he, ye have heard of me. [5] For John truly baptized with water; but ye shall be baptized with the Holy Ghost not many days hence.

The Baptism in the Holy Ghost is a gift from God for the believer. It is important for the reader to understand that when we state "gift," we are not referring to the "gift" of tongues and interpretation of tongues spoken of in 1 Corinthians 12.

There are many people baptized in the Holy Ghost with the evidence of speaking with other tongues that may never be used in the gift of tongues as outlined in Corinthians. One is for personal devotion and a daily walk with Christ. The other is used for corporate worship and for the edifying of the Body. One is a mandate and the other is "as the Spirit wills," according to Scripture.

The reader must understand that at the root of it all, truth faith is the fundamental understanding that the Cross of Christ is the source of ALL things that we receive from God.

True victory never comes without a fight, but it is a fight that has already been won at the Cross through the precious blood of the Lord Jesus Christ. He that the Son has set free is FREE indeed. When we by faith embrace what Christ did for us at the Cross, then the Holy Spirit can work in our lives to bring victory in the areas of our weakness, and we ALL have weakness!

It is when we see our weakness as God sees it which is sin, then we can experience victory through Christ and the power of the Holy Ghost. Christ is the source, His Death, Burial and Resurrection the means, and the Holy Ghost is the power.

Once one is born again, the believer then becomes a candidate to receive the glorious infilling of the Holy Ghost with the evidence of speaking with other tongues as the Spirit of God gives the utterance.

Acts 2:4
And they were all filled with the Holy Ghost, and began to speak with other tongues, as the Spirit gave them utterance.

In 1987, I was glorious baptized with the Holy Ghost for the first time after spending many years in the Baptist Church not even as much as knowing about the Holy Ghost.

I remember the struggle at the beginning when I first started seeking the baptism, and I remember the many obstacles and questions I had as an honest, but frustrated seeker. I remember one night particularly in late 1986, when I went down to the front of my church to have people pray for me to receive the Baptism in the Holy Ghost for the first time. To be frank, I was about as scared as a human being could be.

While growing up in Atlanta, Georgia I remember the first time I ever heard someone speak in tongues. It happened while I was visiting my aunt on my mom's side of the family's church. My first cousin had gone to the altar to be prayed for to be healed and he began to weep, and he began to speak with other tongues. To be frank, as a young Baptist boy, I wanted to run out of the church like a deer. When I went home and told my parents what had transpired, their response was not one that would encourage me to pursue anything that my cousin had experienced. My dear dad; and this is not meant to take a slap at him, believe me, he has come a long way since those days, was probably less encouraging than my mom.

My point in stating this is to comfort those reading this who may have many questions, doubts, and fears about this glorious experience and to let them know they are not alone. Very few seeking the baptism of the Holy Ghost for the first time do it without a bit of fear or trepidation.

There is a particularly good reason why. Most preachers today speak of the baptismal experience of power for the believer in negative tones and connotations instead of preaching faith and encouraging folks to receive! It is terribly sad, but it is the state that the modern church is in. I received the Pentecostal experience at a time when it could not have been worse to be involved in it.

In the late 1980s, the Body of Christ was experiencing one of worst shakings it had experienced in the past 20 years or so. There were sad revelations about many high named Pentecostal preachers. As a former Southern Baptist who had never even as much as heard about the Holy Ghost, I could not have been happier about receiving the Holy Spirit, but I also found out quickly just how friends can become enemies over religious matters. Notice I say "religious" matters, not spiritual ones. However, my little taste of alienation by a few of my good old Baptist "buddies" was nothing compared to the venom and attacks that were experienced by the early church or those associated with the 20th Century outpouring at Azusa Street.

Rev. William Seymour would have men come into his meetings and point fingers in his face, accusing him of everything under God's heaven while calling him every name under the sun. This Pentecostal experience has never come without a price, which makes the modern unbelief of the Church even more sickening and degrading to this writer.

America's mainline Pentecostal denominations, the Assemblies of God, Church of God, Pentecostal Holiness, Foursquare, Church of God in Christ, and a few others, are teetering on a dangerous ledge of no longer being Pentecostal. You must have 51% of your members speaking in tongues to be considered a Pentecostal denomination. Right now, that figure stands at 49% in ALL major denominations!!! The reason for this decline is unbelief in the pulpit and hardness of heart in the pew.

Despite all the enemy's tactics of fear and doubt, I also know that there is NO one and I mean NO one who has experienced the baptism in the Holy Ghost who turned around said, "this is not for today," or "this is of the devil," or "I don't need to speak in tongues to pray."

I believe that Jesus in heaven weeps over these things and He screams from within His heart, "This is WHAT I SHED MY BLOOD FOR!"

It amazes me that 100% of those who resist and reject the mighty baptism in the Holy Ghost are those who know little about what I talk about or who have not experienced the Holy Spirit themselves.

This lesson will help one understand some of the hindrances to receiving the Baptism in the Holy Spirit.

1. Unbelief and Not Yielding Are Two Major Reasons That Keep Some from Not Receiving the Baptism in the Holy Ghost

> **Acts 7:51-53**
> **Ye stiffnecked and uncircumcised in heart and ears, <u>ye do always resist the Holy Ghost</u>: as your fathers did, so do ye. [52] Which of the prophets have not your fathers persecuted? and they have slain them which showed before of the coming of the Just One; of whom ye have been now the betrayers and murderers: [53] Who have received the law by the disposition of angels, and have not kept it.**

There are two factors that can throw up a wall and prevent the believing Christian from receiving the baptism in the Holy Ghost. The first one of these is UNBELIEF. Not yielding one's self to the Spirit's direction and leading is the second.

The person who comes forward to receive the Holy Ghost, while harboring doubts in their heart will go away without receiving!

If one is not sure something is real or for them, they will never pursue and realize the result of what they are seeking! Satan, of course, uses this doubt to prevent many believers from receiving the Holy Ghost thus we must stand on God's Word and proclaim this glorious experience is real despite the enemy's lies. The Christian does not have to entertain Satan's lies but most Christians do. It is a shame that the modern church has more faith in Satan's ability to deceive us than in the Holy Spirit's power to lead us into all truth!

> **John 14:16**
> **And I will pray the Father, and he shall give you another Comforter, that he may abide with you for ever; Even the Spirit of truth; whom the world cannot receive, because it seeth him not, neither knoweth him: but ye know him; for he dwelleth with you, and shall be in you.**

Doubt is removed when we embrace and believe God's WORD about our pursuit of the baptism in the Holy Ghost. Unbelief was Israel's problem in accepting the fact that the power that allowed Christ to perform miracles was from God. Many times, the Pharisees accused Christ of performing miracles by the power of Satan instead of the power by which He performed these miracles, the power of the Holy Ghost.

> **Matthew 12:22-32**
> **Then was brought unto him one possessed with a devil, blind, and dumb: and he healed him, insomuch that the blind and dumb both spake and saw. [23] And all the people were amazed, and said, Is not this the son of David? [24] But when the Pharisees heard it, they said, This fellow doth not cast out devils, but by Beelzebub the prince of the devils. [25] And Jesus knew their thoughts, and said unto them, Every kingdom divided against itself is brought to desolation; and every city or house divided against itself shall not stand: [26] And if Satan cast out Satan, he is divided against himself; how shall then his kingdom stand? [27] And if I by Beelzebub cast out devils, by whom do your children cast them out? therefore**

> **they shall be your judges. [28] But if I cast out devils by the Spirit of God, then the kingdom of God is come unto you.**

Israel had a moment of unprecedented opportunity as a nation when she came out of Egypt. God had ordained the generation led by Moses and Aaron to inherit the promises God made to Abraham, Isaac, and Jacob nearly 250-300 years before.

The Holy Spirit through Paul warns the New Covenant believer as to why Israel failed lest we today in modern times fall into the same trap of unbelief. I must tell you that it is a sad indictment on the modern church that we are so steeped in the same unbelief as Israel of old was.

We have so much more than they did. We have the completed canon of Scripture, the Word of God. We have the gifts of the Spirit. We have great revelatory knowledge of all things. We have been blessed and blessed some more with great financial gain. We have the greatest numbers ever in human history, of people coming and flocking to our church buildings. Yet despite all our modern trinkets, the church does not believe GOD!

Preachers preach unbelief week after week to their flocks and they deny the supernatural working of the Holy Ghost and they refuse to point their listeners to the only source of deliverance for the ills of man, The Cross of Christ.

Some say miracles have passed; others proclaim tongues and the gifts of the Spirit "ceased" with the apostles. Neighbor, if the gifts ceased then God ceased, and God did not cease! How stupid can we get? How so unimpressive can we get with all our education and knowledge yet stand empty, naked, blind, and wretched before a

Holy Creator who cries to His church to just believe what His Word says? He so wants to show us His unparalleled power and grace!

In the book of Romans, Paul warned the Gentiles that if the Lord cut Israel off temporarily because of unbelief, we would be wise to not stand so conceited and arrogant, but FEAR, lest we be cut off too. Despite this warning, the modern church that is comprised now mostly of Gentiles, in these last days CHOKES with unbelief.

> **Romans 11:18-25**
> **Boast not against the branches. But if thou boast, thou bearest not the root, but the root thee. [19] Thou wilt say then, The branches were broken off, that I might be graffed in. [20] Well; because of unbelief they were broken off, and thou standest by faith. Be not high-minded, but fear: [21] For if God spared not the natural branches, take heed lest he also spare not thee. [22] Behold therefore the goodness and severity of God: on them which fell, severity; but toward thee, goodness, if thou continue in his goodness: otherwise thou also shalt be cut off. [23] And they also, if they abide not still in unbelief, shall be graffed in: for God is able to graff them in again. [24] For if thou wert cut out of the olive tree which is wild by nature, and wert graffed contrary to nature into a good olive tree: how much more shall these, which be the natural branches, be graffed into their own olive tree? [25] For I would not, brethren, that ye should be ignorant of this mystery, lest ye should be wise in your own conceits; that blindness in part is happened to Israel, until the fulness of the Gentiles be come in.**

Unbelief permeated the culture of Jesus' day just as it dominates many sectors of our modern world today. Israel's issues of unbelief centered around the validity of the power of Christ!

Think about that and consider the attitude of the church world today towards this same power! Charles Finney once stated the following of preachers who preach unbelief:

> *"One unbelieving soul may do immense evil; especially if he be a minister of the gospel. How easy it is for a blind minister to keep his congregation for ever in darkness, in regard to the meaning of the gospel and the fulness of the salvation provided."*

Finney goes on to say:

> *"A mind under the influence of unbelief, is a very dangerous interpreter of the word of God. Without faith, no man discovers the true meaning of the Bible. Nor can he by any possibility discover its spiritual import, without the state of mind which is always implied in a right understanding of the word of God. The Church is robbed of its inheritance by unbelief. Inasmuch as the promises are conditioned upon faith, and cannot in their own nature be fulfilled where there is not faith, how immense is the evil of unbelief in the Church of God? Gospel rest and salvation lie before them in all their fulness, completeness of Christian character in Christ Jesus, and the sanctification of body, soul, and spirit, are proffered to them and urged with infinite sincerity upon them; but all are rejected through unbelief. Those who are unbelieving in regard to the fulness of Christ's salvation, take away the key of knowledge. They neither enter into gospel rest themselves, and those that would enter they hinder;*

especially is this true of those ministers who call in question the attainability of entire consecration to God in this life."

Unbelief, whether it is unbelief by the sinner regarding salvation, or that of a Christian not believing in the supernatural power of God through the ministry of the Holy Ghost, is eminently a willful sin.

When it comes to the baptism in the Holy Ghost, this writer has seen through the years that it is exceedingly hard to make men believe in this powerful work of the Spirit when they are unwilling to believe. Sadly, when the will is strongly opposed to any truth, it is next to impossible to retain the confidence of the mind in that truth. In other words, if a person's mind is made up, they are not going to change their mind "even if one came back from the dead," to tell them what they are doubting is real and right.

Finney added this comment on unbelief which sums up best how most people see the baptism in the Holy Ghost:

> *"But what must be the strength of depravity in that heart—what must be the power of prejudice, what invincible strength must there be in the opposition of that will, when the confidence of the mind is not secured by infinite evidence; when the mind can look over the whole field and see mountains of evidence piled upon mountains, and yet feel not a particle of inward confidence and resting of heart in the character and word of the blessed God."*

In other words, despite everything the Word of God says about the baptism in the Holy Ghost and the fact that untold MILLIONS have received this glorious infilling, many will still not believe!

A drunkard does not believe that alcohol is poison. A Universalist does not believe that there is any hell. A tea and coffee drinker will not believe that those substances are injurious. That does not change the fact these things are so.

When it comes to faith as it relates to the Baptism in the Holy Ghost, just because one does not believe it, that does not make the experience false.

That brings us to the second interfering factor that causes many not to receive the Baptism in the Spirit which, is in many ways much harder to banish from the equation and that is the matter of yielding.

Part of the issue is that we want to be in control of our own emotions, desires, and actions individually. That is great in the real world, but when it relates to the Holy Spirit, we cannot be self-led, we must be SPIRIT-led! Unfortunately, this human tendency becomes so ingrained that we find it difficult, when confronted with the necessity of yielding our will to that of God, to give up our lifelong search for "independence."

God does not want us independent of Him! He is the Loving Father of our souls who wants us to turn TO HIM for our every living need.

This is the damnable result of the invasion of New Age Humanistic thinking into the modern church world. The modern gospel teaches people to "take control and keep control" of every facet of their lives. The Holy Spirit speaks to us and says, "Give in and throw yourself on the mercy of God." Herein lies the great conflict, not just for the sinner seeking salvation, but also for the seeking believer who is hungry and thirsty for the baptism in the Holy Ghost.

For those seeking the baptism, many feel a strange pressure growing within, a bubbling up of a force that demands expression. What is one to do? Are we to "keep control of ourselves," as we have always been taught, or are we to capriciously throw ourselves down a new path which leads to who-knows-where?

The business of speaking in other tongues is not something that can be easily and logically explained within the perimeters of our overly sophisticated and scientifically oriented world AND church system! Perhaps this is the very reason God has set things up in this way. Many times, He offends the minds of men to lay bare the motives of their heart! The Cross of Christ falls into the same category in many ways.

There is an offense attached to the Cross that many reject. that is why Paul said, "not many mighty, not many noble," are called. The Spirit bids ALL men to come to Christ, but few receive this invitation. As it relates to the believer, the same is true when it comes to the baptism in the Holy Ghost! The Lord Jesus bids ALL men to come to Him and receive the infilling of the Holy Ghost but precious few hear the voice of our Lord and receive this glorious infilling.

> **John 7:37-39**
> **In the last day, that great day of the feast, Jesus stood and cried, saying, If any man thirst, let him come unto me, and drink. [38] He that believeth on me, as the scripture hath said, out of his belly shall flow rivers of living water. [39] (But this spake he of the Spirit, which they that believe on him should**

> receive: for the Holy Ghost was not yet given; because that Jesus was not yet glorified.)

Paul explains in Ephesians 3:19 that God's standards and the world's standards are in conflict where the areas of wisdom and foolishness are concerned. God laughs at the things that mankind values as great wisdom. Conversely, mankind in its smugness, laughs at those who believe the simple unvarnished or untarnished Word of Almighty God!

> **Ephesians 3:10-19**
> **To the intent that now unto the principalities and powers in heavenly places might be known by the church the manifold wisdom of God, [11] According to the eternal purpose which he purposed in Christ Jesus our Lord: [12] In whom we have boldness and access with confidence by the faith of him. [13] Wherefore I desire that ye faint not at my tribulations for you, which is your glory. [14] For this cause I bow my knees unto the Father of our Lord Jesus Christ, [15] Of whom the whole family in heaven and earth is named, [16] That he would grant you, according to the riches of his glory, to be strengthened with might by his Spirit in the inner man; [17] That Christ may dwell in your hearts by faith; that ye, being rooted and grounded in love, [18] May be able to comprehend with all saints what is the breadth, and length, and depth, and height; [19] And to know the love of Christ, which passeth knowledge, that ye might be filled with all the fulness of God.**

What could be more natural then for God to choose something which could be basically "embarrassing" (and capable of being scoffed at by the world) as the benchmark of submission to His will? On the surface, what could seem *less* logical than uttering words we do not understand?

Yet this is exactly that God has chosen as HIS documentation of OUR willingness to YIELD the moment-to-moment control of our lives to Him. The question to the reader is simply this. Are we willing to stand up and make ourselves "fools for Christ," as Paul did?

> **1 Corinthians 4:10**
> **We are fools for Christ's sake, but ye are wise in Christ; we are weak, but ye are strong; ye are honorable, but we are despised.**

Of course, once one is across that great divide and he receives the Holy Ghost, "old things are suddenly passed away" and that (which moments before may appeared to be foolishness) suddenly becomes a bubbling forth of "living waters," a praise song from the innermost foundation of our being. Jesus documented the validity of all this when He spoke of "rivers of living water" springing up "out of the belly." Many things in the Bible are symbolic and "belly" certainly points to the very center of our spiritual and worldly life. Where else then should we expect to feel these first stirrings of a NEW language crying out to be released and freed to praise the God who saved us?

Once you are over this hurdle, I can tell you firsthand that all of that which this writer is trying to convey makes perfect sense! However, BEFORE stepping across that line, it can be frightening, and it can be confusing. When we, for the first time in our lives, feel a compulsion to open our mouths and speak forth supposedly unintelligible phrases or sounds, the first rational inclination is to clamp our mouths shut so no one will suspect that there is something wrong with us. That of course, is precisely the wrong reaction!!

The Holy Ghost will not speak for you! When one is prayed for to receive the Holy Ghost, we must not fight God's leadings. If we will but yield our tongues to the leading and direction of the Holy Ghost, HE WILL SPEAK through us using OUR VOICE and give the utterance!!!! That has been the pattern since the Day of Pentecost, and it is the pattern for today!

The problem, of course, is that all too many Christians simply do not know how to **YIELD**. We are beset on all sides by worldly considerations. What will our neighbors think? What will the family think? What do I think? I know that the hardest person I faced right after I was baptized in the Spirit was my father who was a Southern Baptist preacher at the time. I had never heard one positive thing in our household about speaking in tongues or the baptism in the Holy Ghost!!

Speaking in tongues just does not seem to make sense to most people. When we read the Word of God however, we see that worldly wisdom is foolishness to God and Godly logic is foolishness to the world.

> **1 Corinthians 1:18-31**
> **For the preaching of the cross is to them that perish foolishness; but unto us which are saved it is the power of God. [19] For it is written, I will destroy the wisdom of the wise, and will bring to nothing the understanding of the prudent. [20] Where is the wise? where is the scribe? where is the disputer of this world? hath not God made foolish the wisdom of this world? [21] For after that in the wisdom of God the**

world by wisdom knew not God, it pleased God by the foolishness of preaching to save them that believe. [22] For the Jews require a sign, and the Greeks seek after wisdom: [23] But we preach Christ crucified, unto the Jews a stumblingblock, and unto the Greeks foolishness; [24] But unto them which are called, both Jews and Greeks, Christ the power of God, and the wisdom of God. [25] Because the foolishness of God is wiser than men; and the weakness of God is stronger than men. [26] For ye see your calling, brethren, how that not many wise men after the flesh, not many mighty, not many noble, are called: [27] But God hath chosen the foolish things of the world to confound the wise; and God hath chosen the weak things of the world to confound the things which are mighty; [28] And base things of the world, and things which are despised, hath God chosen, yea, and things which are not, to bring to nought things that are: [29] That no flesh should glory in his presence. [30] But of him are ye in Christ Jesus, who of God is made unto us wisdom, and righteousness, and sanctification, and redemption: [31] That, according as it is written, He that glorieth, let him glory in the Lord.**

The message of the Cross in general is foolishness to a world that perishes through its rejection of its power through unbelief! The tenet that the Holy Spirit cannot be divorced from the Cross, nor can the Cross be divorced from the Holy Ghost, is rejected on the same grounds! Sometimes however, in our Christian walk, there are times when we must just "LET GO AND LET GOD!" We must take a giant step of faith forward into the unknown, trusting God for the result before we can document the result based on our experience.

When Thomas stood before Jesus doubting the resurrection because he had not seen proof, Jesus said, "thrust your hand Thomas into My side and stop your DOUBTING!!!" Jesus responded to this event by telling Thomas that "blessed" are those who believe WITHOUT previous proof!

> **John 20:29**
> **Jesus saith unto him, Thomas, because thou hast seen me, thou hast believed: blessed are they that have not seen, and yet have believed.**

This is exactly the situation when God prompts us to open our mouths and VOICE the stirrings within us!

This is done by faith just as it was when we stepped out of our lives as sinners into the glorious liberty of Christ at conversion! The very moment a believer asks the Lord Jesus to fill him with the Holy Ghost, and he or she is sincere in heart, God's promises WILL work! Down inside there will be words or phrases or "sounds" that will start to form and seek expression. This is the Holy Ghost "giving the utterance!"

We are not in any shape or form telling you that an individual can stand in front of you and tell you what to say. Charismatics who do such stupid and foolish things hurt the cause of Christ and many times they add to the anxiety of the sincere seeker who is scared to death because of the horror stories the unbelieving tells them of such events.

The Charismatic world has done itself NO favors when it comes to this message of the Holy Ghost believe me. I am what you may call a Bapticostal, and in many ways, I am thankful for that. I do not buy into all the Charismatic foolishness no more than I buy into the denominational world's unbelief and hardness of heart in resisting and rejecting this glorious experience.

The baptism in the Holy Ghost is REAL, and it is for today, and you as a reader need to be filled with the Spirit with the evidence of speaking with other tongues! But that said, always remember that the Holy Ghost is, number one a gentleman, and number two He is God. As both, He will never lead the seeker of His power down a path of error, foolishness, or stupidity as I have witnessed in certain circles of the Charismatic camp the past 20 years.

I will say this; however, just because there are a few morons out there who do foolish things, we do not need to reject the Holy Ghost or blame Him for that!

When the Holy Spirit "gives the utterance," that is as far as He will go! From this point on, it is up to the believer! This is the point where YOU the sincere seeker must take over and do your part! It is up to YOU to part your lips, expel your breath, and VOICE the sounds crying out for expression within you! It will no doubt sound unlike anything you have ever heard before. It will no doubt sound different from what YOU expected it to sound like. Satan will no doubt intrude and say, "but surely this isn't the way it should sound!" IGNORE SATAN and IGNORE your own natural skepticism!

This IS the Holy Spirit giving the utterance. Just open your mouth and start to speak out and at that precise moment you will have received the Baptism in the Holy Ghost!

Many Christians who seek the baptism believe, erroneously, that there is some type of coercion or possession involved in speaking in tongues. They believe that some strange trance descends on the baptized Christian and he MUST bring forth the message stirring inside him, whether he wants to or not. This simply is NOT the case.

A Spirit-filled Christian always retains full control of ALL his faculties. God's Holy Spirit is the ultimate example of propriety, courtesy, and restraint. The Holy Spirit does not impose, He suggests. No leading of the Spirit will ever cause any Christian to do anything improper. By the same token, the Holy Ghost will never FORCE anyone to speak in tongues. ALWAYS, with no exceptions, this is under the control of the individual. Of course, the question then arises, "But if it is up to me to speak in tongues, then it will be me speaking in tongues and not of the Lord." What the believer must realize is this.

Who reaps the benefits of you speaking in tongues? The Lord's situation and the Lord's plans will proceed apace whether you speak in tongues or not. YOUR plans and situation, on the other hand, will be dramatically affected by your speaking in tongues. Let us look to Scripture to demonstrate what I am saying.

Acts 2:4 says, "And they were all filled with the Holy Ghost and began to speak with other tongues." Notice the pronoun "THEY" appears once, but only because the second writing of it would be redundant. The COMPLETE passage might read, "And they were filled with the Holy Ghost and **they** began to speak with other tongues."

Acts 2:4
And they were all filled with the Holy Ghost, and began to speak with other tongues, as the Spirit gave them utterance.

Notice that this passage does NOT say, "They were filled with the Holy Ghost and the Holy Ghost started to speak through them." It is quite clear THEY WERE FILLED, and THEY spoke with tongues.

The Spirit GAVE the utterance. They had to speak! Again, the important, critical point to remember is that the Spirit gives the utterance. He plants the "message" within the believer, but the believer does the speaking!

There is no place in the Bible where a single word expresses the thought that the Holy Spirit either speaks in tongues, or forces anyone else to.

In Acts 10:46 it says:

Acts 10:46
For they heard them speak with tongues and magnify God. Then answered Peter,

Peter heard "THEM" speak with tongues and magnify God! The "them" is the people in the house of Cornelius, not the Holy Ghost. The Holy Ghost was the source of the utterance when this glorious outpouring was first given to the Gentiles!

In Acts 19:6 we see a similar statement concerning the disciples upon the Ephesus coast:

Acts 19:6
And when Paul had laid his hands upon them, the Holy Ghost came on them; and they spake with tongues, and prophesied.

This issue of yielding is one of the greatest single hindrances to one receiving the Holy Ghost! We are not a spiritual robot with buttons that God pushes, and then we do certain things. He created us with a WILL that either obeys the Spirit of God or resists the Spirit of God. Some believe that the Spirit will take control of their tongue or put them into some type of "possession" or trance.

Possession is the domain of the devil! God respects our free will, even when it gets us into trouble! God does not overwhelm us with His power and "take over" our normal functions.

Many of you reading this journal WANT to be baptized in the Holy Ghost. Some of the frustration is that many do not realize that THEY are the ones who must OPEN their mouths and EXPRESS the utterance formed inside them by the Holy Ghost. We ask the Lord Jesus to baptize us, then we open our mouths as the Spirit of God gives the utterance!

Are you seeking the baptism in the Holy Ghost today?

How many times have you sensed God's presence? You WANT to be baptized in the Holy Ghost and sense God moving in your life. His presence has flooded and overflowed you. Deep down inside there were stirrings of words you did not recognize as English or any other language you have ever heard. If that is the case, then take the POSITIVE STEP of opening your mouth to "speak out" that which is inside.

As Jesus said, the baptism in the Holy Ghost is like "RIVERS OF LIVING WATER," that flow from your inner most being! Jesus should know because HE IS THE BAPTIZER IN THE HOLY GHOST!

The Holy Ghost is the one giving the utterance, YOU are the one who will do the speaking. To be frank, EVERY CHRISTIAN is ready to receive the baptism in the Holy Ghost. The only thing that hinders this glorious process is the reluctance, lack of awareness, or knowledge to go ahead and speak out what is bubbling up inside of them! God has given the promise neighbor, the SPIRIT will descend. Jesus is the baptizer and He WANTS you to have this.

Chapter Five

THE INITIAL EVIDENCE ONE HAS RECEIVED THE HOLY SPIRIT- PART ONE

TEXT: Acts 2:4– And they were all filled with the Holy Ghost, and began to speak with other tongues, as the Spirit gave them utterance.

As we continue our third installment in this series on the baptism in the Holy Ghost, let me lay a quick foundation of what our ministry believes concerning the infilling of the Spirit for believers AFTER they come to Christ at salvation:

- **We teach and believe FROM THE WORD OF GOD that speaking in tongues is a valid, scriptural expression given by the Holy Spirit. As such, it is relevant to the day and age we live.**
- We do NOT believe that speaking in tongues will automatically produce a better Christian.
- We do not believe or teach that anyone must speak in tongues to be saved or make heaven their eternal home.
- We do not believe or teach that anyone becomes more saved because of speaking in tongues. When a person accepts Christ as His Lord and Savior HE IS SAVED, period. Prayerfully however, this same believing sinner, who now is a believer in Christ, will GROW in his walk with the Lord, but at the moment of salvation he is as saved as he will ever be.
- We DO believe that speaking in tongues is ordained by God.
- We DO believe that it was a COMMON manifestation in the early church, and it is just as widespread and proper today as it was then. The reason for the lack of this manifestation in the church as recorded church history would indicate before 1903 is that the subject was NEVER PREACHED or TAUGHT on from behind

pulpits. After Azusa Street in Los Angeles, California in 1903, the Holy Ghost seemed to rev up His engine and started raising up SCORES of men of God who began to preach and teach on the baptism of the Holy Ghost. Men like Charles Spurgeon, Billy Sunday, and others, including the Wesley Brothers and George Whitfield had supernatural experiences in their Christian lives but did not have a name for it because prior to 1903 there was no name attached to these things. It is recorded history that Spurgeon moved in the prophetic many times in his meetings as well as people, that heard him during his personal prayer time pray in other tongues. Sounds like the baptism of the HOLY GHOST to me!!! Sounds like the Spirit of God made intercession for the saints through Charles Spurgeon and others and empowered them for service and for witnessing!

- We DO believe this a valid manifestation and demonstration of the INITIAL infilling with the Holy Ghost.
- We DO believe tongues are a great HELP to the believer, a giver of strength, and a BUILDER OF FAITH. (Jude 23-24, 1 Cor. 14:1-3)

1 Corinthians 14:4-10
He that speaketh in an unknown tongue edifies himself; but he that prophesies edifies the church.

Speaking in tongues is the initial physical evidence one has received the Baptism in the Holy Spirit! We feel confident in knowing that the Word of God teaches that the way one can be assured they have been baptized in the Holy Ghost is speaking with other tongues as the SPIRIT OF GOD gives the utterance!

Please understand we are not saying "tongues" are the ONLY evidence one is walking in a Spirit-filled manner; what we are saying is the INITIAL PHYSICAL EVIDENCE one has been baptized in the HOLY GHOST will be when that believer speaks with other tongues in a language other than their native one. The part of this that is key is simply this: "THE SPIRIT OF GOD GIVES THE UTTERANCE." This is nothing man can generate on his own other than lending a voice to the utterances of the Spirit in other languages; both heavenly and earthly.

One cannot say I have "joy" so that means I am Spirit-filled; one cannot say I am this or that or a myriad of other things and say that's how I know I've been filled with the Spirit.

The ONE WAY one can know for sure they have experienced the baptism in the Holy Ghost is by what took place with individuals who were baptized in the Holy Ghost according to the book of Acts. They spoke with tongues as the Spirit of God gave them the utterance.

There are **FIVE** separate incidents in the book of Acts which describe individuals being baptized in the Holy Ghost that cover a period of over 20 years.

There is a lengthy dissertation on the Holy Spirit through Paul that he penned in the 14th chapter of 1 Corinthians concerning the spiritual "GIFT" of tongues and interpretation of those tongues used in utterances to the corporate body. Some of what the Holy Spirit had Paul write in 1 Corinthians also holds instructions for the individual believer who has received the Baptism in the Holy Ghost and now has a prayer language they can sing and pray with in the Spirit.

Acts 2:4
And they were all filled with the Holy Ghost, and began to speak with other tongues, as the Spirit gave them utterance.

This verse states that, "And they were ALL filled with the Holy Ghost and began to speak with other tongues as the Spirit of God gave them utterance." This needs no further explanation. it is clear, concise and to the point. As the late Donald Gee once wrote, *"a large part of the distinctive witness of the Pentecostal revival today is that the supernatural STILL accompanies the Christian gospel."*

When the Holy Spirit came at Pentecost, there were supernatural events taking place! The SAME SPIRIT that came at Pentecost is HERE TODAY friend, so common sense would tell us that He has not stopped producing SUPERNATURAL results NOW, despite the clamor from some camps that "All of this went away with the apostles."

These critics are hard-pressed to find New Testament grounds for these theories mind you, yet they scream them anyway from behind pulpits and the unbelieving masses in the church clamor after them with glee.

I can assure you today that despite this clamoring unbelief, we are going to preach and teach the mighty baptism of the Holy Ghost with the evidence of speaking with other tongues as the Spirit of God gives the utterance! We are going to cry out to God for another Pentecost that will shake us to our core and bring us to our knees in intercession and prayer! **No true message of the gospel is ever be void of the power of God.**

We preach CHRIST CRUCIFIED and because we preach Christ Crucified, we also preach the POWER of His resurrection and the power of the HOLY GHOST!

The evidence that those gathered at Pentecost were filled is stated WITHOUT debate. **"They began to speak with other TONGUES as the SPIRIT OF GOD gave them the utterance."**

> Acts 8:16-23
> (For as yet he was fallen <u>upon</u> none of them: only they were baptized in the name of the Lord Jesus.) [17] Then laid they their hands on them, and they received the Holy Ghost. [18] And when Simon saw that through laying on of the apostles' hands the Holy Ghost was given, he offered them money, [19] Saying, Give me also this power, that on whomsoever I lay hands, he may receive the Holy Ghost. [20] But Peter said unto him, Thy money perish with thee, because thou hast thought that the gift of God may be purchased with money. [21] Thou hast neither part nor lot in this matter: for thy heart is not right in the sight of God. [22] Repent therefore of this thy wickedness, and pray God, if perhaps the thought of thine heart may be forgiven thee. [23] For I perceive that thou art in the gall of bitterness, and in the bond of iniquity.

In the 8th Chapter of Acts, we read of a tremendous revival that took place under the ministry of Philip. Souls were saved, miracles occurred, and they were baptized in water "in the name of the Lord Jesus." They were "born again" just as Jesus said in John 3:3-8.

The Spirit of God came inside to dwell these Samaritan believers JUST as He comes inside any New Covenant believer today. This event took place AFTER the Cross, which as we have stated numerous times was the earmark event that made it possible for the Holy Ghost to dwell in man and man to become a habitation of God through His Spirit.

> **Ephesians 2:22**
> **In whom ye also are builded together for an habitation of God through the Spirit.**

After this great revival, Peter and John came from Jerusalem and prayed for the Samaritans to **receive the Holy Spirit**. We have established the fact that the baptism in the Holy Ghost is a separate and distinct work of grace AFTER salvation.

Luke records what took place in verses 16-23 by stating that the Holy Ghost "had not 'fallen' upon them i.e. they had not been baptized in the Holy Ghost but they HAD BEEN SAVED and Baptized in WATER in the name of the Lord Jesus. The term "upon" is the same term used in Acts 1:8 that describes what will happen when the Holy Ghost will come UPON any believer who asks and seeks His help and power:

> **Acts 1:8**
> **But ye shall receive power, after that the Holy Ghost is come upon you: and ye shall be witnesses unto me both in Jerusalem, and in all Judaea, and in Samaria, and unto the uttermost part of the earth.**

While Luke said nothing about the Samaritans speaking in tongues, he did state in verse 18 and 19 that Simon the Sorcerer SAW that through the laying on of apostles' hands, the Holy Ghost was given, and as a result, he offered Peter and John money so that he might also have this **power** that HE might lay his hands on people so that they would receive the Holy Spirit.

It seems obvious to any normal minded person that this greedy individual would not offer money if there had not been some **tangible manifestation of results** that day when Peter and John laid hands on those who had believed Philip's preaching and had been born again. If the laying of hands had no VISIBLE and AUDIBLE results following it, why would he offer to pay the apostles for their "secret?" Peter's rebuke gives us insight that something happened when he said, "YOU HAVE NO PART NOR LOT IN THIS MATTER," meaning "Simon, what you are witnessing is SUPERNATURAL and of God, not men!"

> Acts 4:21-23
> <u>Thou hast neither part nor lot in this matter: for thy heart is not right in the sight of God.</u> [22] Repent therefore of this thy wickedness, and pray God, if perhaps the thought of thine heart may be forgiven thee. [23] For I perceive that thou art in the gall of bitterness, and in the bond of iniquity.

The logical conclusion one can easily draw if one is honestly seeking truth as to what took place in Samaria is that those Peter and John prayed for, "spoke with other tongues as the Spirit of God gave them utterance," just as they did on the Day of Pentecost!

> Acts 9:17
> And Ananias went his way, and entered into the house; and putting his hands on him said, Brother Saul, the Lord, even Jesus, that appeared unto thee in the way as thou camest, hath sent me, that thou mightest receive thy sight, and be filled with the Holy Ghost.

A third occurrence where tongues were involved after someone received the Holy Ghost was what took place when Saul of Tarsus, the killer of Christians, became Paul, and in time one of the greatest apostles who ever lived.

Saul was saved on the road to Damascus when the bright light of the Lord's glory shone around him and he was blinded by its radiance. The Lord spoke to a man named Ananias to go find Paul in a 'street called straight' and lay hands on him that he might "receive his sight and be filled with the Holy Ghost."

We read in Acts 9:17 that when Ananias obeyed the Lord and put his hands-on Saul, Saul was filled with the Holy Ghost. Again, it does not specifically state in this passage that Paul spoke with tongues when this occurred.

HOWEVER, based upon what we read about what happened in Samaria and on the Day of Pentecost, we can conclude that it was at this point that Paul DID speak in tongues because he would write later in his first letter to the Corinthians, "I speak with tongues MORE THAN YE ALL."

1 Corinthians 14:18
I thank my God, I speak with tongues more than ye all:

That leaves the reader NO DOUBT as to whether Paul was Pentecostal or not. I heard the other day one Baptist radio preacher in our fair city proclaim glibly that his church was opposed to ALL manifestations of the Holy Ghost including and especially, speaking in tongues, which he of course labeled as being of Satan. He went on to state that "even if the Apostle Paul came into our meetings speaking in tongues, we would kick him out." I heard chuckles in the background when he said this, so I am sure his people glibly went along with this unbelieving preacher's view of Scripture.

Friend, Paul received this tremendous gift which would enable Him to write 3/4 of the BIBLE we read today! The HOLY GHOST power of Pentecost is what birthed the Scriptures we read and call the INSPIRED WORD OF GOD!

I would love to look this brother in the eye and ask him, "would you really kick the man who wrote 3/4ths of the Bible out of your church because he spoke with tongues?"

We have no problem when these same preachers embrace the seed of Satan that comes into their churches through this ungodly entertainment we call "Christian Rock" and they do not stand up and call it for what it is; EVIL, WICKED, SINFUL, DARKNESS, FULL OF THE DEVIL, and anything you want to add to that list you can. But they seem to find so much courage to stand up against those who speak in tongues and are filled with the Holy Ghost.

Paul spoke with tongues as the Spirit of God gave him the utterance, and Jesus through the Spirit of God, is STILL giving those who are hungry for more of Him those same utterances today! Jesus is the Baptizer in the Holy Ghost!

> **Acts 10:44**
> **While Peter yet spake these words, the Holy Ghost fell on all them which heard the word.**

The Bible describes, in the 10th chapter of Acts, the circumstances of what took place when the Holy Spirit fell upon the household of Cornelius under the preaching of the Apostle Peter.

The Bible says that the Jewish brethren were astonished because "on the Gentiles was also poured out the GIFT of the HOLY GHOST." It then says in the 46th verse, which is one of the most interesting to this writer in all the book of Acts:

Acts 10:46
For they heard them speak with tongues and magnify God. Then answered Peter,

The reason those with Peter were astonished was because they heard them SPEAK with tongues and MAGNIFY God! **The Holy Spirit left NO ROOM for debate or question as to how Peter and those with him KNEW Cornelius's house had received the Holy Ghost.** Incidentally, this took place nearly 20 years after Pentecost.

As Peter was preaching, Cornelius and his household got saved and were filled almost instantaneously with the Spirit AND SPOKE WITH TONGUES as a VISIBLE initial sign they had been empowered as prophetic witnesses to the gospel. The tongues were not a sign that they had gotten saved but were a sign they had been baptized with the Holy Ghost "as they were on the Day of Pentecost."

Acts 10:47
Can any man forbid water, that these should not be baptized, <u>which have received the Holy Ghost as well as we</u> (speaking of those with Peter who had been part of the 120 on the Day of Pentecost)?

This same empowering is available to ALL today who will hear and believe the word of God as Cornelius did.

I have an extraordinarily strong feeling that Peter's message was not one laced with unbelief or questioned as to whether tongues were "for now," or whether they had passed away at Pentecost. Had the modern church structure been in place THEN as it is today, Peter may not have even been allowed to preach Pentecost, or even to go to Cornelius' house. He would have told Cornelius he needed to have psychological counseling for denying Christ.

Cornelius experienced the grace of the Spirit by being born again, and because of that, he and his household received the baptism OF the Spirit. This event was important to MOST of us reading this journal today for it was here that the outward sign of tongues confirmed **that God had accepted and equipped the Gentiles for service.**

Peter did not explicitly mention tongues in his message but without a doubt they were alluded to in his message concerning Pentecost!

> **Acts 11:15-18**
> **And as I began to speak, the Holy Ghost fell on them, as on us at the beginning. [16] Then remembered I the word of the Lord, how that he said, John indeed baptized with water; but ye shall be baptized with the Holy Ghost. [17] Forasmuch then as God gave <u>them the like gift as he did unto us, who believed on the Lord Jesus Christ;</u> what was I, that I could withstand God? [18] When they heard these things, they held their peace, and glorified God, saying, Then hath God also to the Gentiles granted repentance unto life.**

Acts 10:47
Can any man forbid water, that these should not be baptized, which have received the Holy Ghost as well as we?

Peter's defense of what took place at Cornelius' house is our defense today for the fact that the **INITIAL physical evidence of the baptism in the Holy Ghost is speaking with other tongues as the spirit of God gives the utterance.**

As Peter retold the Gentile Pentecost, he stressed the similarity between the outpouring of the Spirit in Caesarea and IN Jerusalem, as well as repeating the promise of Jesus who uttered it many times:

Acts 11:15
And as I began to speak, the Holy Ghost fell on them, <u>as on us at the beginning</u>.

Acts 11:17
Forasmuch then as God gave them the like gift as he did unto us, who believed on the Lord Jesus Christ; what was I, that I could withstand God?

Acts 11:16
Then remembered I the word of the Lord, how that he said, John indeed baptized with water; but ye shall be baptized with the Holy Ghost.

Peter asked a question that this writer asks the modern church, "who or what was I, that I could withstand God?"

WHO AND WHAT ARE WE today that we think we can withstand God on this matter of the Baptism of the Holy Ghost? Modern preachers think "well I just will not preach about it or talk about it to my people and nothing will happen."

Guess what? They are RIGHT!!! NOTHING WILL HAPPEN IN THEIR CHURCHES AND NOTHING DOES HAPPEN. If a mouse squeaks, half the congregation dies of a heart attack for the noise. I remember hearing the late R.W. Schambach once say that *"people are scared to praise God because they think God is deaf."* He then said, *"God isn't nervous either."*

Despite this modern resistance, God is raising up a generation of HOLY GHOST filled preachers, many of them young men for sure. There are also a few of us old folks who have been set aside for many years in the wilderness getting our hearts right and our heads on straight for this last battle for the hearts and soul of a generation before Jesus comes back. For those who will but hear what the Word of God is saying on these matters and simply believe, they are going to see mighty things in these last days prior to the Rapture of the Church.

You ask, "well, what's going to happen to those who resist this message of God's power?" I cannot say and will not say for sure, but as Peter's question insinuates, "are we stupid enough to withstand God?"

Stephen asked the religious of Israel, "How long do you resist the Holy Ghost, you stubborn and stiff-necked?"

> **Acts 7:51**
> **Ye stiffnecked and uncircumcised in heart and ears, ye do always resist the Holy Ghost: as your fathers did, so do ye.**

Let the reader be clear on this all-important point about what took place at Cornelius' house and the Day of Pentecost:

Speaking in tongues was the important link in this affirmation since the Spirit had also likewise manifested himself earlier. NO VALID ARGUMENT could be made against what happened either at Pentecost or at the house of Cornelius!

The experience of tongues was evidence that Cornelius and his friends were IMMERSED, FILLED, and BAPTIZED, IN THE HOLY GHOST and more importantly this tremendous gift was now available to not just Jewish believers, but to Gentile believers as well! Hearing of what happened, the critics stopped their criticism!

I wish things were that simple in modern times. Despite the fact that untold SCORES of MILLIONS of born-again believers have been gloriously baptized in the Holy Ghost with the evidence of speaking with other tongues, there are SCORES of voices behind pulpits who criticize, lampoon, make fun of, mock, and deny that the baptism in the Holy Spirit is a valid part of the Christian experience and walk with God. Some are seriously seeking what God has for them but because of the lack of preaching, they are somewhat in the dark or as some would say, ignorant of the subject. God has patience beyond what we mere mortals have, and He gives great space to those who are seeking and are not yet totally versed in all things spiritual.

There are two types of ignorance. One is seeking, without proper knowledge. There is another type of ignorance that is more deadly, and it is more prevalent in the modern church that is choking out the power of God from our churches and lives today. It is called WILLFUL ignorance.

The term ignorance itself means to "ignore" that which is before one to either believe or not believe. What is before us is the TRUTH! We have the Word of God. It is what Paul alluded to in the book of Acts when he rebuked the idolatry in Athens:

> **Acts 17:31-32**
> **Truly, these times of ignorance God overlooked, but now commands all men everywhere to repent; because He has appointed a day on which He will judge the world in righteousness by the Man whom He has ordained. He has given assurance of this to all by raising Him from the dead." And when they heard of the resurrection of the dead, some mocked, while others said, "We will hear you again on this *matter*."**

The patience of God runs deep for the seeking heart and He will understand those who are truly trying to understand His Word.

What God does not do however is wink at or condone WILLFUL ignorance where there is no hunger to know the truth of His Word. It is an arrogance that declares that man knows more than God and that he can sit on the fence wondering if he needs to believe in His power or not.

Without the Holy Spirit working in our churches friend there is no Church! There is no conviction, no healing, no deliverance, no true worship, no revelation, no doctrine, no prophecy, NOTHING!

The Purpose Driven Life and other self- help manuals have replaced the Bible in most churches. Millions of Christians gleefully cheer the type message Joel Osteen and other self-help gurus preach to stadiums, and then by extension, millions more on television. This is one reason why the mainstream media embraces these ministers and holds them up to the nation as shining examples of "faith," when in fact they are shining examples of false doctrine and error!! When the world embraces your message friend, you are not preaching the right message! When the world applauds you, heaven turns it back. When heaven applauds you, the world will hate you. The world loves its own and hates those who are not of it.

The lack of the Holy Spirit and His power is why the church sinks into apostasy. It is headstrong and it does not even blink an eye by accepting false doctrine and courting the powers of darkness. It is why we invite so-called Christian "rock" bands into our church and pay them money to perform for our youth in hoes of "getting" the young people out to our church. Let this writer make it clear, man of God, that your job is NOT to get the young people out to your church, but to preach this mighty gospel under the anointing and infilling power and grace of the HOLY GHOST where conviction is so strong in your church that people feel like they are hanging over hell on a broken stick!

If the Holy Ghost could come into our churches as He so desperately wants to, NONE OF THAT WOULD GO ON WITHOUT even a mention or the mere prick of our conscience! Individuals living in sin, while professing they know Christ, would come under so much conviction, would either leave our churches or they would find an altar and REPENT!

Mock the Holy Ghost pastor all you want to. Mock the Holy Ghost all you want to unbeliever. Mock the Holy Ghost all you want to teacher. Mock the Holy Ghost all you want to church leader and denominational head. Make fun of us who speak in tongues as the Spirit of God gives the utterance. Make fun of all this as jibber-jabber, some of you call "just unknown gibberish," as I heard one ignorant individual tell me the other day on how she viewed tongues, or "the rantings of the mentally disturbed," as I read on one Independent Baptist website just a little over a month ago.

Friend, if the power of God that sets the captive free and gives us a prayer language that produce rantings of the mentally disturbed, I want to be as disturbed as possible. You see, Satan knows that when we pray in tongues, this power rips the powers of HIS kingdom to shreds and it tears town strongholds from out of the heavenlies through the power and unction of the Holy Ghost!

These "fundamentalists" who attack this are bound with the same powers of darkness that the enemy knows are broken through the power of Holy Ghost praying and preaching. Some of these fundamentalists are just "mentalists" themselves and quite frankly, they need to get saved.

Church leaders who fight against the Holy Spirit need to do some **SOUL SEARCHING and then BIBLE SEARCHING to allow the HOLY GHOST to reveal TRUTH to them in the most powerful and earnest of ways.**

Sit back and grit your teeth and say "he's just way off base and in error" if you want to. I am not writing from a book here friend. I have ONE book open at the present time; THE WORD OF ALMIGHTY GOD and I am giving you what it has to say in various passages concerning this great outpouring of the Holy Ghost and why the evidence of tongues is so vitally important to the live and walk of the believer in Christ!

> **Acts 19:1-6**
> **And it came to pass, that, while Apollos was at Corinth, Paul having passed through the upper coasts came to Ephesus: and finding certain disciples, He said unto them, Have ye received the Holy Ghost since ye believed? And they said unto him, We have not so much as heard whether there be any Holy Ghost. And he said unto them, Unto what then were ye baptized? And they said, Unto John's baptism. Then said Paul, John verily baptized with the baptism of repentance, saying unto the people, that they should believe on him which should come after him, that is, on Christ Jesus. When they heard *this*, they were baptized in the name of the Lord Jesus. And when Paul had laid *his* hands upon them, the Holy Ghost came on them; and they spoke with tongues, and prophesied. And when Paul had laid his hands upon them, the Holy Ghost came on them; and they spake with tongues, and prophesied.**

The final passage in Acts that shows tongues are a sign that one has been baptized in the Spirit as found in Acts 19 where Paul came upon the disciples he found in the upper coasts of Ephesus and asked them "Have you received the Holy Spirit since you believed?"

In the original language, this is literally "having believed, did you receive." These men were already saved because they were called "disciples." Every time the word "Disciples" is used in the Book of Acts, it refers to individuals who have accepted Christ. Paul could tell that these individuals, although Saved, had not yet been baptized with the Holy Spirit.

When they said "we have not as much as heard whether be any Holy Spirit, "it did not mean that they did not know of the existence of the Holy Spirit, but they were not aware that the Age of

The Spirit had come, and that Believers could literally be baptized with Him. At Salvation, the Holy Spirit baptizes believing sinners into Christ. At the Spirit baptism, Jesus baptizes Believers in the Holy Ghost!

> **Matthew 3:11**
> **I indeed baptize you with water unto repentance: but he that cometh after me is mightier than I, whose shoes I am not worthy to bear: he shall baptize you with the Holy Ghost, and *with* fire:**

When Paul explained this to these men, he laid his hands on them in verse 6, and the Holy Spirit came upon them just as He did in Acts 8:17, 9:17-18, and for the fifth time in Acts, it confirmed the fact that the initial physical evidence that one has been Baptized with the Holy Spirit is speaking with other tongues. Sometimes there is prophecy at the same time and sometimes there is not. There will ALWAYS be the initial evidence of speaking in tongues!!

In the Mouth of Two Witnesses

> **Deuteronomy 19:15**
> **One witness shall not rise up against a man for any iniquity, or for any sin, in any sin that he sinneth: at the mouth of two witnesses, or at the mouth of three witnesses, shall the matter be established.**

In the Old Covenant the book of Deuteronomy declares that in the mouth of two or at three witnesses ALL matters shall be established.

In the case of tongues as recorded in the Book of Acts, we see tongues mentioned directly in THREE of the FIVE passages where it is confirmed that when it involves the infilling of the Holy Spirit, it says that they SPOKE WITH OTHER TONGUES as the SPIRIT OF GOD gave the utterance!

Even in the two cases of Acts 8 and 9 where there was no direct mention of tongues, it was STRONGLY implied this is what took place, especially in the case of Paul who later wrote he "spoke in tongues more than ye all!"

The issue in this lesson and journal is that any honest seeker after the truth, and upon studying the WORD OF GOD in this regard, he will come to the conclusion that SOMETHING happened when these individuals were filled with the Holy Ghost. That "something" was that they SPOKE WITH TONGUES as the Spirit of God gave them the utterance!!

Just because something is not mentioned, as with the case of tongues and the Samaritans, Theologian Stanley Horton makes a wonderful point when he says,

> *"Luke often did not explain everything when it was clear elsewhere in his accounts; For example, he does not mention water baptism every time he tells about people believing or being added to the Church, but it is clear that the failure to mention this is not significant nor does it mean it didn't take place each time someone got saved and came into the church; for this reason we can say that the fact Luke does not mention speaking in tongues with the Samaritans is not that significant and certainly does not imply they did not speak with other tongues as Peter and John came down and laid their hands on them."*

In the three accounts in Acts where the baptism of the Spirit is mentioned, the terms "they spoke," are uniform. In Ephesians 5:18-19 the command to "speak" to ourselves is also tied into the command to be "continually filled with the Spirit!"

- Acts 2:4–""they.... began to <u>speak</u>."
- Acts 10:46–"they heard…them <u>speak</u>."
- Acts 19:6–"they <u>spake</u>."
- Ephesians 5:18-19–"<u>SPEAKING</u> TO YOURSELVES."

Ephesians 5:18-19
And be not drunk with wine, wherein is excess; but be filled with the Spirit; [19] Speaking to yourselves in psalms and hymns and <u>spiritual</u> songs, singing and making melody in your heart to the Lord;

I mention Ephesians 5:18-19 because this is the passage where we are COMMANDED to be filled with the Spirit. Even the COMMAND from the Holy Ghost through Paul in Ephesians carries connotations of SPEAKING to ourselves IN THE SPIRIT and WITH OUR OWN UNDERSTANDING!

When we say we "pray in the Spirit," or "sing in the Spirit," we mean we pray or sing with other tongues **as the SPIRIT OF GOD GIVES THE UTTERANCE!**

There are times I also sing and pray with my own understanding as well. This is a matter we will take up in the next installment of this lesson series.

Without argument, bottom line is that the INITIAL PHYSICAL EVIDENCE THAT ONE HAS BEEN BAPTIZED IN THE HOLY

GHOST is the fact that they will speak with other tongues as the Spirit of God gives the utterance!

Some try and tie the baptism in the Spirit into the graces of the Fruit of the Spirit saying that the initial evidence that one has been filled is that they develop better character. That "new character" should **already** be taking place through the manifestation of the Born-Again experience in Christ! When we are saved, CHRIST is formed IN US through the power of His Spirit.

The FRUIT of the Spirit and the manifestation of the Spirit's POWER are two totally different distinct operations of God. The fruit of the Spirit is the proof of our walking in the Spirit, as ALL Born again believers should do; be they spirit filled or not. It is NOT the proof of the baptism in the Holy Ghost! Fruit always takes time to grow. The divinely appointed proof of the coming of the COMFORTER can be and **IS GIVEN instantly! (GEE)**

We never read in the New Testament, NEVER, that they put Cornelius or others on any type probation for a time to see by their lives whether they had received the Holy Ghost!!

Rather, His Coming was something to which God gave witness **instantly and convincingly.** <u>**God's DIVINELY CHOSEN SIGN OF THE COMING OF THE HOLY GHOST IN THE LIFE AND HEART OF THE SEEKING BELIEVER IS A SUPERNATURAL MANIFESTATION GIVEN AT THE MOMENT; none other than SPEAKING WITH OTHER TONGUES AS THE SPIRIT OF GOD GIVES THE UTTERANCE.**</u>

Yet They Would Not Hear

> Isaiah 28:11-12
> **For with stammering lips and another tongue will he speak to this people. [12] To whom he said, <u>This</u> is the rest wherewith ye may cause the weary to rest; and this is the refreshing: yet they would not hear.**

> Acts 2:4
> **And they were all filled with the Holy Ghost, and began to speak with other tongues, as the Spirit gave them utterance.**

Of all the things that took place on the original Pentecost, the final choice of the HOLY GHOST both THEN and NOW, was then and is now, speaking with new tongues as the Spirit of God gives the utterance.

God has chosen it for HIS SIGN and we as believers would be wise to ACCEPT it HUMBLY and CHEERFULLY!

Isaiah the prophet prophesied that it would be a sign to unbelieving Israel that it would be the REST and REFRESHING to those who would heed and listen, but for all of this, ISRAEL would not hear, and the modern church for all this IS NOT hearing today but rejecting this very message I speak of!

> Isaiah 28:11-12
> **For with stammering lips and another tongue will he speak to this people. [12] To whom he said, <u>This</u> is the rest wherewith ye may cause the weary to rest; and this is the refreshing: yet they would not hear.**

The condition of being filled with the SPIRIT is recognizable and AUDIBLE! We cannot receive this experience and not know it.

I want to state that again. One cannot be baptized in the Holy Ghost and not be sure that they have received this gift or not. If you spoke with other tongues as the Spirit of God gave the utterance, FRIEND YOU HAVE BEEN FILLED! If you have not spoken with other tongues, then friend, you have NOT BEEN FILLED with the Spirit according to what the Bible declares.

I know there is strong disagreement on this point. Some teach (and I heard a well-meaning man of God say this just a few weeks back), that the sign one is spirit-filled is that we become "witnesses," of Jesus. That is true, but it is not the INITIAL physical evidence that the people received in the book of Acts when they got baptized in the Holy Ghost.

It does not say when the day of Pentecost was come, they began to "be witnesses."

NO! It says they "began to SPEAK with other tongues as the Spirit of God gave them the utterance!"

Some say the sign one has been filled is joy and cheerfulness. That may be one of many other signs one is WALKING in the Fullness of the Spirit of God without a doubt, but neighbor, it is not the INITIAL physical evidence on has been baptized in the Holy Ghost!

There was joy in Samaria BEFORE Peter and John ever showed up at the preaching of Philip. If joy was all that was required to be filled with the Spirit, Peter and John wasted their trip from

Jerusalem to come there, and it was not a short trip in those days. NO! Again, laying hands on the Samaritans was not for them to receive more joy but for them to receive the infilling of the Holy Spirit accompanied by speaking with other tongues as the Spirit of God gave them the utterance.

Going back to the Samaritan revival, one of the Southern Baptist's leading commentators, F.F. Bruce, agrees with Horton's assessment of the Samaritan revival:

> *"The context leaves us in NO DOUBT that their reception of the Spirit was attended by EXTERNAL manifestations such as had marked His descent on the earliest disciples at Pentecost."*

Mr. Bruce, if you were still alive today, I would shake your hand, friend and ask you to visit about 99% of the denominational churches in this city and nation and, to be frank, repeat what you just said. The revival at Samaria **was** marked by supernatural manifestations that marked the Spirit's FIRST descent at Pentecost; the main one being "and they began to speak with other tongues as the Spirit of God gave them the utterance."

> **Acts 2:4**
> **And they were all filled with the Holy Ghost, and began to speak with other tongues, as the Spirit gave them utterance.**

Isaiah the prophet sadly declared the end that yet through ALL of this "yet they would not hear." Paul restated this in his declaration to the Corinthian Church in 1 Corinthians 14 tying the 8th and 9th gifts of the Spirit into the prophecy of Isaiah!

Being Filled with The Spirit is Vital to Church Leadership

Acts 6:3-5
Wherefore, brethren, look ye out among you seven men of honest report, <u>full of the Holy Ghost</u> and wisdom, whom we may appoint over this business. [4] But we will give ourselves continually to prayer, and to the ministry of the word

We established quite clearly in this series of study that we do not in any way, shape, form, or fashion, believe or teach that one must speak in tongues to be saved. HOWEVER, when one IS saved, we have established the fact also that we believe the Word of God CLEARLY teaches that those who ask the Lord to fill them with His Spirit will speak with other tongues as the Spirit of God gives them the utterance! This is not given in some abstract place in Scripture. It is ALL over the New Covenant.

The apostles told the Jerusalem church to select seven men "of honest report, full of the Holy Ghost," a condition that had to have been easily detectable among the early apostles! How could they have picked them out if they had not known who was filled?

Sadly, the church world today does not make being full of the Holy Ghost a requirement any longer for people to be in leadership! That is why church pulpit committees many times bring in hirelings instead of shepherds. That is why pastors go out and pick demon-inspired worship leaders instead of SPIRIT-FILLED worship leaders to lead their church, because we do not make being spirit-filled a priority!

NEIGHBOR, the church needs to get back to the power and moving of the HOLY GHOST!

The Evidence of Tongues

> Acts 2:7-11
> **And they were all amazed and marveled, saying one to another, Behold, are not all these which speak Galileans? [8] And how hear we every man in our own tongue, wherein we were born? [9] Parthians, and Medes, and Elamites, and the dwellers in Mesopotamia, and in Judaea, and Cappadocia, in Pontus, and Asia, [10] Phrygia, and Pamphylia, in Egypt, and in the parts of Libya about Cyrene, and strangers of Rome, Jews and proselytes, [11] Cretes and Arabians, <u>we do hear them speak in our tongues the wonderful works of God</u>.**

What is behind this tremendous gift of tongues one receives when they are baptized in the Holy Ghost?

Some speak despairingly of this great gift by saying it is nothing more than babble, chatter, or incoherent jabbering. However, one should be careful, and I mean VERY careful in saying anything about the Holy Ghost!

The very fact that each time the term "and they spoke with tongues as the SPIRIT OF GOD gave the utterance," should give us pause right there to know that the SPIRIT OF GOD is the one doing the talking through the individual who is speaking! The individual is lending their voice yes, but the SPIRIT OF GOD IS DOING THE TALKING!! For that reason, we can easily conclude that speaking in other tongues is **not** gibberish, jabber, babble, or incoherent prattle as some misguided individuals declare.

Speaking in tongues is generally a language spoken SOMEWHERE in the world and known by some people in the world OR in heaven! These are both earthly and heavenly languages.

I want to say that again. Speaking in tongues as we just stated, are tongues spoken by the Spirit of God and are generally a language spoken SOMEWHERE in the world and known by some people in the world OR they are known in heaven but they are not the original dialect of the one doing the talking!

We are given insight in the 2nd chapter of Acts that there were devout men from every nation under heaven and this, of course, referred to the world known in those days. It says they had come together and were confounded because, "how hear we every man in our own TONGUE, wherein we were born?" It then goes on to list the people who were there. This included:

- **Parthians**
- **Medes**
- **Elamites**
- **At Least 13 Additional Nationalities**

Yet, ALL these disparate people in that day said, "We do hear them speak in our tongues the wonderful works of God!"

Now these individuals gathered on the of Pentecost (the 120) were NOT preaching to these people to become saved. They were merely praising the Lord in other tongues and speaking a language they had not learned. Some skeptics have tried in vain to explain away as it was some language the 120 just learned in the natural. In other words, according to those who are wrong in their thinking, they had suddenly become linguists and were praising God in languages other than Aramaic, Hebrews, or Greek which were the common local tongues. **THIS IS NOT TRUE!** These were uneducated Galileans who were NOT students of languages. They were fishermen in most cases.

Even the Pharisees and Sadducees who would later try to kill them for their message and testimony of Christ declared them to be "unlearned and uneducated men," yet they knew they had been with Jesus! Oh, Praise the Lord!

> **Acts 4:13**
> **Now when they saw the boldness of Peter and John, and perceived that they <u>were unlearned and ignorant men</u>, they marveled; and they took knowledge of them, that they had been with Jesus.**

Of course, this is the way it ALWAYS is when individuals speak in tongues. There are hundreds and perhaps THOUSANDS of languages and dialects in this world, and many of them sound very strange to our ears. They are not strange however, to the people who routinely converse in them. So, it is NOT just jabber, gibberish, chatter, or idle babble. It is always a Language that is spoken supernaturally by the believer and understood somewhere in this world, but NOT spoken and understood by the individual who has been filled with the Holy Ghost.

Another tactic of skeptics is to use this supernatural gift to say that when missionaries go to school and learn other languages, the Holy Spirit fills them with these new languages through education and that is what "speaking in other tongues," really means in Scripture. That is absurd and again it is the rantings and ravings of the unbelieving, not the heartfelt knowledge of the honest seeker of truth!

Let the reader beware that there is SO much out there that is stated in the negative about the baptism in the Holy Ghost that it is not remotely funny in the least, but it is very sad.

If one will notice, whenever it was time to preach to these people about the Lord Jesus Christ and give an invitation to be saved, guess what, SIMON PETER DID NOT CONTINUE SPEAKING IN OTHER TONGUES, but he preached in the common language of the day, which was either Aramaic or Hebrew.

> **Acts 2:14**
> **But Peter, standing up with the eleven, lifted up his voice, and said unto them, Ye men of Judaea, and all ye that dwell at Jerusalem, be this known unto you, and hearken to my words:**

Of course, ALL those present understood. It is easy to see how so many people could know the Hebrew language being Jews themselves and it was the language of the country in which they resided. This is common among many people today. And it is also possible that SOME of the 120 had learned more than one language, BUT the LANGUAGE they spoke as they were baptized in the Holy Ghost was NOT a language that was known to them. It was a SUPERNATURAL UTTERANCE, given by the HOLY GHOST, which always accompanies this glorious baptism of power! Tongues refers then to languages known either on this earth or in heaven.

Tongues of Men and Of Angels

> 1 Corinthians 13:1
> Though I speak with the tongues of men and of angels, and have not charity, I am become as sounding brass, or a tinkling cymbal.

In 1 Corinthians 13:1, Paul speaks of tongues of men and of **angels**, which in essence describes other tongues on which he gives an extensive dissertation later in the 14th chapter. This dissertation deals with both CORPORATE and INDIVIDUAL tongues or as one commentator put it; "DEVOTIONAL" and "CORPORATE" tongues.

One is for the individual believer; the other is for corporate worship services. Let the reader be sure he/she does not confuse the two, for many do, and they get all sorts of confused theology in their brain as a result.

Many times, Paul addressed tongues in what seems to be a negative way, but he was merely addressing the abuses of tongues in PUBLIC worship, not private devotion! One big thing we will briefly mention is the role of the interpreter when one is speaking with other tongues.

If one is in private devotion or praising God in tongues as unto the Lord, they do not need an interpreter present to do so!!

I never will forget my brother telling me of a recent evangelistic crusade he attended when the evangelist spoke in tongues during the message when a person behind him started speaking out "well my Bible tells me he needs an interpreter to be doing that." NO, he did not need an interpreter for that! If he were addressing the crowd with a MESSAGE in tongues, which is the "GIFT OF TONGUES and INTERPRETATION," as recorded in 1 Corinthians 12, THEN the role of the interpreter would have been an issue.

For the evangelist to be preaching and just start praising God in tongues, there was no need for an interpreter. The praise he was given was between him and God. The LORD knew exactly what He was saying and there was probably a small chance that someone in the audience could have been present who understood that language he was speaking and understood it. My brother did not' indicate anything like that took place but I have seen that and been part of such an experience.

In 1994 I was privileged to host a Spanish speaking exchange student who was not saved but went to church with me one Sunday. One morning our pastor got up and did basically the same thing that this brother did at the crusade my brother spoke of. He praised God in tongues. No one in the audience said a word. They just joined with him in praising God as well. Our guest however, sat on the back row of that church that morning and began to weep as the Spirit of God dealt with her heart through what our pastor spoke while speaking in tongues.

She came to me later that day crying and said, "the man with the Bible in his hand up front this morning said to me "Praise the Lord Jesus Christ, Who IS The Only God and Lord of all " and kept repeating it in Spanish–how did he know Spanish?" It shook her up so badly that she wound up in tears. Our family told her about Jesus that day and planted a seed. She would not give her heart to the Lord then, and I have not heard from her since she left in early 1995 to go back home to Spain, but we can only pray that the seed that was planted on that Sunday morning BY A MAN OF GOD obeying the Spirit of God and speaking in a tongue not known to him, but known to a Spanish exchange student from Barcelona visiting a church for the **first time, will spring forth one day before it's too late and she will come to Christ and become a light to nation bound by the powers of darkness!**

That is why, neighbor this is important what I write to you about today.

That, sadly, is the state of mind of MILLIONS of disengaged Christians from the realities of the Word of God and what it says on this matter.

I am giving scripture references left and right in this lesson series, but I encourage you to study this out for yourself if you do not feel that you can believe what I am writing. READ THE BOOK for yourself and hear what the Spirit of God says about this!

Stop listening to unbelieving preachers who sadly, themselves, plainly need to get saved to begin with!

On a humorous note, my brother said it took everything in him not to turn around and say, "Lady, here is the interpretation of that message" and let her know in no uncertain terms how she needed to get her heart right with God. Of course, he said the Holy Ghost in him said "NO, let ME deal with her, not you."

There are times when people speak in tongues that are heavenly languages that are not known on this earth. Paul used the term "tongues of angels," which gives weight to that thought. Either way, whether it be tongues of men or tongues of angels, ALL utterances given to the believer as a result of being baptized in the Spirit are given by the SPIRIT Himself and they always "glorify God," and magnify His wondrous works!

> **Acts 2:11**
> **Cretes and Arabians, we do hear them speak in our tongues the wonderful works of God.**

Why Tongues?

As we close this current lesson of this series, let me take a brief look at why the Lord choses "tongues" for the sign one has been filled with His Spirit.

God has certainly good reasons for doing ALL the things He has done over the millennia, and the same is true in this matter. One must remember that what took place at Pentecost was prophesied by both JOEL and ISAIAH.

Joel prophesied the outpouring and Isaiah prophesied that through TONGUES the Lord would speak to His people and that men would "with stammering lips and unknown tongue," speak to nations!

> **Isaiah 28:11-12**
> **For with stammering lips and another tongue will he speak to this people. [12] To whom he said, This is the rest wherewith ye may cause the weary to rest; and this is the refreshing: yet they would not hear.**

1 Corinthians 14:21
In the law it is written (referring to Isaiah 28:11-12), With men of other tongues and other lips will I speak unto this people; and yet for all that will they not hear me, saith the Lord.

Isaiah went on to add that even though the Lord would arrange this mighty sign, **men would not listen to Him**, which is a terrible indictment against the human race even today. It was an indictment against the nation of Israel in Isaiah's day, and it is an indictment against the apostate church today!

Following are some of the reasons on what the Word of God says are reasons why God chose speaking in tongues as the INITIAL sign pointing to one who has been baptized in the Holy Spirit:

- **Supernatural**–First it is ALWAYS a supernatural utterance that takes place when a person is baptized in the Holy Ghost. It must be exercised by FAITH, but it not of the individual's doing; it comes from the Lord Jesus Christ and was promised long ago as Isaiah who pointed to its tremendous importance.
- **Given by God**–Careful reading of 1 Corinthians 14:21 and Isaiah 28:11-12 would infer that when men speak with other tongues it is actually GOD speaking THROUGH them to the people. When something is given by God Himself friend, we would be rather wise not to reject what He is offering for in rejecting His gift, we are rejecting HIM! The church world says, "Oh, we want God to be part of our religious activity," but in the same breath it rejects the gift of the Holy Spirit. God will not set aside His programs for our carnal, selfish, and unbelieving hearts. We either take

ALL that He has to offer, or we take NONE of what He has to offer, plain and simple.
- **Universal**–This is a single evidence the world over; it is not one evidence for one country and something else for another as again some foolishly insist. It is the same evidence everywhere. It was the same evidence in the New Testament days as it is today. It is the same in England as it is here in America and vice versa.
- **Instantaneous**–The MOMENT the baptism of the Holy Spirit comes to the individual, he starts to speak with other tongues. It happens that same way with everyone. It is not something that involves an interaction with other individuals. It is STRICTLY a personal experience with GOD and the individual! And when it occurs, you do not need an interpreter around to tell you what you are saying as some foolishly insist either. Once you are baptized in the Holy Ghost, the Spirit of God may choose to use you in a deeper way through corporate utterances that WILL require you pray for and seek after an interpretation; but praising God and receiving the initial infilling of the Spirit have nothing to do with corporate utterances. These are two different types of tongues. One is devotional and the other is corporate. We believe that the Word of God clearly establishes the fact that tongues take place the MOMENT the baptism in the Spirit occurs in the heart and life of the believer.
- **The Tongue Is A Most Unruly Member** – James tells us that of all the members of our body the tongue is the hardest to tame! When God sanctifies our tongue neighbor, He has sanctified us! When the Holy Ghost is in control of the tongue, we will use our tongues for the blessing of others, not the cursing of others! (James 3)

In Summary

Once again, to make these points as clear as we can make them: at salvation, the believing sinner is influenced by the Holy Ghost through the Spirit's work of conviction. When the sinner is saved, the Holy Ghost takes up permanent residence in that person's heart and life as one is BORN of the Spirit.

Yes, the Spirit of God indwells us at salvation but without the believer moving on to the baptism of the Holy Ghost, the Spirit of God at salvation becomes stagnant and many times He is hindered to do any more. After Salvation when we are endued with power for service, He is released in our heart and lives to do what is necessary to make us witnesses for CHRIST!

Salvation and the baptism in the Holy Ghost are two separate and distinct experiences FOR TODAY. They are different to source, time, and nature. One must be saved FIRST, THEN that one can experience the mighty baptism in the Holy Ghost.

We are told by the Spirit of God to be "FILLED with the Holy Ghost," and filled we must be. You cannot fill a bottle or well that is already full! That should tell us that believers are not automatically "filled" with the Spirit at salvation but are commanded to be so AFTER they get saved.

Friend, we all need the baptism in the Holy Ghost today!

HE (JESUS) will baptize you with the Holy Ghost and with FIRE! He so wants you to ASK Him to do that today. For those who have been filled and need a fresh touch from heaven, He wants to RE-FILL those who need a refreshing.

Isaiah called it just that; "a refreshing" and a "rest," of which He will cause the weary to rest.

It's a GRAND and GLORIOUS feeling as the old gospel says and neighbor, this writer is not ashamed to lay his heart out before you and tell you The Holy Ghost is REAL and this experience is REAL and it is for YOU today! I leave you with the words of a precious song that has been ringing in my heart for weeks:

He will fill your hearts today with overflowing
Bring your vessels not a few, As the Lord commanded you
He will fill your hearts today with overflowing
With the Holy Ghost and Fire

Chapter Six

AS THE SPIRIT OF GOD GIVES THE UTTERANCE

TEXT: Acts 2:1-4–And when the day of Pentecost was fully come, they were all with one accord in one place. [2] And suddenly there came a sound from heaven as of a rushing mighty wind, and it filled all the house where they were sitting. [3] And there appeared unto them cloven tongues like as of fire, and it sat upon each of them. [4] And they were all filled with the Holy Ghost, and began to speak with other tongues, as the Spirit gave them utterance.

What took place on the Jewish Feast of Pentecost is what must take place today in the modern church!

The Feast of Pentecost is a day that commemorates the giving of the Law by God to Moses on Mt. Sinai. It also commemorates the day Holy Spirit fell upon 120 men and women gathered on the Jewish Temple Square in Jerusalem as recorded in the Book of Acts. This event ushered in the Church Age with a dynamic that was unknown to man up to that time. That unknown was speaking with other tongues as the Spirit of God gave the utterance as well as, the Holy Spirit is now LIVING inside the redeemed. This was something that He could not do with those under the Law!

What took place on the Day of Pentecost has challenged religious spirits in every movement and entire denominations ever since. Remember this friend. True Christianity is more than just a formal exercise of ritual and ceremony. It is more than just attending a local church, singing in the choir, teaching Sunday School, or even preaching a sermon, as wonderful and honorable as all of that is.

True Christianity does not reside in a building, but in the hearts and souls of every true born-again child of God, who have come to faith in Christ by placing that faith in what He did for us at the

Cross. All must come to Him through the work of the convicting power of the Holy Spirit. It is of utmost importance the Holy Spirit does the convicting and the bringing, not man!

Many have had emotional experiences and they have thought that those experiences in and of themselves have "saved" them. Many go to the altar under a cloud of guilt, shake a preacher's hand, sign a church pledge card, join a denomination, and do all sorts of other religious activity. Others have confessed their sins to a priest thinking that by doing so to another man in authority that this somehow "saves" them. NONE of these things have ever saved a single soul, and none of these things ever will!

We must be BORN AGAIN as Jesus said in John 3. He must become LORD of our lives in totality and not just in a religious way where we remain living to ourselves and not unto God!

Once we are saved however, the work of the Holy Spirit does not cease or stop. His work is just beginning! The next step, after salvation, according to the Word of God is for every believer is to be baptized in the Holy Ghost with the evidence of speaking with other tongues.

Speaking in tongues is the most talked about phenomena in Christianity today. The Pentecostal and Charismatic movements have brought speaking in tongues to the forefront and they have made these movements some of the fastest growing movements worldwide since the turn of the Century. Simply put, the Pentecostal movement is by far the largest, and most important religious movement to originate in the United States.

Recent studies indicate that nearly 35% of ALL those who profess Christ as Savior have been gloriously baptized in the Holy Spirit after salvation, with the evidence of speaking with other tongues. Some believe that these movements that were birthed in the fire of the Spirit have impacted the world far greater than the Reformation did.

This has taken place even though these same movements are facing the greatest persecution and ridicule. This goes back to the days of Azusa Street. Sadly, much of this persecution has come from mainline Christian denominations that refuse to believe in the baptism in the Holy Ghost as a Biblical experience and that it is one for today. Instead of embracing what the Word of God says about tongues, these same unbelieving movements have declared all-out war on those who believe and teach the Baptism in the Holy Spirit.

Dr. Vinson Synan, who this writer met once in person in the early 1990s, was a pioneer of the Holy Ghost movement that touched America. He rightly points out in a great deal of his writings, that the original theology that produced the foundation for the Azusa Street outpouring, was not set forth by a Pentecostal, but by the founder of the United Methodist Church, John Wesley.

From John Wesley, the Pentecostals inherited the idea of a subsequent crisis experience called "entire sanctification, "perfect love," "Christian perfection," or "heart purity." It was John Wesley who posited such a possibility in his influential tract, "**A Plain Account of Christian Perfection**" (1766).

It was from Wesley that the Holiness Movement developed the theology of a "second blessing." However, it was Wesley's colleague, John Fletcher, who first called this second blessing a "baptism in the Holy Spirit;" an experience which brought spiritual power to the recipient as well as inner cleansing. This was explained in his major work, "**Checks to Antinomianism**." (1771).

At least three movements, the Methodist/Holiness movement, the Catholic Apostolic movement of Edward Irving, and the British Keswick "Higher Life" movement prepared the way for what appeared to be a spontaneous outpouring of the Holy Spirit in America.

Perhaps the most important immediate precursor to Pentecostalism was the Holiness movement which issued from the heart of Methodism at the end of the Nineteenth Century. During the Nineteenth Century, thousands of Methodists claimed to receive this experience, although at the time, no one saw any connection with this spirituality and speaking in tongues or any of the other charismas.

Then beginning in 1901, with only a handful of students in a Bible School in Topeka, Kansas, the number of Pentecostals increased steadily throughout the world during the Twentieth Century throughout the mid-1990s and became the largest family of Protestants in the world.

This destroys the smug and arrogant attitudes and feeling held by some that tongues began with a few ignorant and uneducated few in America who had mental problems. John Wesley did not have mental problems. He founded the United Methodist Church, one of the most powerful denominations in America. And to just clarify for the spiritually ignorant, He founded the UMC with a Holy Ghost anointing that set this nation's soul on fire in the late 1800s and early 1900s. We need that fire to be rekindled in this hour!

However, as silence regarding spiritual gifts has descended across pulpits in America, very few understand the operation and ministry of the Spirit regarding tongues in these modern times. Other than the Second Coming of Christ, most people desire to know more about the subject of tongues than any other subject in the Bible.

If speaking in tongues was even mentioned once in the Word of God, it would be an important subject to discuss and understand. However, the Bible mentions speaking in tongues thirty-five times, including the words of Jesus Himself, who promised that it would be one of the signs that would follow those who believed in Him. He said, "they would speak with new tongues."

That did not and still does not mean that speaking in tongues is requirement for salvation. However, tongues are a sign to those who come to Christ in faith, and upon asking, are filled with the Spirit of God.

> **Mark 16:17-18**
> **And these signs shall follow them that believe; In my name shall they cast out devils; they shall speak with new tongues; [18] They shall take up serpents; and if they drink any deadly thing, it shall not hurt them; they shall lay hands on the sick, and they shall recover.**

Many of the "newer" translations are literally taking this verse out of the context of Scripture. Some translations already have tried to remove the idea that the valuable part of the New Testament believer's walk is being baptized in the Holy Ghost with the evidence of speaking with other tongues. These SIGNS shall follow them which believe; they shall speak with new tongues. Those are the words of Jesus, not man!

It boggles this writer's mind that so-called educated men with doctorate degrees can take an eraser and erase the thoughts of God as if man has a supposed, yet misguided, superior knowledge as to what God is saying. God calls man's wisdom "foolishness," and as Paul said in 1 Corinthians, the "foolishness" of God is always going to be WISER than men. The greatest of man's wisdom pales in comparison to the foolishness of God.

Some call speaking in tongues, "foolish," yet God uses it to destroy the wisdom of men! Oh, Glory to God! I feel a shout coming on!

Mockers hear this writer. Call those of us who speak in tongues ignorant, demonic, backwoods, and uneducated if you like; mock, make fun, twist scripture and the truth to your own peril; laugh, lampoon and snicker at all of which I speak. Your problem is the sin of unbelief, plain and simple.

These mockings and false twisting of scripture are a compliment coming from most, who if pressed, probably could not even tell you why they do not believe in tongues other than, "I heard my pastor say this," or "I heard a relative say that."

Years ago, in a small Bible study that I was leading at a local homeless ministry, there was a lady in the crowd who smirked and mocked what I speak of, saying, "I watched 'The Exorcist' and the demon possessed girl spoke in tongues; I guess that means speaking in tongues is evil." I could somewhat understand this poor individual's ignorance because she was not saved. What I could NOT understand was that the leader of this ministry who was hosting the Bible study agreed with this woman by laughing at what she said. Incidentally, I was asked, not so nicely, to leave a few weeks after this.

I would rather be looked on as foolish and be called names while knowing that I know I am born again and FILLED with the HOLY GHOST! If speaking in tongues is PART of "God's FOOLISHNESS," then please sign me up.

> **1 Corinthians 1:25**
> **Because the foolishness of God is wiser than men; and the weakness of God is stronger than men.**

There are many modern ministers who constantly brag of their education yet deny everything supernatural they can at every given moment they can. They are worse than the Pharisees of Jesus' day who later said the same of Peter and John after they had come from the fresh encounter with the Holy Ghost on the Day of Pentecost. These religious leaders mocked the outpouring of the Spirit calling Peter and John "unlearned," and "ignorant." They may have been, but one thing is for certain, they also could not deny this fact and stated such in saying, "they had been with Jesus!"

> **Acts 4:13**
> **Now when they saw the boldness of Peter and John, and perceived that they were unlearned and ignorant men, they marveled; and they took knowledge of them, that they had been with Jesus.**

Salvation is God's greatest gift to the world through the shed blood of the Lord Jesus Christ. The Baptism in the Holy Spirit is God's greatest gift to His children, the Church.

The Baptism in the Holy Ghost might be also and properly be called the Baptism of POWER and as such, this experience is an invaluable asset to the Christian committed to seeking the furtherance of God's plan for the world.

To state it again so as to be clear, you do not have to speak in tongues to be saved; this experience is for those already saved and wanting to do more for the Kingdom of God than just sit on their thumbs and go through the motions of religion, week in and week out. We need to be more worried that people know we have been with Jesus than worry about whether they mock us and call us unlearned and ignorant.

I know what it is like to feel the presence of Almighty God flow over me like a river. I know what it feels like to have His glory touch me in such a way that I have not been able to do anything but lay flat on my face and just weep without being able to say a word. I know what it feels like to speak in tongues to the point I must go down to my knees under the power and weight of God's Glory.

I am NOT ASHAMED OF THE HOLY GHOST. I AM NOT ASHAMED TO STAND UP AND FIGHT FOR THE TRUTH OF THIS. I am not ashamed to take to task the denominational world, especially the Southern and Independent Baptists for their unbelieving, hard-hearted, rejecting attitudes that deny the power of God, JUST AS THE PHARISEES OF OLD DID.

Some reading this may not agree or have experienced what this writer is talking about. Some may not even want to experience what I am talking about nor do they care one iota about anything that is spiritual.

Let me warn you however, that to continue the insidious doctrine and theology that those who speak in tongues are demon possessed is to stand on dangerous grounds in heaven.

A few years ago, a well-known late evangelical leader who was President of one of the biggest Baptist theological seminaries in America died just four months after he had stated such doctrine in a morning college devotional service. In addition, this same leader kicked four students out of his seminary when he found out that they had spoken in tongues. I am not going to question his salvation, but I will tell you this. Wherever he is in eternity, he learned quickly that tongues were not of Satan, but of God!

There are many like him who are going to be held accountable before Almighty God one day for what they have taught and stated to others as "Scripture."

The Apostle Peter said men "wrestle" with the scriptures to their own destruction; and sadly, many are doing that even today. This attitude comes from a religious spirit that seeks to oppose the Spirit of Truth and that which is of God.

I have felt the sting personally through the years of what it is like to come up against this spirit and attitude and it is not pretty. It hurts to hear someone who claims they are saved verbally espouse such stupidity and do it gleefully and cheerfully mocking not only the experience, but equating those who do with drug pushers, alcoholics, and whoremongers.

Neighbor, one is treading on DANGEROUS grounds and he needs to understand that he is precariously close to BLASPHEMING THE HOLY GHOST when he says things like "tongues are of Satan," and "those who speak in tongues are demonic."

If that is the case, then Paul was demonic; Peter was demonic; John was demonic; Mary the Mother of Jesus was demonic; Luke was demonic; Matthew was demonic; Mark was demonic; James was demonic! Are you hearing me neighbor? Are you hearing me so-called preacher of the gospel?

I would rather go home to South Georgia, and stand in the middle of the barn of my late grandfather's house and listen to donkeys' bray in the middle of a hot South Georgia summer day, than to hear some of the stupidity and moronic chatter that comes from the mouths of those who claim to be so educated theologically, yet they have a heart so full of unbelief and arrogance when it comes to the power of God that it would choke those donkeys.

We believe every Christian who receives the Baptism in the Holy Ghost speaks in other tongues AS THE SPIRIT OF GOD GIVES THE UTTERANCE. We believe speaking in tongues is the INITIAL physical evidence that one HAS received the Holy Ghost. It is certainly not the ONLY evidence, but we believe it is the INITIAL evidence.

It is sad that the church rejects this teaching as being from Satan yet embraces the myriad of human and even demonic fads that are sweeping the church, and it says those are of God. I hear such things like this all the time: "they are just so uplifting and encouraging" and this and that, and this and that, ad nauseum." I do not care how uplifting something is in the natural; if it is not birthed by the Spirit of God, it will do the hearer and the one embracing such foolishness absolutely NO GOOD! IT IS DEATH, and it will KILL people if it is not produced by the Spirit of God.

Churches embrace these fads like candy in a candy shop, then have convulsions when the matter of tongues are brought up among their midst. God help us.

We are not serving or worshipping new age gurus parading as spiritual leaders. We are not worshipping as 12-step program or the local rehab center's technique. We are worshipping the Risen Christ, the Lamb of Glory, the Baptizer in the HOLY GHOST with Fire.

> Luke 3:16-17
> **John answered, saying unto them all, I indeed baptize you with water; but one mightier than I cometh, the latchet of whose shoes I am not worthy to unloose: he shall baptize you with the Holy Ghost and with fire: [17] Whose fan is in his hand, and he will thoroughly purge his floor, and will gather the wheat into his garner; but the chaff he will burn with fire unquenchable.**

Sending a Christian into the world without the Holy Spirit is like sending a soldier into battle without a weapon!

When a person is saved, he becomes a Christian just as a person becomes a soldier the moment he is sworn into a military Army. But in the Army or any other branch of the military, the inductee is not ready for battle until he has basic training and has been issued his weapons. The Christian is in the same condition at the time of salvation. If he is not encouraged to receive the baptism in the Holy Ghost that prepares him for the ever-coming and the ever-continuing battle against Satan, he is being sent out into a battlefield WOEFULLY unprepared.

We were told recently by someone they did not "need to speak in tongues to pray," brushing aside the importance of this great experience available to ALL who will believe. This individual made the experience of tongues to be no more than "gibberish, and babble," as they put it by saying, "the only people I know who speak in tongues are speaking in tongues one minute and smoking crack the next."

I am sure the Holy Spirit was incredibly pleased with this individual insinuating that all those who spoke in tongues are no better than a person who smokes crack.

Folks like this will not believe, even if someone came back from the dead and told them otherwise.

These type of individuals usually quote one or two scriptures and twist them in a negative way to make it seem like the Bible discourages speaking in tongues when in fact, there are THIRTY-FIVE verses and passages of Scripture, both in the OLD and the NEW Covenant, relating to this great experience!

If you do not understand the ministry of tongues, it is best to keep your mouth shut about it and simply acknowledge your ignorance before the Lord. He has a way of answering those who humbly admit they do not know everything there is to know about certain doctrinal issues. They do not want to find themselves fighting something that is of God by labeling it of Satan or lumping those who speak in tongues into a group, as this individual did, with those who are not even saved, and basically insinuating a correlation between those who speak in tongues and those with serious spiritual and mental problems.

I am here to declare to you that MILLIONS have been gloriously baptized in the Holy Ghost and they are not crack addicts, prostitutes, whoremongers, or any other type of emotionally disturbed people.

These millions include MANY in the early Church who were present on the day of Pentecost including PETER, John, James, Luke, and Mary the Mother of Jesus. Later, the Apostle Paul received this glorious experience after the Lord sent Ananias to him to lay his hands on him to "receive his sight and receive the Holy Spirit."

He did not lay his hands on the Apostle to be saved; that had already taken place on the Road to Damascus. Paul received the baptism in the Holy Ghost with the evidence of speaking with other tongues AS THE SPIRIT OF GOD GAVE THE UTTERANCE.

> **Acts 2:4**
> **And they were all filled with the Holy Ghost and spoke with tongues as the Spirit of God gave the utterance.**

Paul under the inspiration of the Holy Ghost in 1 Corinthians said, "if any man wishes to be ignorant (speaking of spiritual gifts and in the 14th chapter he as addressing tongues and prophecy), LET HIM BE IGNORANT!"

This subject should not be cast lightly aside as unimportant to the Church. God does not fill His book with things of minor importance. Many people who have never spoken in tongues speak as though they are experts in this field, when, they teach only from theory and from their own bias and unbelief AND NOT from Scripture.

Let us look at some general questions about speaking in tongues and why the utterance the Holy Spirit gives those who are baptized in Spirit is important!

What Good Is Tongues?

The Apostle Paul writes, "He who speaks in tongues edifies himself...I would like every one of you to speak in tongues" (1 Corinthians 14:4,5). With these positive statement about tongues, the question must be asked, "why do so few Christians speak in tongues?" I believe the answer is because there is little sound, logical, and scriptural teaching as to the scope and value of speaking in tongues.

Recently I spoke to a group of widows of deceased veterans and shared my testimony on how God saved and filled me with the Holy Spirit with the evidence of speaking in tongues. After the talk, the number one question that most of the group asked was on speaking in tongues. One inquisitive student asked, "What does speaking in tongues do for you?" I answered, "It does exactly what the Bible says it does: He who speaks in tongues edifies himself."

The word "edify" means to "build up" or "charge up," much like charging up a battery. We all need a spiritual charge. All of us at times feel spiritually drained. One of God's ways to charge your spirit is through speaking in tongues.

This charging up is spoken of in Jude saying that it "build up our most holy faith," through praying 'in the Holy Ghost. Paul said in Romans that the SPIRIT HELPS us to pray with "groanings and moanings that cannot be understood." This intercession is according to the WILL OF GOD!

> **Jude 1:20-21**
> **But ye, beloved, building up yourselves on your most holy faith, praying in the Holy Ghost, [21] Keep yourselves in the love of God, looking for the mercy of our Lord Jesus Christ unto eternal life.**

> **Romans 8:26-27**
> **Likewise, the Spirit also helpeth our infirmities: for we know not what we should pray for as we ought: but the Spirit itself makes intercession for us with groanings which cannot be uttered. [27] And he that searches the hearts knoweth what is the mind of the Spirit because he makes intercession for the saints according to the will of God.**

Many people inaccurately define speaking in tongues as "speaking gibberish" or "talking nonsense." The truth is, speaking in tongues is the most intelligent, perfect language in the universe. It is God's language.

What language do you suppose people speak in heaven?

Languages are given their name based on the countries they come from. For example, English comes from England. Spanish comes from Spain. Italian comes from Italy.

Well, where do tongues come from? Well they come from Heaven! Tongues are both an earthly and a heavenly language. Regardless of the source, these are languages of what is spoken in heaven!! The only difference is that the people in heaven understand what they are saying. Here on earth Paul says, "For anyone who speaks in tongues does not speak to men but to God. Indeed, no one understand him; he utters mysteries with his spirit" (1 Corinthians 14:2).

1 Corinthians 14:2
For he that speaketh in an unknown tongue speaketh not unto men, but unto God: for no man understandeth him; howbeit in the spirit he speaketh mysteries.

The Rev. Tom Brown of El Paso, Texas, made this statement about tongues which I say a hearty "Amen" to:

> *"Jesus says that those who believe in Him will "speak in new tongues" (Mark 16:17). The word "new" means appearing for the first time. No one had spoken these languages before. Contrary to bad theology tongues is not an ability given to preach the gospel in the language of foreigners. This would make tongues 'old' languages. It is only appropriate that 'new tongues' should be spoken by those of the "new birth." It is natural and normal to speak in the language of your birth. We are born again from above, therefore we should speak the language from above—that language is called 'new tongues.'"*

> **Mark 16:17**
> **And these signs shall follow them that believe; In my name shall they cast out devils; they shall speak with new tongues;**

It is God's wish and command that EVERY Christian should be filled with the Holy Spirit.

Therefore, anyone working against this infilling, whether consciously or through erroneous doctrine, is in effect working at cross purposes to the will of God! We are in such desperate need of what the Lord Jesus Christ spoke of through Luke in Acts 1:8 when He said, "you shall receive POWER after that the HOLY GHOST comes upon you!"

> **Acts 1:8**
> **But ye shall receive power, after that the Holy Ghost is come upon you: and ye shall be witnesses unto me both in Jerusalem, and in all Judaea, and in Samaria, and unto the uttermost part of the earth.**

We need the POWER of the Holy Ghost if we are to work effectively against the forces of darkness of the enemy.

Anyone hindering the Christian in any way, as he enters this battle, is tacitly working FOR Satan, even though he might be appalled at the thought of doing so.

If one will think of what Jesus said they will see too that the promise in Acts 1:8 was in context a part of the LAST message Jesus preached to His disciples before He was taken away.

> Acts 1:4-9
> **And, being assembled together with them, commanded them that they should not depart from Jerusalem, but wait for the promise of the Father, which, saith he, ye have heard of me. [5] For John truly baptized with water; but ye shall be baptized with the Holy Ghost not many days hence. [6] When they therefore were come together, they asked of him, saying, Lord, wilt thou at this time restore again the kingdom to Israel? [7] And he said unto them, It is not for you to know the times or the seasons, which the Father hath put in his own power. [8] But ye shall receive power, after that the Holy Ghost is come upon you: and ye shall be witnesses unto me both in Jerusalem, and in all Judaea, and in Samaria, and unto the uttermost part of the earth. [9] And when he had spoken these things, while they beheld, he was taken up; and a cloud received him out of their sight.**

Why would this be His last message to His chosen followers?

The Lord was leaving the earth. His lifetime of work completed. He was about to depart for Heaven where He would remain for about 20 centuries! This would be the last time He would be physically present to advise His disciples and other followers. This unique situation stamps His words with unusual importance. He might have spoken of prophecy, salvation, worship, and a myriad of other things but He mentioned NONE of these things. Being God, who knew and knows everything, He told them they should attempt NOTHING concerning the salvation of the world, until they would receive the PROMISE of the Father.

Acts 1:4
And, being assembled together with them, commanded them that they should not depart from Jerusalem, but wait for the promise of the Father, which, saith he, ye have heard of me.

In view of the dramatic circumstances surrounding this pronouncement, we can assume that EVERY word contained within these verses, was among the most important ever uttered by our Lord and Master.

Salvation equips us to enter the presence of God after mortal life is over. The baptism in the Holy Ghost equips us to live faithfully (and happily) during those years BEFORE we go to be with God. To willingly eschew this God-given assistance, is to HANDICAP at best, ourselves, and those we may teach and preach to, throughout our Christian lifetime.

Yet despite clear scriptural guidelines and TRUTH that the Bible lays out for those willing to take the time to study, great controversy swirls about the Baptism in the Holy Ghost with the evidence of speaking with other tongues. It is not surprising, perhaps, that this should be so. Satan hates with all his being, seeing individuals and churches transformed and set on fire by the filling of the Holy Spirit and revival. It is not surprising that he would promote doctrines that suggest this phenomenon "is not for today." Believe me, if the devil had his way and say, it would not have been for ANY day.

But SCRIPTURE DOES NOT AGREE with what Satan tries to promote through those controlled by the spirit of his false doctrines.

Misguided Christians who even ADMIT tongues were an evidence of the Baptism in the Holy Ghost during the apostolic days, say, "It ended when the last apostle died, this isn't for today."

My response to that is simply this–did the HOLY SPIRIT end His ministry to believers when the last apostle died?" Of course not. It is absurd for one to remotely believe such foolishness. It is just as absurd to take this ministry that was foretold by the prophets to take place from the Holy Spirit coming at Pentecost and going all the way through the Great Tribulation period and Israel's travail in returning to Christ and say it all ended 2,000 years ago when there is NOT ONE SINGLE SOLITARY SCRIPTURE to back such claim up! NOT ONE!

> **Joel 2:28-29**
> **And it shall come to pass afterward, that I will pour out my spirit upon all flesh; and your sons and your daughters shall prophesy, your old men shall dream dreams, your young men shall see visions: [29] And also upon the servants and upon the handmaids in those days will I pour out my spirit.**
>
> **Isaiah 28:11-12**
> **For with stammering lips and another tongue will he speak to this people. [12] To whom he said, This is the rest wherewith ye may cause the weary to rest; and this is the refreshing: yet they would not hear.**

Through Joel, Almighty God SPOKE about a great outpouring of His Spirit "upon ALL flesh," which was quoted by Peter during His great sermon at Pentecost:

> Acts 2:17-21
> **And it shall come to pass in the last days, saith God, I will pour out of my Spirit upon all flesh: and your sons and your daughters shall prophesy, and your young men shall see visions, and your old men shall dream dreams: [18] And on my servants and on my handmaidens I will pour out in those days of my Spirit; and they shall prophesy: [19] And I will show wonders in heaven above, and signs in the earth beneath; blood, and fire, and vapor of smoke: [20] The sun shall be turned into darkness, and the moon into blood, before that great and notable day of the Lord come: [21] And it shall come to pass, that whosoever shall call on the name of the Lord shall be saved.**

The Father further confirms this again in Acts 2:38-39.

> Acts 2:38-39
> **Then Peter said unto them, Repent, and be baptized every one of you in the name of Jesus Christ for the remission of sins, and ye shall receive the gift of the Holy Ghost. [39] For the promise is unto you, and to your children, and to all that are afar off, even as many as the Lord our God shall call.**

What promise was Peter referring to? He was referring to the PROMISE OF JOEL 2:28-29 and that which he had spoken under the Spirit's unction and anointing in Acts 2:17-21.

Peter said that this glorious power would be for YOU (those living in Jerusalem at the time), and to your children (generations that would follow), and to ALL that are afar off (MEANING THE GENTILES which includes every single one reading this journal), and as MANY as the Lord our God shall call!

If you have been born again then you have been called and you are a candidate to receive the mighty baptism of the Holy Ghost!

This does NOT sound like an offer with an expiration date stamped on it! Why does Satan fight so hard to discredit the Baptism? Sadly, because the enemy knows far better than most Christians know, the frustration that he faces when the mighty Holy Ghost power falls upon a group of ineffectual, Christ-denying "churches. These same places are suddenly turned into bastions of POWER for the Lord and they shake the gates of hell to its core when they see souls saved, believers delivered, sick bodies healed, and demonic bondages BROKEN, all by the power of God. Weak and frightened Christians become raging lions for the cause of Christ. People who could not be persuaded to tell others about their Savior are now suddenly turned into powerful Holy Ghost fire filled witnesses. Backsliding Christians suddenly straighten out their lives and become examples of righteous Christian living! This does not take place because of man-made fads or slick written books detailing how we can grow our churches through slick marketing schemes! This comes because of HOLY GHOST POWER that is available to ALL those who will but believe and receive!

As far as the church is concerned, the HOLY SPIRIT is the single most important factor in the world today. WITHOUT HIM, the church becomes nothing more than what is has become today; a marketing scheme that circumvents the Cross and the power of the Holy Ghost. With the HOLY GHOST, we become effective, dedicated, productive cross-bearers for Christ!

The Utterance of Tongues

This writer wants to make two things crystal clear again.

One, speaking in tongues is NOT a requirement for one to be saved; we're not saved because we speak in tongues, but because we've placed our faith in the blood of the Lord Jesus Christ and have repented of our sins. Our faith must be in His Finished work on the Cross, plain and simple!

Secondly, and this is just as important to understand. Speaking in tongues is NOT in itself an experience that is an end all to all spiritual experiences and encounters with God. This is not going to zap one into spiritual maturity.

What IS important is YIELDING our most unruly member, the tongue, to the control of God's Spirit.

I heard someone say the other day that the hardest things the Holy Spirit deals with in controlling us as believers is our tongues and our wallets! This individual is correct on both counts. James, the half-brother of Jesus, had a lot to say about the tongue is his epistle.

> **James 3:1-8**
> **My brethren, be not many masters, knowing that we shall receive the greater condemnation. [2] For in many things we offend all. If any man offends not in word, the same is a perfect man, and able also to bridle the whole body. [3] Behold, we put bits in the horses' mouths, that they may obey us; and we turn about their whole body. [4] Behold also the ships, which though they be so great, and are driven of fierce winds, yet are they turned about with a small helm, whithersoever the governor listeth. [5] Even so the tongue is a little member, and boasteth great things. Behold, how great a matter a little fire kindle's! [6] And the tongue is a fire, a world of iniquity: so is the tongue among our members, that it defiles the whole**

> body, and setteth on fire the course of nature; and it is set on fire of hell. [7] For every kind of beasts, and of birds, and of serpents, and of things in the sea, is tamed, and hath been tamed of mankind: [8] But the tongue can no man tame; it is an unruly evil, full of deadly poison.

It is remarkably like salvation. The act of PUBLICLY confessing our acceptance of Christ by walking forward to an altar, accomplishes nothing by itself.

One must be BORN AGAIN by the Spirit of God to be saved. We are not saved because we come down to the altar, shake a preacher's hand, and sign a membership pledge card as so many sadly think. However, it is crucially important within the context of our ACKNOWLEDGING the Lordship of Christ. This does not mean that public acknowledgement of our acceptance of the Lord is not that important. Jesus said otherwise.

> **Matthew 10:32**
> Whosoever therefore shall confess me before men, him will I confess also before my Father which is in heaven.

Our willingness to yield our unruly member, the tongue, to the Holy Spirit is exactly parallel to the act of walking forward at the time of salvation.

The new Christian in the first instant of submission is embarrassed, frightened, and reluctant to get up out of his seat and make a public display of his surrender to a greater power. He could submit to the Lord quietly in his seat and be as committed as he is when he walks to the front but the act of coming forward is an act of faith that witnesses to others of the moment of salvation. It serves as a tangible, definite dividing line between the prior indecision and the new commitment.

Giving up our tongues and voices to the use of God's Spirit is the same principle. "Speaking in tongues," sets us apart, not only from the unsaved, but from other Christians as well. Relinquishing our will to God to allow this radical departure, serves as a sign. It is a sign not only to us, but to God as well, that we are finally ready to yield our will to Him.

This is the foundational and fundamental reason tongues are important even though the reader must understand there is MUCH more to the baptism in the Holy Ghost than just speaking in tongues.

Never forget this. The Bible is God's Holy Inspired Word, written by the Holy Ghost as He moved upon the men of old. The Bible must be the Christian's final authority on any topic or manifestation for it is the Bible that was given by inspiration of God.

One's denomination or even a pastor's opinion of things may or may not be inspired by God even though the pastor may speak eloquently and sway the crowds with his brilliance. God is not looking for eloquence behind the pulpit. He is looking for Holy-Ghost filled preachers to stand up under the anointing of the Spirit and declare "thus saith the Lord," no matter the cost or how many religious devils may get stirred up in the process. Tongues are not an issue in the mind of God. He ordained them to be a means of speaking to His people in ages past according to the great prophet Isaiah, yet, as the prophet also stated, "they would not hear."

> **Isaiah 28:11-12**
> **For with stammering lips and another tongue will he speak to this people. [12] To whom he said, This is the rest wherewith ye may cause the weary to rest; and this is the refreshing: <u>yet they would not hear</u>.**

The "they" in this passage that the Holy Spirit through Isaiah was referring to was National Israel at the time. This passage carries prophetic overtones regarding the coming Great Tribulation period, as well as a warning to the modern church world which by and large, has rejected the mighty baptism in the Holy Ghost.

Despite a clear statement that this is a "REST" and a "REFRESHING," millions within the denominational world refuse to believe and "yet will not hear."

For the child of God there is no greater joy of refreshing than one being baptized in the Spirit! One simply cannot live for God without the ministry and help of the Holy Ghost. One cannot experience the Rest wherein we rest in the Finished work of Christ except through the power and ministry of the Holy Ghost. One simply cannot experience true abundant life except one experience the infilling of the Holy Ghost who alone fills one's heart with an intimate love for Jesus Christ and burns within us a Godly zeal to live righteous, holy lives before the Father.

One may ask, "well are you saying if I reject tongues, then I am rejecting the work of the Holy Ghost?" Well, how can you not be? We cannot pick and choose what ministries of the Holy Ghost we want to operate among our churches and which ones we want to resist and reject.

Let us just put it this way.

Many believers have come to Christ in faith but have not sought after the baptism in the Holy Ghost for a myriad of reasons. I am thinking of a well-known Baptist evangelist who has been dead many years now, who I respect and read behind often. He loved the Lord with all his heart, but he never felt there was a need for him to go on and receive the baptism in the Holy Ghost. Did I think the man was saved? Absolutely! He preached the Cross as the only way for men to be saved and he did not flinch from that one iota. I cannot help but wonder however, what would the Lord have done through him had he believed in receiving this glorious infilling of the Spirit.

Tongues are not an issue as to whether one is saved. There are some denominations that make that an issue, but they are just as wrong as those who outright reject and deny that tongues are needed for the believer today.

There are many diverse and different ministries of the Holy Ghost without a doubt, but there are none so polarizing as speaking in other tongues as the spirit of God gives the utterance. I cannot help but think that if I were Satan, I would want to create as much polarization as I could over this because when ANY believer kneels down and prays in the Spirit, they are wreaking havoc on his kingdom!!!!

I go back to the sardonic tone of the individual who said, "well I can pray without speaking in tongues. We do not need any of that for God to hear us." That attitude is one that lays bare the motive of those who do not believe!

I have come to realize that if a person has legitimately made up their mind that they are not going to believe in this experience (speaking with other tongues when filled with the Holy Ghost), then it may be wise to not waste your time or theirs in discussing this with them.

Jesus said, blessed are those who HUNGER AND THIRST after righteousness. If one is not hungry and thirsty for more of God, one will not be filled. Speaking in tongues will not catch anyone off guard. No one can make you thirsty and no one can make you hungry.

In 1 Corinthians 14:26, Paul is talking about public ministry gifts that are manifested in the church, "as we come together." These gifts are not the private devotional and intercessory work of the Spirit in the believer. ALL can speak in tongues if they so desire and ASK. NOT all who speak in tongues will be used in public utterances and interpretation.

> **1 Corinthians 14:26**
> **How is it then, brethren? when ye come together, every one of you hath a psalm, hath a doctrine, hath a tongue, hath a revelation, hath an interpretation. Let all things be done unto edifying. [27] If any man speaks in an unknown tongue, let it be by two, or at the most by three, and that by course; and let one interpret. [28] But if there be no interpreter, let him keep silence in the church; and let him speak to himself, and to God.**

Paul clearly tells us that if we come together and someone gives a public utterance in tongues "as the Spirit of God," speaks through us in other tongues, let it be done in the purpose of LOVE and edification of the church. There is NOWHERE in this passage where Paul is discouraging speaking in tongues. He even says if there is not an interpreter, (v. 28) "let him keep silence IN THE CHURCH AND let him speak to himself AND to God.

What Paul was saying in that passage is that without an interpreter, that individual's message in tongues will not edify anyone and it will be better for him to keep quiet if what he says is not going to edify others PUBLICALLY. If that person wishes to worship in tongues in a public gathering, let him do it to "himself and to God."

God is not upset with us worshiping in tongues because by doing so we are PRAISING and SPEAKING to HIM!

READ THE BIBLE and stop listening to the lies of the devil child of God.

Paul was not talking about tongues as the initial sign of the baptism in the Spirit, nor was he talking about tongues as a private, devotional, prayer language. You can recognize this by simply looking at the language Paul uses concerning speaking in tongues. When Paul asks the question, "Do all speak in tongues?" he was referring to the public manifestation of the spiritual gift of tongues, which enables a person gifted in the interpretation to speak out the meaning of the tongue. Not all have been given this gift of "different kinds" of tongues. This is instruction for public gatherings, not private prayer times.

The SPIRIT OF GOD gives the UTTERANCE! These utterances are not from Satan, nor from man, nor from some gibberish and babble as some sad folks may surmise.

Let the unbelieving stay in their unbelief if they wish; we cannot force anyone to believe; to be frank God cannot make us do that either.

That is OUR part in this great fight of faith. We must simply believe.

The SPIRIT OF GOD gives the UTTERANCE! He gave the utterance 2,000 years ago on the Day of Pentecost and He has been giving the utterance ever since. He wants to fill you today with overflowing.

When you came to Christ at salvation, the Holy Spirit baptized you into Christ. When you get baptized in the Holy Ghost, Jesus is the one who does the baptizing! That is powerful.

Neighbor, in these perilous last and prophetic days where apostasy reigns and every demon of hell has been unleashed upon Planet Earth and even here in America, we need something more than a book report on Sunday to get us through. We need the power of Almighty God. The power of God is found in the preaching of the Cross of Christ which includes the mighty baptism in the Holy Ghost with the evidence of speaking with other tongues.

It is time we stop beating around the bush and get to the brass tacks of seeing God move in our nation and world. The clock says, "ten to midnight," if not later and without the help of the Holy Spirit, we are doomed to lose an entire generation to the powers of darkness. It is not by might, not by power, but by my Spirit says the Lord of Host!

Zechariah 4:4-6

So I answered and spoke to the angel that talked with me, saying, What are these, my lord? [5] Then the angel that talked with me answered and said unto me, Knowest thou not what these be? And I said, No, my lord. [6] Then he answered and spake unto me, saying, This is the word of the Lord unto Zerubbabel, saying, Not by might, nor by power, but by my spirit, saith the Lord of hosts.

It is not by might, nor by power, but BY MY SPIRIT saith the Lord. In these last hours before the Lord comes, these are our battle weapons and weapons we must use NOW, not later!

Chapter 7

The Benefits of Speaking in Other Tongues

TEXT: 1 Corinthians 12:1-3–Now concerning spiritual gifts, brethren, I would not have you ignorant. [2] Ye know that ye were Gentiles, carried away unto these dumb idols, even as ye were led. [3] Wherefore I give you to understand, that no man speaking by the Spirit of God calleth Jesus accursed: and that no man can say that Jesus is the Lord, but by the Holy Ghost.

1 Corinthians 14:1-4
Follow after charity, and desire spiritual gifts, but rather that ye may prophesy. For he that speaketh in an unknown tongue speaketh not unto men, but unto God: for no man understands him; howbeit in the spirit he speaketh mysteries. But he that prophesies speaketh unto men to edification, and exhortation, and comfort. He that speaketh in an unknown tongue edifies himself; but he that prophesies edifies the church.

Isaiah 28:11-13
For with stammering lips and another tongue will he speak to this people. To whom he said, This is the rest wherewith ye may cause the weary to rest; and this is the refreshing: yet they would not hear. But the word of the LORD was unto them precept upon precept, precept upon precept; line upon line, line upon line; here a little, and there a little; that they might go, and fall backward, and be broken, and snared, and taken.

Many have asked the question, "How can speaking in other tongues be of any help or service to anyone?" Most of the time these questions are asked in laughter, sarcasm, mocking, and in most cases to speak despairingly of this great gift.

Some say speaking in tongues is nothing more than just babble, chatter, or incoherent jabbering. I can assure the reader that is the furthest from the truth!

In addition, the issue of the Baptism in the Holy Ghost was not and IS not a humorous matter to Jesus. Prior to His ascension, He commanded His followers to tarry in Jerusalem to be endued with power from on high, calling this great infilling of the Spirit, the "Promise of the Father." He even quoted John the Baptist who foretold that Jesus was the baptizer in the Holy Ghost!

> **Acts 1:4-5**
> **And, being assembled together with them, commanded them that they should not depart from Jerusalem, but wait for the promise of the Father, which, saith he, ye have heard of me. [5] For John truly baptized with water; but ye shall be baptized with the Holy Ghost not many days hence.**

> **Luke 24:49**
> **And, behold, I send the promise of my Father upon you: but tarry ye in the city of Jerusalem, until ye be endued with power from on high.**

Jesus' blood paid the price, not only for man to be redeemed from the powers of darkness but it paid for man to become a habitation of the Spirit of God and be gloriously baptized in the Holy Ghost and fire!

We mentioned in an earlier chapter that terminology trips many people up when trying to understand this powerful experience available to all believers.

When we say "baptized in the Holy Ghost," many tie their arguments against this enduement to the fact that the Bible teaches there is only ONE baptism into the Body of Christ and that is where you receive this "baptism of the Spirit" at salvation. That is both right AND wrong! The Spirit of God does baptize us INTO CHRIST when we get saved, but AFTER we get saved, it is CHRIST who then baptizes us WITH the Holy Ghost and immerses us with His power for us to be powerful tools of grace for the Kingdom of God.

While there will be some who say "ok" I see that; the next statement we make is what makes the religious even madder.

Because we feel the Bible shows us this, we believe and teach that the INITIAL physical evidence that one has received the infilling of the Spirit after salvation is that they will speak with other tongues as the Spirit of God gives them the utterance. Tongues brings on the fire to the debate so to speak and pardon the pun. Let me assure those in the church world who mock and lampoon those who speak in tongues according to Acts 2:4 that God is not laughing. There was a terrible price that was paid for man's redemption AND for man to be filled with the Spirit!

The baptism in the Holy Spirit was FIRST experienced on the Day of Pentecost which Luke described in Acts 2:1-4 and it is really the foundational passage for all those who have received this glorious enduement of power for service.

> **Acts 2:1-4**
> **And when the day of Pentecost was fully come, they were all with one accord in one place. [2] And suddenly there came a sound from heaven as of a rushing mighty wind, and it filled all the house where they were sitting. [3] And there appeared**

> unto them cloven tongues like as of fire, and it sat upon each of them. [4] And they were all filled with the Holy Ghost, and began to speak with other tongues, as the Spirit gave them utterance.

The promised blessing of the Father for those who obeyed Christ and waited for it, CAME in the form of the Holy Ghost.

Let the writer make this truly clear to the reader:

We cannot divorce God the Father from God the Son. So many attempt to do that by seeking a myriad of ways of salvation to God other than through Christ. There IS no other way to God except through the Son. Jesus is the Way.

While we cannot divorce Christ from God the Father, we also cannot divorce the HOLY SPIRIT from the ministry of Christ THEN, and from HIS ministry to us today! It was through the anointing of the HOLY GHOST that Christ did EVERYTHING that He did on Earth as a man anointed by the Holy Ghost thus he became our example of what He would shed His blood for to achieve ministry through ALL those who come to Him in faith!

> **Acts 10:38**
> **How God anointed Jesus of Nazareth with the Holy Ghost and with power: who went about doing good and healing all that were oppressed of the devil; for God was with him.**

People want to worship a Jesus that is more of a historical figure than a LIVING Savior and Redeemer, seated at the Right Hand of the Heavenly Father, interceding for the saints and releasing POWER upon the earth through the work of the Spirit. NOTHING friend and I mean NOTHING we get from God comes to us except it come through the means of the Holy Ghost!

> **1 Corinthians 2:12**
> **Now we have received, not the spirit of the world, but the spirit which is of God; that we might know the things that are freely given to us of God.**

We cannot know God except we know Him through the office and work of HIS SPIRIT which operates within the parameters of what the SON accomplished on the Cross of Calvary 2,000 years ago.

To state it again. We cannot divorce Christ from the Spirit as sadly, the modern church does. IN addition to this, we cannot divorce the Holy Spirit, from HIS WORK and MINISTRIES that He does either, and those ministries and gifts are recorded for us in the WORD OF GOD, which incidentally was WRITTEN BY MEN INSPIRED BY THE SPIRIT OF GOD!

We cannot say "we believe in the Holy Spirit, but we do not believe in speaking with other tongues."

Why you may ask?

Because everyone who spoke with other tongues in scripture SPOKE in tongues as the SPIRIT OF GOD gave them the utterance! It was the HOLY GHOST speaking through the voices of those obeying His unction and in reality, one could easily say it was GOD speaking through their voices because the Holy Spirit IS GOD!

Isaiah said that with stammering lips and an unknown tongue "I will speak to this people," yet they will not hear. Paul would quote this passage in Isaiah in the 14th chapter of 1 Corinthians when he gave an entire chapter dissertation on the matter of speaking with other tongues both publicly in the church and in one's private prayer language that we have already covered.

We must understand that MOST, not all, of what Paul wrote in 1 Corinthians 14 was addressed to the Corinthian CHURCH BODY to correct abuses in PUBLIC WORSHIP services that were taking place by those at Corinth. These were Spirit-filled believers who spoke in tongues but because of arrogance and pride they had forgotten the fundamental reason for ALL that the Spirit of God does. He leads us to all TRUTH which is basically Christ. Jesus told the Disciples in John 16:13 that "He (the Holy Spirit) shall speak of ME!"

As CHRIST edified the Church through His selfless sacrifice of His own flesh and blood for the salvation of fallen humanity, so too does the Holy Spirit seek for the edification of the Church today!

If one sits down and reads 1 Corinthians 14 with an unbelieving heart or if he does not understand the text and the setting from which Paul was speaking, one may come away from 1 Corinthians thinking "well Paul was admonishing the church to shun tongues all together," which again, is the furthest from the truth. Paul never once told the Corinthians that they should shun spiritual gifts. Instead he said, "COVET earnestly the best gifts," including speaking with other tongues.

One may say, "well he said that we should prophesy," instead of speak in tongues, yet that too was not an admonition against tongues, but to let the Corinthians know that unless tongues were interpreted in a public setting, no one would be edified! He was not denigrating tongues nor was he telling them to not be baptized in the Spirit. He would say in this same chapter, "I speak in tongues more than ye all!"

When one prophesies, it is a spiritual utterance in one's native language. When one speaks in another tongue, it would be obvious that they are speaking in a language not known the hearer and, likely, not the hearer as well. If that takes place, the only way for the hearer to be edified is for that message in tongues to be interpreted. Divers kinds of tongues and interpretation of tongues are two gifts of the Spirit that are listed separately in 1 Corinthians 12:8-12. So, for one to argue that Paul is admonishing the church to abandon this glorious gift, it is not scripturally correct.

There are others who will glibly argue, "Well Jesus never spoke in tongues so why should we?" That is what one may call an argument from silence and it is never a good idea to base one's theology on an argument of silence. It is also not a good idea to base one's faith on this type argument as well. Are we 100% sure Jesus did not speak in tongues? NO! Jesus was the son of Man and the Son of God. All the things He did on this earth were done as a man anointed by the Holy Ghost. The Holy Spirit in Him was the same Holy Spirit that we have today!!

The Holy Spirit through the writer of Hebrews speaks of "strong crying," and "tears," the Lord offered up throughout His earthly life to the Father in light of the coming Cross.

> **Hebrews 5:7**
> **Who in the days of his flesh, when he had offered up prayers and supplications with strong crying and tears unto him that was able to save him from death, and was heard in that he**

feared; [8] Though he were a Son, yet learned he obedience by the things which he suffered;

When He prayed in the Garden of Gethsemane, His prayer became so intense that drops of blood began to fall from His brow. No, the Bible does not tell us that He spoke in tongues during those times, but it never says He never spoke in tongues either.

In Romans 8 we see that one of the ministries of the Holy Spirit is "travail and intercession with GROANINGS that cannot be uttered." The term "uttered," is a verb used from the same word used in the original language for "UTTERANCES," as found in Acts 2:1-4 and the term "groanings," carries similar connotations as that of the "prayers and supplications," spoken of in Hebrews 5.

Just as the gospels did not record everything that Jesus did, neither did Acts record everything that the apostles did. So, just because it never says, "Peter spoke with tongues," or "John spoke with tongues," it does not mean they did not. Peter and John were among the 120 on the Day of Pentecost so, to be frank, I can assure you they did!!

Whether Jesus spoke in tongues or not while on Earth is irrelevant to TODAY.

Jesus ministered under the Old Covenant, but because of what HE DID FOR US AT THE CROSS. We have been given a BETTER COVENANT BUILT UPON BETTER PROMISES! It is called the NEW COVENANT and it was established so that men could be BORN AGAIN and be filled with the HOLY GHOST.

Speaking in tongues was not available under the Old Covenant because the sin debt humanity owed God could not be paid with the blood of "bulls and goats" under the Law. But when Jesus went to glory and presented HIS BLOOD before the Father for ALL THOSE who would come to Him in Faith, the door was swung wide open for the HOLY GHOST to INDWELL the believer and FILL those who come to Christ with HIS POWER!!!

The Holy Spirit with His gifts and ministries could not come until Jesus paid this price and presented His blood to the Father in heaven! He now has done all that is necessary to save us and give us both the indwelling presence of the Spirit at salvation and the enduement of power by the Spirit after salvation!

> **Acts 2:32- 33**
> **This Jesus hath God raised up, whereof we all are witnesses. [33] Therefore being by the right hand of God exalted and having received of the Father the promise of the Holy Ghost, he hath shed forth this, which ye now see and hear. [34] For David is not ascended into the heavens: but he saith himself, The Lord said unto my Lord, Sit thou on my right hand, [35] Until I make thy foes thy footstool. [36] Therefore let all the house of Israel know assuredly, that God hath made that same Jesus, whom ye have crucified, both Lord and Christ.**

When Jesus went to Father, He received the Promise of the Holy Ghost and SHED HIM FORTH on the Day of Pentecost which ISRAEL both SAW and HEARD.

How did they hear?

Because those filled with the mighty baptism in the Holy Ghost spoke with other TONGUES as the SPIRIT OF GOD gave the utterance!

He That Speaks in An Unknown Tongue

> **1 Corinthians 14:2**
> **For he that speaketh in an unknown tongue speaketh not unto men, but unto God: for no man understandeth him; howbeit in the spirit he speaketh mysteries.**

As we have laid out earlier in this book, unknown tongues are generally a language or languages spoken somewhere in this world OR in the heavenlies! Paul speaks of "tongues of Angels" in 1 Corinthians 13, thus that leads us to believe that there are certain languages that are not of this earth!

We are given insight to this when it states that the languages heard on the Day of Pentecost were languages from EVERY NATION UNDER HEAVEN, especially those nations known to the disciples during the time this great event took place.

It says they had come together and were confounded because "how hear we every man in our own tongue, wherein we were born?"

> **Acts 2:7-9**
> **And they were all amazed and marveled, saying one to another, Behold, are not all these which speak Galileans? [8] And how hear we every man in our own tongue, wherein we were born? [9] Parthians, and Medes, and Elamites, and the dwellers in Mesopotamia, and in Judaea, and Cappadocia, in Pontus, and Asia,**

Acts 2:11
Cretes and Arabians, we do hear them speak in our tongues the wonderful works of God.

It then goes on to list the people who were there; Parthians, Medes, Elamites, and at least 13 additional nationalities. Yet all these disparate people said, "we do hear them speak in our (own) tongues the wonderful works of God."

Now these individuals were not preaching to these people to be saved. They were merely praising the Lord in other tongues and speaking a language they had not learned. Some skeptics have tried to explain this away as some language the 120 had just learned prior to the day of Pentecost. That neighbor is absurd, and it speaks to how unbelief can cause educated preachers to say some of the stupidest things!

If we are to believe the skeptics, then we must assume that 120 fishermen and common people suddenly become linguists in a matter of minutes and were praising God in other languages other than Aramaic, Hebrew, or Greek which were the common local tongues. That argument would hold a bit of water without this one glaring fact that stares even the most casual student of the Bible in the face; these were uneducated Galileans and NOT students of languages. Most, if not all, were mainly blue-collar workers, fishermen by trade, including Peter and John who were labeled "uneducated and unlearned," by the religious of Israel following the powerful preaching of Peter under this newfound anointing. This was a sound from HEAVEN and 2,000 years later, this "sound" of heaven is still being heard throughout the world by those who are filled with the Holy Ghost!

> **Acts 4:12 -13**
> **Neither is there salvation in any other: for there is none other name under heaven given among men, whereby we must be saved. [13] Now when they saw the boldness of Peter and John, and perceived that they were unlearned and ignorant men, they marveled; and they took knowledge of them, that they had been with Jesus.**

This is the way it ALWAYS is when people speak in tongues. There are hundreds and perhaps thousands of languages and dialects in this world and many of them sound very strange to our ears. Of course, they are not strange to the people who routinely converse in them.

It is always a language that is spoken somewhere in the world but not known by the individual speaking in other tongues. If you will notice, when it came time to preach to these people about the Lord Jesus Christ and give an invitation to be saved, Peter did not continue speaking in tongues.

Peter preached in the common language of the day, which was either Aramaic or Hebrew. Of course, all those present understood it. It was not the same language they heard when the people were praising God earlier. These were supernatural utterances given by God.

In addition to earthly languages the Apostle Paul mentions in 1 Corinthians 13:1, there are also "tongues of angels," which would also indicate that these were some heavenly languages that people receive when they are baptized in the Holy Ghost.

There are some languages heard in heaven and not on earth.

So, before one is quick to criticize and judge tongues as being unknown gibberish and jabber while denying their significance for today, I would ask one simple question. What type language do you think is going on in heaven? Do you think God just speaks American English? Do you think He speaks only in YOUR dialect? Paul mentions "tongues of men, AND OF ANGELS."

The language of heaven is the language of the Spirit and the language of the Spirit is given to a believer when that believer is baptized or endued with power from on high!

Common sense tells us that if it is the SPIRIT giving the utterance, which is ALWAYS the case, then it should be not hard to comprehend that men may speak in a heavenly or angelic, unearthly language at times.

The Benefits of Speaking in Tongues

There is MUCH good accomplished when one speaks in tongues.

The first benefit of speaking with other tongues is they are the INITIAL sign one has been filled with the Holy Ghost. They literally usher in the baptism of the Spirit into the life of the believer. Let us look at other benefits point by point:

Tongues Are A Refreshing to the Believer

In Isaiah 28:11-12, which was quoted by Paul in I Corinthians 14:11-13, Isaiah mentions something of extreme importance: "This is the rest wherewith ye may cause the weary to rest; and this is the refreshing.

When one receives that baptism in the Holy Ghost and begins to speak in tongues on a regular basis, this enduement of power becomes like a spiritual recharging of one's spiritual batteries daily.

All the religious activity in the world will never do that! The Holy Ghost can do that for us 24 hours a day, seven days a week, at no cost to the believer except FAITH and allowing the Spirit of God to pray through us as only HE can!

In this vein, one must understand that praying in tongues builds up the believer spiritually as the Holy Spirit tells us through Jude.

> **Jude 1:24**
> **Now unto him that is able to keep you from falling, and to present you faultless before the presence of his glory with exceeding joy,**

Speaking in Tongues Helps One to Pray

> **Romans 8: 8:26-28**
> **Likewise the Spirit also helpeth our infirmities: for we know not what we should pray for as we ought: but the Spirit itself maketh intercession for us with groanings which cannot be uttered. [27] And he that searches the hearts knoweth what is the mind of the Spirit, because he makes intercession for the saints according to the will of God. [28] And we know that all things work together for good to them that love God, to them who are the called according to his purpose.**

Paul wrote an entire chapter of Romans (Romans 8) laying out spiritual victory over sin. In this chapter, he also deals with the will of God and the intercessory work of the Holy Spirit through the believer. He tells us that when we pray, we pray for things we ought not. When the Holy Ghost prays through us, we pray the mind of the Spirit AND the will of God for our lives!

The Greek says that the "groanings that cannot be uttered" in verse 26 are sounds, words and utterances "which cannot be articulated in a normal or natural voice." That sounds like speaking in other tongues to me. Through these unknown utterances or tongues, the Holy Spirit helps us pray because, in essence, He is doing the praying for us!

When we do not know how to pray about a certain situation, it is often because we do not recognize the complexities of the problem. God does. The Holy Spirit does.

Thus, when we go before God in the natural, many times we ask for what WE see as the solutions but in fact, they are not the right solutions.

When we pray in the Spirit, which should be everyday as believers in Christ to be frank with you friend, or in other words when we pray in other tongues, the Holy Spirit brings not only a great refreshing, but a great assurance of knowing that God the HOLY GHOST is praying through us, and He is always praying according to the will of God.

The Spirit says things to the Heavenly Father that we would not know what or how to say in our human, natural ability, but they are always in the best interest of the believer because that is what the Spirit's job is about on Planet Earth. To be frank, we probably do not even want to know what the Spirit of God is praying through us!

This ministry of the Spirit is to SEAL US until the day we see Jesus at the Judgment Seat of Christ! His work in us is eternal, not temporal, and what He has begun, He will FINISH and not QUIT until the job is done! We can truly KNOW that ALL things are working together for the GOOD of them who love God and are CALLED according to His Heavenly Purpose!

> **Romans 8:28**
> **And we know that all things work together for good to them that love God, to them who are the called according to his purpose.**
>
> **Philip. 1:6**
> **Being confident of this very thing, that he which hath begun a good work in you will perform it until the day of Jesus Christ:**

The Lord Jesus makes intercession for us in heaven. The Holy Spirit makes intercession for us here on earth and that intercession, whether by Christ in heaven, or the Holy Ghost on Earth, is ALWAYS according to the will of God.

Why is that so vitally important one may ask?

Because according to what the Holy Spirit wrote in John's first epistle, we know that when we pray ACCORDING TO GOD'S WILL, we can be 100% assured God HEARS US and He answers whatsoever we ask and desire of Him! Friend, now that is PRAYER!

That is powerful intercessory, life-changing, nation-changing, church-changing, family-changing, household changing, spouse-changing, boss-changing, work-changing PRAYER!

Neighbor, this is how nations are brought to Christ through revival and the outpouring of the Holy Ghost! When we pray in the HOLY GHOST, or pray in other tongues as the Spirit of God gives the utterance, we do not "think" but we "KNOW" that we are praying according to the will of God and He will hear and ANSWER us!!

> I Jn. 5:14-15
> **And this is the confidence that we have in him, that, if we ask any thing according to his will, he heareth us: And if we know that he hear us, whatsoever we ask, we know that we have the petitions that we desired of him.**

Tongues Are A Sign to the Unbeliever

> 1 Cor. 14: 24
> **Wherefore tongues are for a sign, not to them that believe, but to them that believe not: but prophesying serves not for them that believe not, but for them which believe**

Thirdly, tongues are a sign to the unbeliever.

Joel said that "in the last days I will pour out My Spirit upon ALL flesh." When one hears someone or they themselves speak in other tongues, they are witnessing a sign and hearing audibly that we are living in the last days! This is a warning to the unbeliever to get right with God! It is a sign to a backslidden church to come back to God and return to the foot of the Cross! It is harvest time neighbor and the outpouring of the Holy Ghost on the Day of Pentecost that has empowered the church since then is a sign that we are living in days that are growing late and quickly are reaching their end.

Another way that this may be a sign is that an unbeliever may hear these unknown tongues spoken in their own language and what is being said may be something that brings them to God!

This happened to an exchange student from Spain named Maggie, who I had in my home almost 30 years ago. During a church service she attended with our family at the time, she heard two men speaking in other tongues during the prayer time. When she got home, she asked me if those men were from Spain. I told her "no," they were speaking with other tongues because of the Pentecostal experience. She began to weep and say, "Mr. Chris, I heard them saying, "Alleluia to the Christ," over and over and I want to know more about this Christ. Maggie came from a place of deep witchcraft and it was an opening for our family to share the gospel with her. While she did not accept Christ that day, the seed was planted for her to take back to her homeland that she had heard the truth about Jesus. Had those men not spoken in tongues, Maggie would have never asked me that question.

That is how tongues can also be used a sign to the unbeliever.

Speaking in Tongues Edifies the Believer

1 Cor 14:4
He that speaketh in an unknown tongue edifies himself; but he that prophesies edifieth the church.

Paul said in 1 Corinthians 14:4 that a person speaking in tongues is edifying himself. Some have tried to use that statement to make tongues out to be a selfish act on behalf of those who have been baptized in the Holy Ghost. Nowhere in that statement does Paul say this is wrong. Friend, unless you are SUPERMAN or God, which you and I are NEITHER, we need to have our faith BUILT UP daily due to the onslaught of the Satanic forces around us and the powers of darkness seeking to kill us and bring us into captivity. Now if there are any reading this that do not feel their faith needs building up daily, then tongues are probably not for you, friend.

I need HIM every day of my life, every second of every minute of every hour of every day of every week of every year of every century of every millennium for all eternity to HELP me while I am here on this earth. I cannot walk this Christian walk except the Holy Ghost walk it for me. In my flesh is NO GOOD THING, and the second I depend on my flesh to get me out of trouble, I usually just fall further into that trouble headlong and into even worse oblivion.

Speaking in tongues not only strengthens the believer, it builds one's faith, and edifies one's heart as the Bible says. This edification is not in selfishness - but just the opposite - in Spirit bathed humility that reveals to us who believe our utter hopelessness outside CHRIST. The Holy Spirit never does that. The Holy Ghost always does this in a healthy manner and He never makes a mistake by edifying the believer in a way that would corrupt the carnal ego.

Jude exhorts us to PRAY in the HOLY GHOST, building UP OUR MOST HOLY FAITH! This faith is MOST HOLY and because it is MOST HOLY, the HOLY GHOST is connected to us because of our faith which is always to be in CHRIST and HIM CRUCIFIED! That is why it is holy; because it is anchored in the MOST HOLY ONE of all, the LORD JESUS CHRIST. Praise the name of the Lamb forever and forever.

Jude 1:24
Now unto him that is able to keep you from falling, and to present you faultless before the presence of his glory with exceeding joy,

Tongues Are A Divine Form of Communication

1 Cor 14:14-15
For if I pray in an unknown tongue, my spirit prayeth, but my understanding is unfruitful. What is it then? I will pray with the spirit, and I will pray with the understanding also: I will sing with the spirit, and I will sing with the understanding also.

When our spirit unites with the Holy Spirit and the Spirit of God prays through us, it is a direct line of communication to God. When we pray in the Holy Spirit, our understanding may be unfruitful, but there are times when we need to get a hold of God immediately. Paul said there would be needful times to pray both in the Spirit and with our own understanding. When we are praying in the Spirit, even Satan does not understand what we are saying! Think about it. The only time when the enemy cannot interfere with the flow of prayer between you and God is when you are praying in the Holy Ghost.

Doesn't this make the arguments against the Holy Spirit seem so childish? We are fighting the very one thing that can connect us to God and get an answer to our needs as the church. No wonder the enemy has blinded so many to this experience and he has deluded others into attacking it. You need the baptism in the Holy Spirit! You need to be filled with the Holy Ghost as they were on the day of Pentecost. You need this experience. It is for today!

Do All Speak with other Tongues?

A lot of confusion and controversy arises over Paul's statement to the Corinthians that he would rather speak five words of understanding in his own language than 5,000 in another tongue. Many people have taken this statement and argued that this validates the fact that some will not speak in tongues because not all will be given the "gift." Others say, "well, you are not supposed to speak in tongues if you do not have an interpreter," and a myriad of other excuses as to why we do not want to believe that tongues are for today and relevant to the Spirit's ministry to the believer.

Others say, "Well, the Bible says, if a man does not have an interpreter present, "he should just keep silent." Sad to say, that is what most of us do in our church gatherings whether there is an interpreter present or not. We keep silent and NEVER utter a word of praise or thanks to God and we act like some corpse down at the local morgue until we get home and get in front of our television sets to cheer on our favorite team. The people who state such do not care one iota whether an interpreter is present or not, and if you pressed them, they do not even know what the role of the interpreter IS to begin with when dealing with spiritual gifts.

We do open our mouths from time to time in church to cut down and tear down the preacher or our neighbor! This modern brand of Christian tends to have a great capacity to worry about an interpreter being present when someone allows the Spirit of God to speak through them. I am just wondering if they are worried as much about that interpreter being present instead of being worried about the gossiping, slandering, cursing, and backbiting that comes out of most of our church member's tongues? Let me give you a memo: praying in the HOLY GHOST as the Spirit of God gives the utterance and/or worshipping, singing and praising God in tongues is NOT of Satan. Backbiting, gossiping, slandering, murmuring, complaining; THOSE THINGS ARE OF SATAN!

The fact is that ALL can speak in tongues if they so desire but not all will. The question Paul was addressing deals with two different types of tongues: devotional tongues and the gift of tongues as outlined in 1 Corinthians 12 and 14. We teach and preach that every recipient of the Holy Spirit, without exception, speaks with other tongues as he is baptized in the Holy Spirit. However, the initial physical evidence of this experience (as recorded in Acts 2:4) should not be confused with the experience and operation Paul spent three chapters on discussing in 1 Corinthians 12-14.

The GIFT of TONGUES and INTERPRETATION of TONGUES are two of the nine gifts of the Spirit. Admittedly, everything received from God is a gift, but there is a difference in the devotional, infilling of the Holy Spirit that is a gift to all believers who come to Jesus and asked to be filled, and the use of tongues in corporate gatherings where the Body of Christ comes together to be ministered to and the spiritual "GIFT" of tongues is in operation as outlined in 1 Corinthians 12:10.

> **1 Corinthians 12:10**
> **To another the working of miracles; to another prophecy; to another discerning of spirits; to another divers' of tongues; to another the interpretation of tongues.**

A person who speaks in tongues every day of his life (and he should do this), may never be used in the gift of tongues. A person who is used in the gift of tongues in corporate settings should pray and ask that God also give him the gift of interpretation. These experiences are similar, yet different. One is for personal worship. The other (1 Cor. 12) is for events that transpire when the Body of Christ comes together in corporate times of fellowship and union when the Lord may want to speak a message to the Body through a tongue and interpretation of that tongue.

When the Bible says, "not all speak with tongues," it is not saying that when you are baptized in the Holy Ghost you will not speak in tongues. It is saying that the Holy Spirit has given special gifts to people in the body and some may be used in the gift of speaking in tongues to the Body corporately and some will not. ALL who receive the initial infilling of the HOLY GHOST WILL SPEAK WITH OTHER TONGUES WITH NO EXCEPTIONS!

When we say the gift of tongues, we are talking about the experience where the Spirit of God moves on an individual, and that person gives a message in the body from the Lord. When the person finishes speaking the message in tongues, another should interpret what has been said. If an interpretation does not come forth, then the body has not been edified because NO ONE HAS UNDERSTOOD WHAT WAS SAID. When Peter preached the message of Pentecost, he had just come from the most powerful outpouring of the Holy Spirit in the history of the church. Yet, when he addressed those gathered, he did not give the message in tongues, he spoke in his natural language so that all could understand. This is what Paul is referring to when he says, "I would rather speak five words of my own understanding." If we read just a few verses down we'll see that Paul was in no way demeaning tongues for he says, "I speak in tongues MORE THAN YE ALL," and "I would that YOU ALL spoke with tongues," meaning I would that ALL of you would be baptized in the HOLY GHOST AND FIRE and be filled with the Spirit of God and allow Him to give you a prayer utterance that is vital to your Christian walk and faith! Friend, we cannot walk this Christian walk without the HOLY GHOST!

Look at 1 Corinthians 14 with me a bit and let us break this down line by line, verse by verse.

> **1 Corinthians 14:4-28**
> **He that speaketh in an unknown tongue edifies himself**

(when he is praying privately in his personal devotional time with God).

> **but he that prophesies edifies the church**

(this is where the gift of 1 Corinthians 12:10 comes into play).

I would that ye all spake with tongues, but rather that ye prophesied: for greater is he that prophesies than he that speaketh with tongues, except he interpret, that the church may receive edifying (Paul is saying if there is no interpreter present it's better to give a word of prophetic utterance than go off in an unknown tongue and no one know what you are saying; he is not saying that prophesying is better than tongues, he's just saying that when we come together in corporate worship it's important for the BODY to be edified not just the individual).

> **Now, brethren, if I come unto you speaking with tongues, what shall I profit you, except I shall speak to you either by revelation, or by knowledge, or by prophesying, or by doctrine?**

(This is the foundation for ALL True prophetic utterances–a "revelation," "by knowledge i.e. something we learn about Christ, a "prophesying," or utterance that encourages, edifies or exhorts, or a doctrine, which may take the form of an exhortation to hold fast in the faith or beware of some false doctrine. THE HOLY GHOST IS ABLE TO DO ALL THESE THINGS IF WE LET HIM!)

> **And even things without life giving sound, whether pipe or harp, except they give a distinction in the sounds, how shall it be known what is piped or harped? For if the trumpet give an uncertain sound, who shall prepare himself to the battle? So likewise ye, except ye utter by the tongue words easy to be understood, how shall it be known what is spoken?**

(HE IS SPEAKING OF GIVING A MESSAGE IN TONGUE IN CORPORATE WORSHIP, NOT PRIVATE DEVOTION HERE)

> **for ye shall speak into the air.**

(IF someone speaks in tongues in a service and no one interprets it will be just like that; someone speaking into the air)

> **There are, it may be, so many kinds of voices in the world, and none of them is without signification. Therefore if I know not the meaning of the voice, I shall be unto him that speaketh a barbarian, and he that speaketh shall be a barbarian unto me.**

(Some have taken Paul's words here and used them to mean that those who speak in tongues are as barbarians; how foolish and utter nonsense that spews sometimes from the darkened hearts of unbelievers, many who are "believers" but just do not want to believe in the power of God!)

> Even so ye, forasmuch as ye are zealous of spiritual gifts, seek that ye may excel to the edifying of the church.

(THIS IS THE KEY TO ALL SPIRITUAL MINISTRY)

> Wherefore let him that speaketh in an unknown tongue

(IN CORPORATE WORSHIP)

> pray that he may interpret. For if I pray in an unknown tongue, (INDIVIDUALLY in our private prayer time) my spirit prayeth, but my understanding is unfruitful. What is it then? I will pray with the spirit,

(I will pray at times in tongues)

> and I will pray with the understanding also:

(Because there are seasons, we need to understand what we are asking the Lord for; other times there are needs only the HOLY GHOST can meet through His work of Intercession)

> I will sing with the spirit, and I will sing with the understanding also. (The same can be said of singing in the Spirit and singing with my understanding)

> Else when thou shall bless with the spirit, how shall he that occupies the room of the unlearned say Amen at thy giving of thanks, seeing he understands not what thou sayest? For thou verily gives thanks well, but the other is not edified. I thank my God, I speak with tongues more than ye all: Yet in the church I had rather speak five words with my understanding,

> that by my voice I might teach others also, than ten thousand words in an unknown tongue. Brethren, be not children in understanding: howbeit in malice be ye children, but in understanding be men. In the law it is written, With men of other tongues and other lips will I speak unto this people;
>
> (Quoted from Isaiah 28:11-12)
> and yet for all that will they not hear me, saith the Lord. Wherefore tongues are for a sign, not to them that believe, but to them that believe not: but prophesying serves not for them that believe not, but for them which believe.

(When those that believe not hear a message in tongues they are hearing the warning from heaven the last days outpouring is here and time is short; when prophetic utterances are given in corporate worship those are always for specific needs/areas the Holy Ghost is addressing within the Church)

> If therefore the whole church be come together into one place, and all speak with tongues, and there come in those that are unlearned, or unbelievers, will they not say that ye are mad? But if all prophesy, and there come in one that believeth not, or one unlearned, he is convinced of all, he is judged of all: And thus are the secrets of his heart made manifest; and so falling down on his face he will worship God, and report that God is in you of a truth. How is it then, brethren? when ye come together, every one of you hath a psalm, hath a doctrine, hath a tongue, hath a revelation, hath an interpretation. Let all things be done (in corporate worship) unto edifying. If any man speak in an unknown tongue,

(give a message in tongue to the corporate gathering i.e. the whole church who has come together in one place)

> **let it be by two, or at the most by three, and that by course; and let one interpret. But if there be no interpreter, let him keep silence in the church; and let him speak to himself, and to God.**

(i.e.–keep your message in tongue to yourself until there is surety the BODY will be edified–this is NOT talking about individual worship or prayer!)

> **As one can see, a great deal of this 14th chapter of Corinthians speaks of CORPORATE worship, not our individual prayer lives and intimate walk with Christ.**

If a person is just speaking in his own devotional language, worshipping the Lord, there is seldom, if ever, a need for interpretation. The GIFT OF TONGUES is not in operation. Sometimes in worship situations, a person hears someone speaking in tongues and wonders what is called for. I have been preaching at times when the Spirit of God will give an utterance of worship through me. I am not giving a "message" in tongues to those I am preaching to, I am worshipping the Lord.

When I do this, there is no need to stop the message and get an interpretation. I had a lady just recently who watched a video of a message I preached some years ago and when I was preaching, I began to speak in other tongues as the Spirit of God gave the utterance. Seeing the video, the dear lady in question said, "He was speaking in tongues on that video and that is wrong since he did not have an interpreter present." No, it was not wrong since I was not addressing the congregation in other tongues. I was praising the Lord in tongues, but I was addressing the congregation in English. Had it been the other way around then it would not have been edifying to the congregation listening to me preach so THEN it would have been wrong!

On the other side of this coin, I have been in Pentecostal churches where the preacher cannot even finish his message because everyone wants to interpret every utterance in tongues he gives. The gifts of the Spirit are given for our edification, comfort, and MATURITY in the Lord. Tongues are not a sideshow to show off one's spirituality or lack of common sense. Paul said that unless he spoke to them by revelation, doctrine, and in their own understanding, he would be speaking into the air and it would seem to those who do not know any better like a barbarian.

> **1Corinthians 14:6-12**
> **Now, brethren, if I come unto you speaking with tongues, what shall I profit you, except I shall speak to you either by revelation, or by knowledge, or by prophesying, or by doctrine? And even things without life giving sound, whether pipe or harp, except they give a distinction in the sounds, how shall it be known what is piped or harped? For if the trumpet give an uncertain sound, who shall prepare himself to the battle. So likewise ye, except ye utter by the tongue words easy to be understood, how shall it be known what is spoken? for ye shall speak into the air. There are, it may be, so many kinds of voices in the world, and none of them is without signification. Therefore if I know not the meaning of the voice, I shall be unto him that speaketh a barbarian, and he that speaketh shall be a barbarian unto me. Even so ye, Forasmuch as ye**

are zealous of spiritual gifts, seek that ye may excel to the edifying of the church.

This dissertation in 1 Corinthians 14 is NOT a message against speaking in tongues. If preachers would stop and think for three seconds and THINK, they would realize how stupid it sounds that the HOLY GHOST, who is the author of 1 Corinthians 14, not PAUL, would have him write against the very thing the HOLY GHOST WANTS TO DO IN THE HEARTS AND LIVES OF EVERY SINGLE BELIEVER who has come to CHRIST!

The Holy Spirit was setting forth guidelines for those who would be used in the gift of tongues and interpretation as recorded in 1 Corinthians 12:10-12.

Sadly, many argue against the entire experience of tongues with these scriptures. Just remember: a Spirit-filled person who has been baptized in the Holy Ghost may and should speak in tongues every day of his life, and he may well do so, but that does not mean necessarily they will EVER move in the "GIFT of tongues as outlined in 1 Corinthians 12 and 14. One is for devotion, the other is for the Body. Paul was giving correction, not a stoplight. The Corinthians had allowed confusion to intrude into their worship services. The Holy Spirit through Paul was saying, "Let it be done in order." The Holy Spirit would NOT have had Paul admonish them to stop HIS work among them!! God forbid!

1 Corinthians 14:18-24
I thank my God, I speak with tongues more than ye all: Yet in the church I had rather speak five words with my understanding, that by my voice I might teach others also, than ten thousand words in an unknown tongue. Brethren, be

> not children in understanding: howbeit in malice be ye children, but in understanding be men. In the law it is written, With men of other tongues and other lips will I speak unto this people; and yet for all that will they not hear me, saith the Lord. Wherefore tongues are for a sign, not to them that believe, but to them that believe not: but prophesying serveth not for them that believe not, but for them which believe. If therefore the whole church be come together into one place, and all speak with tongues, and there come in those that are unlearned, or unbelievers, will they not say that ye are mad? But if all prophesy, and there come in one that believeth not, or one unlearned, he is convinced of all, he is judged of all:

Some of you reading this journal are at a crossroads. You have been saved by the blood of Jesus. If you died or Jesus came right now, you would be taken to heaven to be with Him eternally. You love Him with all your heart. For whatever reason, be it ignorance, fear, traditional teaching, or just unbelief, you have not received this glorious experience we have talked about and you want to. It is just a matter of asking and allowing the Holy Spirit to anoint you with power. It has already been paid for, just as your salvation was paid for at Calvary. In a later journal we are going to talk about how one actually receives the Holy Spirit.

We do not have to beg God for this experience! He wants to baptize us with HIS power. He wants His Spirit to come upon you just like it did His Son, Jesus Christ some 2,000 years ago.

The only prerequisite for receiving the baptism of the Holy Spirit is salvation. Nothing more, nothing less. You cannot make yourself anymore worthy to receive this blessed gift than you are now. However, there are some factors that will keep one from receiving, which are basically unbelief, and not yielding our tongue to the Lord. There are others who may have unforgiveness in their heart towards others and that too hinders the flow of the Spirit.

I am not one of those who believe you must clean yourself up FIRST before the Holy Spirit will fill you. If you are struggling with a bondage, then YOU friend, are the very one HE wants to assist and deliver! There is nothing you can do to save yourself and there is sure nothing you can do to FREE yourself from the bondage you find yourself in.

The church world has erroneously taught folks that "God helps those who help themselves." That is a fairy tale, not scripture! God helps those who ASK for His help! We had to BY FAITH ask the Lord Jesus into our heart at salvation; He did not bust our hearts door down and just come in; there had to be a willingness and confession that we could not save ourselves and we needed Him. Well the same is true when One is seeking the Holy Spirit.

As believers we are born again but we are not saints YET! There are many flaws still in our lives that the Holy Spirit is called upon to deal with through the process of sanctification. This is not a wham-bam in your face one moment experience. For most of us, it is a lifelong walk and sometimes it is one that is marked by failure and disappointment. If we are struggling, then we NEED TO CONFESS our struggle and ask the Lord Jesus to baptize us in the Holy Ghost and with Fire! He WILL do that, and the Holy Spirit will be more than willing to take up the task of changing and conforming us into the image of the Lord Jesus Christ.

The very moment a believer asks the Lord Jesus to fill him with the Holy Spirit, God's promise of the Coming Comforter will work.

Down inside there will be words or phrases or sounds that will start to form and seek expression. The Holy Ghost is giving utterance. The Holy Ghost will not speak for You!

That is as far as the Holy Ghost will go! The rest is up to you the believer. This is the point where you must take over and open your mouth and speak those things, and voice the sounds crying out for expression within you.

I have never met two people with the same prayer language, and I have never met two people with similar expressions or experiences when it comes to being baptized in the Holy Ghost. We are all different. God created us that way. Your experience may not be like mine, but YOU WILL SPEAK IN OTHER TONGUES! Ignore the voice of the skeptics. Ignore Satan telling you "this surely is not the way it should sound." Friend, the HOLY SPIRIT is the one GIVING you this utterance, not man. You cannot learn this in school or seminary. As you feel these impressions and "words" in your innermost being, just open your mouth and start to speak; the Holy Spirit will do the rest. You have asked your Heavenly Father for the Holy Ghost. Now rest in HIM for He will not give you a stone or a serpent instead.

> **Luke 11:11-13**
> **If a son shall ask bread of any of you that is a father, will he give him a stone? or if he ask a fish, will he for a fish give him a serpent? [12] Or if he shall ask an egg, will he offer him a scorpion? [13] If ye then, being evil, know how to give good gifts unto your children: how much more shall your heavenly Father give the Holy Spirit to them that ask him?**

The Holy Spirit does not impose. He suggests. He leads and no leading of the Holy Spirit will cause you to do anything improper. You will always retain full control of all your faculties. By the same token, He will not FORCE you to speak in tongues. Notice the passage in Acts 2:4; THEY BEGAN TO SPEAK with other tongues as the SPIRIT GAVE THEM THE UTTERANCE. The Spirit plays a role in this experience, BUT YOU PLAY a role too! Just relax and allow the Lord Jesus to baptize you in His precious Holy Spirit.

It is His plan for your life as His child and just as you came to HIM in childlike faith as a sinner drawn by the Holy Spirit, Jesus now wants to baptize you in this same Holy Spirit who saved you at some point in your past. We receive EVERYTHING from the Lord, including this glorious gift BY FAITH and it is by FAITH one will receive the mighty baptism in the Holy Ghost.

1 Corinthians 14:38
But if any man be ignorant, let him be ignorant

Paul said, let him that wants to be ignorant of these things, BE IGNORANT. This experience is for today and God is still filling people with the Holy Ghost. If you want to fight it, fight it, but you sir, will find yourself happily fighting against GOD! To those reading this who are honestly seeking more of God; believe that Jesus wants you to be filled with the Spirit so that you can become a greater witness for Him. The power of the Holy Ghost can change countries. He can change marriages. He can change schools. He can change churches. He can change YOU!

Chapter 8

THE SECOND WORK OF GRACE AFTER SALVATION

Matthew 3:11

I indeed baptize you with water unto repentance: but he that cometh after me is mightier than I, whose shoes I am not worthy to bear: he shall baptize you with the Holy Ghost, and with fire:

Salvation and the baptism in the Holy Spirit are two separate and distinct experiences when it comes to the believer.

Salvation is the greatest thing that can take place in the life of a believing sinner while the Baptism in the Holy Ghost with the evidence of speaking with other tongues is the greatest thing that takes place in the life of the BELIEVER, AFTER he comes to Christ through salvation! A person may experience salvation, die and make heaven his eternal home without ever receiving or experiencing the baptism in the Holy Ghost.

I know several born again people who, for whatever reason, have never taken that next step in their Christian walk and be filled with the Spirit. The argument would be made by some that they were filled, even though they never spoke with tongues, but that is not so.

This writer grew up as Southern Baptist. I learned about the blood of Jesus and the Cross when I was a young child in a Sunday school class at my dad's Baptist church in Atlanta, Georgia. I learned the foundational truths that have kept me grounded in Christ today from the Baptist church. However, up until 1986, all that I heard about the Holy Ghost was always negative and believe me, NOTHING was said to encourage me to move to seek the baptism in the Holy Ghost. In 1987, that all changed when on a glorious Saturday night in February, I received the infilling of the Spirit with the evidence of speaking with other tongues as the Spirit of God gave the utterance.

In the fall of 1986, I had gone to the altar many times seeking this tremendous gift to no avail. The Lord had to take me to the private kitchen of my now deceased Aunt who was filled to the brim with the Holy Ghost. I remember to this day that as a young child, I would lay in the upstairs room of her house while she knelt downstairs in the late afternoons and cry out to God in intercession and prayer for me and my brother. She kept us when we were children while mom and dad worked. I remember the days when we would hear her pray in English and then all of sudden, we would feel something like electricity fill that small house that she lived in. She would begin to pray in a heavenly language that the angels and God Himself in heaven probably only knew, but we knew she was touching another world and our names were being called out to God.

Friend, children do not escape that type of experience no matter how far from God they try to run later on in life. Parents, we need to be doing the same today with our young people! Instead of spending time in front of that hell-sent NUT BOX called television hours at a time, we need to be on our knees crying out to God in travail for the hearts and souls of our children.

The reader must understand that this writer has been part of both the Pentecostal and non-Pentecostal worlds and I have no bone to pick with either one. I have ministered in just about any type of church one can think of other than a Catholic church and cults like the Jehovah Witness or Mormons, even though if the Lord opened that door, I am sure we would have a ball preaching under the anointing of the Spirit there; they might have to carve out a wall in the back of the church for me to escape from but it would be fun!

That is what actually happened in 1992 when I was preaching at an Independent Baptist church in Mableton, Georgia. As I was preaching, the Spirit of God came upon me and I spoke briefly in tongues and the church devils came out of the wall in a horrible way. My late Uncle Owen (whom I later referred to as Uncle Abraham who rescued Lot that night) stood between me and several churchgoers who were demanding that I tell them what I prayed in tongues. Uncle Owen stood up and rebuked those making a scene reminding them they needed to be careful about resisting the Holy Ghost. I remember him telling them that if all that they were concerned about was the 30 seconds I prayed in tongues and not the message from the Word of God that had been delivered during the sermon, they may need to check their heart. It was at that moment that this writer started looking into bodyguards when he went to preach at Baptist Churches!

I have been around both people who are Spirit-filled and those who have never experienced what I write about and it is a fair statement and assessment that many who have never spoke in tongues sometimes exhibit more of a Christ-like Spirit than most so-called Spirit-filled people do who parade their giftings arrogantly while boasting of their "superior spiritual condition."

I say that to underscore the fact that one can be saved and not speak in tongues but for one to experience the baptism in the Holy Ghost ONE must be BORN AGAIN! Being born again gets one ready for heaven. The baptism in the Holy Ghost gets one ready for service and warfare here on Earth.

One true trait that is always evident in the life of a Spirit-filled believer is humility!

This writer learned this the hard way as pride and arrogance delayed and almost destroyed the call of God on my life many years ago when I was young.

I have always loved a song by one of my favorite gospel singers, John Starnes, entitled "Don't give up on the child of God, he's the one God is keeping." When it looks like we are down for the count friend, God the HOLY GHOST picks us back up and puts us back into the ring to fight on for another day, and another, and another! Praise God.

I know there are people in ALL denominations who truly love the Lord and are saved even though many, either through ignorance or sadly, through unbelief have never and will never go on to receive this mighty infilling of the Holy Spirit that we speak of. The Holy Spirit through Paul said ,"BE FILLED WITH THE SPIRIT!" That message is to believers, not sinners, for sinners my friend, cannot receive the spiritual things of God until they are born again by this same Spirit.

> **Ephesians 5:18**
> **And be not drunk with wine, wherein is excess; but be (continually being) filled with the Spirit;**

The baptism or infilling of the Holy Ghost MUST be preceded by salvation (regeneration); only THEN can the HOLY GHOST flow from us in the fullness of power. He DWELLS within us at salvation without a doubt, but His work is not complete in us when we get saved, it is JUST BEGINNING.

Let me say that again. The indwelling of the Spirit DOES take place at Salvation but it's the ENDUEMENT of power for service that releases the Spirit's indwelling power to MOVE in us, through us and to others after we have been baptized in the Holy Ghost.

In John 4:14, Jesus said that those who come to Him would experience "wells of water springing up unto everlasting life."

In John 7:37-39, The Lord described the baptism of the Holy Ghost as "living waters," that would "flow" out of HIS (CHRIST'S) innermost being to the believer. That represents the fact that Jesus is the baptizer in the Holy Ghost!

The Holy Ghost brings us to Christ at salvation. The LORD JESUS immerses us IN THE HOLY GHOST after we get saved. We have a WELL of water in us at salvation from which we draw from Christ. When we are baptized in the Holy Ghost BY JESUS, we then have rivers of living water FLOWING from within us that reproduces CHRIST in others as we become powerful WITNESSES upon the earth for HIM!

> **Isaiah 12:1-4**
> **And in that day thou shalt say, O Lord, I will praise thee: though thou wast angry with me, thine anger is turned away, and thou comfortedst me. [2] Behold, God is my salvation; I will trust, and not be afraid: for the Lord Jehovah is my strength and my song; he also is become my salvation. [3] Therefore with joy shall ye draw water out of the wells of salvation. [4] And in that day shall ye say, Praise the Lord, call upon his name, declare his doings among the people, make mention that his name is exalted.**

John 4:14
But whosoever drinketh of the water that I shall give him shall never thirst; but the water that I shall give him shall be in him a well of water springing up into everlasting life.

John 7:37-39
In the last day, that great day of the feast, Jesus stood and cried, saying, If any man thirst, let him come unto me, and drink. [38] He that believeth on me, as the scripture hath said, out of his belly shall flow rivers of living water. [39] (But this spake he of the Spirit, which they that believe on him should receive: for the Holy Ghost was not yet given; because that Jesus was not yet glorified.)

Acts 1:8
But ye shall receive power, after that the Holy Ghost is come upon you:

an to the powers of darkness controlling us! When we divorce Christ from the power of the Spirit, we have committed Spiritual adultery and we have in essence apostatized unto "another Jesus," and "another Spirit." What we see paraded in front of us as "evangelical," is nothing but a bastardized version of Christianity and it is NOTHING close to the heart of God. To be frank, this current crop of evangelicals would be the first to drive the nails into the hand of the Lord Jesus were He back on earth today! They resist everything supernatural and Spirit-born and yet still label themselves as "fundamental."

I have a better term for them that I heard from another evangelist recently; "MENTAL!" Not to sound unkind, but it grieves the heart of the Lord to hear the absolute STUPIDITY and MORONIC statements that come from men who call themselves preachers and who lead millions astray to a Christ-less gospel; one that is void of God's power.

> **2 Corinthians 11:3-4**
> **But I fear, lest by any means, as the serpent beguiled Eve through his subtilty, so your minds should be corrupted from the simplicity that is in Christ. [4] For if he that cometh preacheth another Jesus, whom we have not preached, or if ye receive another spirit, which ye have not received, or another gospel, which ye have not accepted, ye might well bear with him.**

Christians want a personal relationship and experience with God. Most grow tired of listening to what their preacher has to say "about" God without experiencing the joy and power of a one on one relationship with the Heavenly Father through the ministry of the Holy Spirit.

It is God's son, Jesus Christ, who reveals Himself to the believer through the power of the intercessory and revelatory work of the Holy Ghost. Jesus said the Holy Ghost would "speak of Me" (speaking of Christ) and REVEAL to the Church that which He takes from Christ and SHOW it unto us, the believer. Again, this is not a promise to the sinner, but to the saved!

> **John 15:26-27**
> **But when the Comforter is come, whom I will send unto you from the Father, even the Spirit of truth, which proceedeth from the Father, he shall testify of me: [27] And ye also shall bear witness, because ye have been with me from the beginning.**

John 16:15
All things that the Father hath are mine: therefore said I, that he shall take of mine, and shall show it unto you.

Even though ALL believers can have this glorious experience if they wish, many reject it outright and they refuse to ask for it because of unbelief. Yes, some reject it out of ignorance, but many times that can be laid at the door of backslidden or in some cases, just plain LOST preachers who refuse to preach on this all important subject.

Very precious few ministers of God give room today in their services and churches for the Lord Jesus to baptize people in the Spirit. If there was more preaching on the Baptism of the Holy Ghost, we would see more people willing to receive this precious gift! Because it is approached with unbelief and hardness of heart, it is inevitable that those who hear such messages will never seek after more of the power of God!

Friend, it is not what your denomination says about this that counts. It is what the WORD OF GOD says and it says, "HE SHALL Baptize YOU WITH THE HOLY GHOST AND WITH FIRE."

Matthew 3:11
I indeed baptize you with water unto repentance: but he that cometh after me is mightier than I, whose shoes I am not worthy to bear: he shall baptize you with the Holy Ghost, and with fire:

At salvation, life is imparted to someone who was formerly dead in sin; the baptism in the Holy Ghost EMPOWERS someone who was formerly a weak, ineffectual Christian. The believer then is fitted for God's service. It is clearly the mandate of God that every Christian SHOULD receive the baptism in the Holy Ghost. Jesus COMMANDED the disciples to WAIT until they received the baptism of the Spirit before starting out in their ministries.

> **Acts 1:4-5**
> **And, being assembled together with them, commanded them that they should not depart from Jerusalem, but wait for the promise of the Father, which, saith he, ye have heard of me. [5] For John truly baptized with water; but ye shall be baptized with the Holy Ghost not many days hence.**
>
> **Luke 24:48-49**
> **And ye are witnesses of these things. [49] And, behold, I send the promise of my Father upon you: but tarry ye in the city of Jerusalem, until ye be endued with power from on high.**

The activities of the Holy Spirit are many and varied. He is a comforter, a teacher, a leader, a communicator, and a guide. He is the director of all of God's activities on the earth today.

When the sinner comes to the moment of salvation, he does "receive" the Holy Ghost within the context of being "born-again," under the INFLUENCE of the Spirit. However, assuming that being born of the Spirit is the same as the "baptism of power," has lead to erroneous doctrine which has caused untold numbers of Christians to fail to receive this deeper relationship with the HOLY GHOST because of this teaching.

Let me tell you something friend. I do not have the answers to the problems of the human race. You do not have the answer to the problems of the human race. We cannot even find the answers to our OWN problems! But there is ONE WHO DOES have the answer and He is the HOLY GHOST who was sent from the throne of God to be a PARACLETE, a COMFORTER, a GUIDE OF TRUTH, and a LEADER and DIRECTOR in all our affairs here on earth if we will but be sensitive to His leading and obey His every command!

John 16:7-11
Nevertheless I tell you the truth; It is expedient for you that I go away: for if I go not away, the Comforter will not come unto you; but if I depart, I will send him unto you. [8] And when he is come, he will reprove the world of sin, and of righteousness, and of judgment: [9] Of sin, because they believe not on me; [10] Of righteousness, because I go to my Father, and ye see me no more; [11] Of judgment, because the prince of this world is judged.

John 14:14-17
If ye shall ask any thing in my name, I will do it. [15] If ye love me, keep my commandments. [16] And I will pray the Father, and he shall give you another Comforter, that he may abide with you for ever; [17] Even the Spirit of truth; whom the world cannot receive, because it seeth him not, neither knoweth him: but ye know him; for he dwelleth with you, and shall be in you.

Look at the progression the Lord Jesus spoke of concerning the Holy Ghost:

- **You KNOW HIM**
- **He shall DWELL WITH YOU**
- **He shall be IN YOU**

There are those who preach that on the Day of Pentecost the Holy Ghost came to dwell with believers. That statement was half right but in a way, half wrong in the way that they present this fact. The Holy Spirit DID come to dwell and stay with believers at Pentecost, but He also came to do a whole lot more than just dwell.

The Spirit of God was already influencing the work of God upon the Earth before Pentecost. It was at the Day of Pentecost when He came with such power and force that 120 ineffectual followers of Jesus were filled with the power of God and became "men who turned the world upside down," for Christ!

Yes, He came to dwell but He also came to EMPOWER and SEND FORTH! Yes, He came to dwell but He also came to KNOCK DOWN THE GATES OF HELL and break the powers of darkness off the face of the Earth! Yes, He came to DWELL but He came to give believers something more than a dead form of religion.

He came to fill us to overflowing with the presence of Jesus and to MOVE in power THROUGH US, TO US, and IN US as the Kingdom of God is revealed to a lost and dying world through those who allow Him to empower them for service!

His work in us is not for us to just sit on a church pew from week to week and listen to sermon after sermon, but to anoint us with the Holy Ghost and with power as God did Jesus who went about doing GOOD and HEALING ALL that were oppressed of the devil for GOD WAS WITH HIM!

The Lord has ordained the church to move in the kind of power Jesus moved in while on Earth and to do His works to heal ALL those oppressed of Satan. That is the ministry of the New Covenant

Church; to do the WORKS of Christ, and without the power of the Holy Spirit present, we can NEVER do the works of Christ or any other works for that matter.

> **Acts 10:38**
> **How God anointed Jesus of Nazareth with the Holy Ghost and with power: who went about doing good, and healing all that were oppressed of the devil; for God was with him.**

> **Ephesians 2:20-22**
> **And are built upon the foundation of the apostles and prophets, Jesus Christ himself being the chief corner stone; [21] In whom all the building fitly framed together groweth unto an holy temple in the Lord: [22] In whom ye also are builded together for an habitation of God through the Spirit.**

God and man were never intended to lead separate existences. We were created to have intimacy and fellowship with the Father. Many people have become so sick and dissatisfied with cold, formal religion and they have hungered for a greater spiritual reality. They long to experience a dynamic Christian life.

Many sit in their churches week in and week out waiting for God to transform their church into a dynamic church. The key to those churches becoming more dynamic is the power and moving of the Holy Spirit. The third person of the Godhead will always move where He is welcomed and allowed to operate whether it be saints or the corporate buildings of true born-again believers that we call the church.

I will tell you this. I have never met anyone YET who was disappointed when they received the baptism in the Holy Ghost. I have met a few individuals that were once filled but they took their eyes off Jesus and put their faith in man and not God and they became disillusioned. They removed their simple childlike faith in the Cross and replaced it with other things. But for those truly baptized in the Holy Ghost there has never been disappointment!

Remember this friend. The foundation of the Holy Ghost baptism is the CROSS OF CHRIST. Being filled with the Spirit does not abrogate our responsibility of taking up our cross and walking after Christ on a daily basis. On the contrary; it actually GIVES us the POWER to take up that cross and WALK in the power of HIS GRACE which is necessary for us to do just that. In Romans 5:1, the Holy Spirit calls this "ACCESS into this GRACE," and power, meaning that for those who come to Christ and are willing to obey the Spirit of God, there is more than abundant grace for the trip ahead and journey to glory.

> **Romans 5:1-2**
> **Therefore being justified by faith, we have peace with God through our Lord Jesus Christ: [2] By whom also we have access by faith into this grace wherein we stand, and rejoice in hope of the glory of God.**

Because of the Cross of Christ, we have been given the power of the HOLY GHOST to STAND in this grace that we have been given and REJOICE in the HOPE of the glory of God! We have been declared "not guilty," because of the blood which has made it possible for us to be filled with the HOLY GHOST, the GRACE, or POWER that makes Calvary and its effects REAL in our hearts and lives.

Whatever God demands, His grace always provides and supplies for in our heart and life. Our job is to BELIEVE on the only TRUE SON OF GOD, THE LORD JESUS CHRIST, and to keep our faith anchored in what He has done for us at the Cross!

The Holy Ghost is more than a religious concept, a vague symbol or even a "force," as some put it. The HOLY GHOST IS GOD, who will drastically transform one's life beyond words! Peter knew this when he declared that the events on the Day of Pentecost were tied to the prophecies of Joel the prophet in the Old Covenant.

> **Acts 2:38-39**
> **Then Peter said unto them, Repent, and be baptized every one of you in the name of Jesus Christ for the remission of sins, and ye shall receive the gift of the Holy Ghost. [39] For the promise is unto you, and to your children, and to all that are afar off, even as many as the Lord our God shall call.**

> **Joel 2:28-32**
> **And it shall come to pass afterward, that I will pour out my spirit upon all flesh; and your sons and your daughters shall prophesy, your old men shall dream dreams, your young men shall see visions: [29] And also upon the servants and upon the handmaids in those days will I pour out my spirit. [30] And I will shew wonders in the heavens and in the earth, blood, and fire, and pillars of smoke. [31] The sun shall be turned into darkness, and the moon into blood, before the great and the terrible day of the Lord come. [32] And it shall come to pass, that whosoever shall call on the name of the Lord shall be delivered: for in mount Zion and in Jerusalem shall be deliverance, as the Lord hath said, and in the remnant whom the Lord shall call.**

Acts 2:16-18

But this is that which was spoken by the prophet Joel; [17] And it shall come to pass in the last days, saith God, I will pour out of my Spirit upon all flesh: and your sons and your daughters shall prophesy, and your young men shall see visions, and your old men shall dream dreams: [18] And on my servants and on my handmaidens I will pour out in those days of my Spirit; and they shall prophesy:

Let me clarify some things again in this study for the reader:

- We do NOT believe that speaking in tongues will automatically produce a better Christian
- We do not believe or teach that anyone has to speak in tongues to be saved or make heaven their eternal home
- We do not believe or teach that anyone becomes more saved as a result of speaking in tongues. When a person accepts Christ as His Lord and Saviour HE IS SAVED, period. Prayerfully however, this same believing sinner, who now is a believer in Christ, will GROW in his walk with the Lord, but at the moment of salvation he is as saved as he will ever be.
- We DO believe that speaking in tongues is ordained by God
- We DO believe that it was a COMMON manifestation in the early church and it is just as widespread and proper today as it was then; The reason for the lack of this manifestation in the church as recorded church history would indicate before 1903 is that the subject was NEVER PREACHED or TAUGHT on from behind pulpits. After Azusa Street in Los Angeles, California in 1903, the Holy Ghost seemed to rev up His engine and started raising up SCORES of men of God who began to preach and teach on

the baptism of the Holy Ghost. Men like Charles Spurgeon, Billy Sunday and others, including the Wesley Brothers and George Whitfield had supernatural experiences in their Christian lives but they did not have a name for it because prior to 1903 there was no name attached to these things. It is recorded history that Spurgeon moved in the prophetic many times in his meetings as well as, people heathat heard him during his personal prayer time heard him pray in other languages to God. Sounds like the baptism of the HOLY GHOST to me!!! Sounds like the Spirit of God made intercession for the saints through Charles Spurgeon and others and empowered them for service and for witnessing!

- We DO believe this a valid manifestation and demonstration of the INITIAL infilling with the Holy Ghost
- We DO believe tongues are a great HELP to the believer, a giver of strength, and a BUILDER OF FAITH

There are tremendous religious forces in ALL denominations seeking to divorce Christ from the Cross, the work of the Spirit's anointing and the ministry of Jesus, and what the Holy Spirit does and the Holy Spirit Himself. We can do none of these things and expect the power of God to move and operate within our churches.

Sadly, so many believers, as well as so-called churches have opted for humanism in place of Holy Ghost power. The prayer meeting has been replaced with fellowship meals and family fun night. Times and seasons of intercession have been replaced by self-help programs, bingo games and softball teams.

Spiritual matters have taken a back seat to other things that matter nothing when dealing with eternity and the state of men's souls.

Friend, the subject of the Holy Spirit is MORE than just a doctrinal argument between the Pentecostal and non-Pentecostal camps within the Body of Christ.

The Holy Spirit is GOD and believe me, there IS NO argument in heaven about Who He is, What He Does, When He Does it and How He Does it.

I've always said that if we don't stop resisting and rejecting the Holy Spirit in our church structures, God is going to remove Himself totally. He has already removed Himself to a degree as we witness this continued slide into apostasy and false doctrine by the church.

When the Holy Spirit is given TOTAL freedom, LIGHT always overrules the darkness. When the Holy Spirit is given some freedom, as He is in some churches, then SOME light exists yes, but there is also darkness.

There are some churches however that the Spirit's power and work has been so pushed aside for the ways of men that LIGHT has left and darkness has taken abode among the leadership and laity of those bodies. The results of this darkness are NO SOULS being saved, altars being empty every Sunday, no sick bodies being healed, no bondages being broken, and in many cases these same bondages are accepted and applauded, i.e. homosexuality and transgenderism, no restoration of broken homes and NO unction and conviction coming from the pulpit.

We're so worried about being "Baptist," or "Methodist," or "Pentecostal," or "whatever else we are," than we are concerned that we are IN CHRIST and FULL OF THE HOLY GHOST!

The church today so needs the Holy Spirit! We need a fresh enduement of Holy Ghost power including many mainline Pentecostal denominations!

The Assemblies of God, Church of God, Pentecostal Holiness, Foursquare, ALL need to come back to the foundation of the Holy Ghost and let Him reenergize us with His power and fire. We so need Jesus to baptize us afresh with the Holy Ghost and with Fire.

Individuals Are Baptized IN the Holy Spirit After Conversion

> **John 3:3-8**
> **Jesus answered and said unto him, Verily, verily, I say unto thee, Except a man be born again, he cannot see the kingdom of God. [4] Nicodemus saith unto him, How can a man be born when he is old? can he enter the second time into his mother's womb, and be born? [5] Jesus answered, Verily, verily, I say unto thee, Except a man be born of water and of the Spirit, he cannot enter into the kingdom of God. [6] That which is born of the flesh is flesh; and that which is born of the Spirit is spirit. [7] Marvel not that I said unto thee, Ye must be born again. [8] The wind bloweth where it listeth, and thou hearest the sound thereof, but canst not tell whence it cometh, and whither it goeth: so is every one that is born of the Spirit.**

As already mentioned, many teach that the Holy Spirit comes automatically after conversion, and there is nothing else to be sought, asked for, or even requested from God. They say, in effect, that once we get saved, then our relationship with God is complete.

While some outright reject the notion of ANY work of the Spirit at salvation, there are some who do believe in a "filling" of the Spirit after conversion and that one must seek the Lord for this and overtly ASK for it. Most of the time however, these folks deny that is is accompanied by speaking in tongues which is false.

When it comes to the second work of Grace by God after one gets saved, we must say again that there is huge difference in what the Holy Ghost does in regnerating the sinner into Christ and Christ than baptizing the believer with the Holy Ghost and fire! To state it a different way; there is a DIFFERENCE between being BORN of the Spirit and being baptized IN the Spirit!

Let's look at some examples.

> **Acts 2:1-4**
> **And when the day of Pentecost was fully come, they were all with one accord in one place. [2] And suddenly there came a sound from heaven as of a rushing mighty wind, and it filled all the house where they were sitting. [3] And there appeared unto them cloven tongues like as of fire, and it sat upon each of them. [4] And they were all filled with the Holy Ghost, and began to speak with other tongues, as the Spirit gave them utterance.**

Acts 2:4 describes the filling of the 120 with the Holy Spirit. These 120 gathered on the day of Pentecost were not gathered to be saved. Acts 1:4-8 tells us that some who were present, including Mary, the mother of Jesus, and the 11 apostles who had actually just chosen the 12th (Matthias).

> Acts 1:12 -14
> **Then returned they unto Jerusalem from the mount called Olivet, which is from Jerusalem a Sabbath day's journey. [13] And when they were come in, they went up into an upper room, where abode both Peter, and James, and John, and Andrew, Philip, and Thomas, Bartholomew, and Matthew, James the son of Alphaeus, and Simon Zelotes, and Judas the brother of James. [14] These all continued with one accord in prayer and supplication, with the women, and Mary the mother of Jesus, and with his brethren. [15] And in those days Peter stood up in the midst of the disciples, and said, (the number of names together were about an hundred and twenty,)**

The list of these in Acts 1:12 do not include those who needed to get saved! In Luke 10:20 the Master told His disciples that when they were rejoicing over the fact of devils being subject to them (within the authority of Jesus), that they should rather rejoice BECAUSE THEIR NAMES WERE WRITTEN IN HEAVEN.

> Luke 10:20
> **Notwithstanding in this rejoice not, that the spirits are subject unto you; but rather rejoice, because your names are written in heaven.**

This of course confirms the fact they were already saved, with their names written in the Lamb's Book of Life. They were receiving the enduement of power for service in compliance with the commandment of the Lord and at the same time witnessing the advent of the Holy Spirit's indwelling power and His fullness.

The outpouring on Pentecost was not to make the 120 "more saved," but it was a baptism of FIRE! This was subsequent to salvation for those who gathered. Mary the mother of Jesus had already tasted a small portion of what took place at Pentecost earlier on when the angels foretold the birth of Christ as a result of the "HOLY GHOST COMING UPON THEE!"

Luke 1:35
And the angel answered and said unto her, The Holy Ghost shall come upon thee, and the power of the Highest shall overshadow thee: therefore also that holy thing which shall be born of thee shall be called the Son of God.

Matthew 1:15-21
And Eliud begat Eleazar; and Eleazar begat Matthan; and Matthan begat Jacob; [16] And Jacob begat Joseph the husband of Mary, of whom was born Jesus, who is called Christ. [17] So all the generations from Abraham to David are fourteen generations; and from David until the carrying away into Babylon are fourteen generations; and from the carrying away into Babylon unto Christ are fourteen generations. [18] Now the birth of Jesus Christ was on this wise: When as his mother Mary was espoused to Joseph, before they came together, she was found with child of the Holy Ghost. [19] Then Joseph her husband, being a just man, and not willing to make her a public example, was minded to put her away privily. [20] But while he thought on these things, behold, the angel of the Lord appeared unto him in a dream, saying, Joseph, thou son of David, fear not to take unto thee Mary thy wife: for that which is conceived in her is of the Holy Ghost. [21] And she shall bring forth a son, and thou shall call his name Jesus: for he shall save his people from their sins.

The SAME HOLY GHOST that came upon MARY giving birth to the Christ, would now COME UPON HER again and IN HER on the day of Pentecost!

Acts Chapter 8

> **Acts 8:6**
> **And the people with one accord gave heed unto those things which Philip spake, hearing and seeing the miracles which he did.**

This same passage speaks of unclean spirits being cast out and of many being healed. There was great joy in the city. Then in verse 12, it tells of the Samaritans believing what Philip was preaching concerning the Kingdom of God and the name of the Lord Jesus Christ and how they were being baptized, both men and women.

This is exactly what the Word tells US to do in John 3:16, Acts 10:42-43, and in other Scriptures.

> **John 3:16-17**
> **For God so loved the world, that he gave his only begotten Son, that whosoever believeth in him should not perish, but have everlasting life. [17] For God sent not his Son into the world to condemn the world; but that the world through him might be saved.**

> **Acts 10:42-43**
> **And he commanded us to preach unto the people, and to testify that it is he which was ordained of God to be the Judge of quick and dead. [43] To him give all the prophets witness, that**

> **through his name whosoever believeth in him shall receive remission of sins.**

When anyone "believes" the things of the Kingdom of God and on the NAME OF THE LORD JESUS CHRIST, that person is saved! So these Samaritans were saved by the blood of Jesus when Philip preached. They were washed in the blood, and their names were written down in the Lamb's Book of Life. Then the 14th verse of this passage talks about the apostles who were in Jerusalem heard about the Samaritans receiving the Word of God. They then sent Peter and John unto them.

In the 15th verse, we are told that Peter and John "prayed that they might receive the Holy Spirit."

> **Acts 8:14-15**
> **Now when the apostles which were at Jerusalem heard that Samaria had received the word of God, they sent unto them Peter and John: [15] Who, when they were come down, prayed for them, that they might receive the Holy Ghost:**

Now, if an individual receives EVERYTHING at conversion, why in the world were Peter and John there? What was the point of going down and preaching the Holy Spirit and praying for them if they had automatically received the Spirit of God in full at conversion as is commonly taught today?

One commentator I read behind on this matter made the suggestion that the Samaritans had not gotten actually born again under Philip's preaching and that John and Peter came down to pray for the Spirit to indwell them. This writer strongly disagrees with that interpretation and I believe the Bible itself disagrees with that as well.

Now, had this event taken place BEFORE the Cross, I would actually agree in part with the Baptist brother. Those who were born again under the Old Covenant could be saved through faith in the Covenant and coming Messiah, but the Spirit of God never "dwelled" inside them as He does us today under the New Covenant.

Acts 8:16
(For as yet he was fallen upon none of them: only they were baptized in the name of the Lord Jesus.)

The Samaritans had been baptized in the name of the Lord Jesus under Philip's preaching; as a result they experienced salvation AFTER the Cross and as a result, all those who received the Word of God were BORN AGAIN and received the Spirit of God at salvation.

They had been saved, but NONE OF THEM HAD BEEN FILLED with the Holy Spirit. They had been baptized in water according to the Scripture passage, but they had not received the baptism IN the Holy Ghost with the evidence of speaking with other tongues. In the 17th verse it says that hands were laid on them and only THEN did they receive the Holy Spirit!

Acts 8:17
Then laid they their hands on them, and they received the Holy Ghost.

Those are two distinct and separate experiences that took place at the Revival in Samaria and those are the two distinct experiences that takes place in the hearts and lives of every single individual who comes to Christ today!

When we are lost, we experience salvation by being BORN OF THE SPIRIT, being dead in trespasses and sin then experiencing NEWNESS of life; after we get saved. We then become qualified to experience the mighty baptism in the Holy Ghost with the evidence of speaking with other tongues as the Spirit of God gives the utterance.

Acts Chapter 9–The Conversion of Saul of Tarsus (PAUL)

The 9th Chapter of Acts describes the conversion of Saul of Tarsus (Paul). The 12th verse recounts God's command to Ananias to go and pray for Paul and put his hands on him that Paul might receive his sight. Ananias was not directed to lay hands on him that he might be saved because Paul had already accepted the Lord Jesus Christ as His Saviour on the Road to Damascus because of the great vision that was recorded in the 3rd through the 7th verses of the 9th chapter of Acts.

> **Acts 9:3-7**
> **And as he journeyed, he came near Damascus: and suddenly there shined round about him a light from heaven: [4] And he fell to the earth, and heard a voice saying unto him, Saul, Saul, why persecutest thou me? [5] And he said, Who art thou, Lord? And the Lord said, I am Jesus whom thou persecutest: it is hard for thee to kick against the pricks. [6] And he trembling and astonished said, Lord, what wilt thou have me to do? And the Lord said unto him, Arise, and go into the city, and it shall be told thee what thou must do. [7] And the men**

which journeyed with him stood speechless, hearing a voice, but seeing no man.

Acts 9:12
And hath seen in a vision a man named Ananias coming in, and putting his hand on him, that he might receive his sight.

The 17th verse states that when Ananias met Saul he called him, "Brother Saul." He would NOT have done so if Paul had not accepted Jesus for it was this same man who hours or days earlier might have KILLED Ananias and every other single Christian he could find. That is what Saul was before he changed his name to Paul. He was a Christian killer!

Acts 9:17
And Ananias went his way, and entered into the house; and putting his hands on him said, Brother Saul, the Lord, even Jesus, that appeared unto thee in the way as thou camest, hath sent me, that thou mightest receive thy sight, and be filled with the Holy Ghost.

Paul was saved. His name written in the Lamb's Book of Life. He was already washed in the blood of the Lamb. The Bible makes it clear that Ananias was sent to pray for him that he might receive his sight again (since Paul's blindness was caused by the great light coincident with the vision on the road), AND that he might be filled with the Holy Ghost!

If one is baptized in the Holy Spirit at conversion, what in the world was Ananias doing and WHY was he praying for Paul? Yes, the Holy Spirit indwells us at salvation, but there is a distinct and more powerful work the Lord Jesus wants to do in our hearts AFTER we get saved and that is to FILL US WITH THE HOLY GHOST!

Acts Chapter 10

In the 10th chapter of Acts, it would seem that the outpouring of the Holy Spirit took place in the home of Cornelius almost immediately after conversion. This immediate outpouring is also a common occurrence today (at least in churches where the Holy Spirit is preached). It should be the NORM instead of the exception.

The things we read about in Acts should be earmarks of our churches today but instead most of what this writer is discussing is shunned, rejected and in some sad cases, labeled to be of Satan. Neighbor, we need the Holy Spirit to come back in His fullness to the church of the Living God!

Acts Chapter 19

The 19th chapter of Acts describes the Apostle Paul as speaking to the disciples of John at Ephesus. He asked them (as recorded in the 2nd verse) "Have you received the Holy Ghost since you believed?" And they replied that they did not even know what Paul was talking about.

That is the state of most churches today as it relates to the baptism in the Holy Ghost! There is certainly a great deal of ignorance concerning this but this ignorance is the result of preachers refusing to preach the whole counsel of God.

I remember discussing this with a minister from Tennessee and he looked at me and said, "Son, you just need to find balance in your beliefs and preaching." Well if balance means preaching a message void of the power of the Holy Ghost, then neighbor, this writer would rather be OUT OF BALANCE and in the will of God rather than have all the balance in the world and be in apostasy!

Preacher, preach the Word. Preach the Holy Ghost. Preach the mighty baptism in the Holy Ghost. Preach the power of almighty God. Preach the anointing and the leading and guiding of the Holy Ghost.

After Paul explained the message of the Holy Ghost to them he laid hands on them, "and the HOLY GHOST came on them."

> **Acts 19:1-3**
> **And it came to pass, that, while Apollos was at Corinth, Paul having passed through the upper coasts came to Ephesus: and finding certain disciples, [2] He said unto them, Have ye received the Holy Ghost since ye believed? And they said unto him, We have not so much as heard whether there be any Holy Ghost. [3] And he said unto them, Unto what then were ye baptized? And they said, Unto John's baptism.**

> **Acts 19:6**
> **And when Paul had laid his hands upon them, the Holy Ghost came on them; and they spake with tongues, and prophesied.**

Now if again, as most preachers want to proclaim, that we get EVERY single thing the HOLY Spirit has for us at salvation, why in the world did Paul even bother to discuss the matter of the Holy Ghost with these brethren? He was not there to get these men saved. He was there to lay hands on them to receive the baptism of the HOly Ghost.

I heard over radio the other day a preacher slur the Apostle Paul by stating that "if the apostle Paul came into his church speaking in tongues, he would kick him out." I do not know who this minister was, but if I had a chance to tell him something, I would tell him that it is not PAUL that he should better be worrying about kicking out. When we blaspheme the HOLY GHOST through our ignorance and unbelief, we kick GOD out of our churches, and when He leaves friend, we are in far worse shape than if Paul or any other human came and attended.

Paul was there to lay hands on them to receive the Holy Spirit, "and they spake with tongues and prophesied."

The Spirit of Sonship, The Power Of The Spirit

> **Romans 8:9**
> **But ye are not in the flesh, but in the Spirit, if so be that the Spirit of God dwell in you. Now if any man have not the Spirit of Christ, he is none of his.**

> **Romans 8:14-16**
> **For as many as are led by the Spirit of God, they are the sons of God. [15] For ye have not received the spirit of bondage again to fear; but ye have received the Spirit of adoption, whereby we cry, Abba, Father. [16] The Spirit itself beareth witness with our spirit, that we are the children of God:**

Every Christian receives the Holy Spirit of adoption into sonship with God at the time of salvation. (Romans 8:9) This was not, however, what Paul was referring to when he addressed John's disciples at Ephesus when he asked them "had they received the Holy Spirit since they believed?" The Apostle was asking about the Spirit baptism John had prophesied and preached about, which goes back to the original text of our journal today: "He shall baptize you with the Holy Ghost and with fire."

Matthew 3:11
I indeed baptize you with water unto repentance: but he that cometh after me is mightier than I, whose shoes I am not worthy to bear: he shall baptize you with the Holy Ghost, and with fire:

John described how Jesus would baptize them AND ALL OTHERS WHO COME TO HIM IN FAITH AND ASKING FOR THIS PRECIOUS GIFT with the Holy Spirit and fire.

John 1:31-34
And I knew him not: but that he should be made manifest to Israel, therefore am I come baptizing with water. [32] And John bare record, saying, I saw the Spirit descending from heaven like a dove, and it abode upon him. [33] And I knew him not: but he that sent me to baptize with water, the same said unto me, Upon whom thou shalt see the Spirit descending, and remaining on him, the same is he which baptizeth with the Holy Ghost. [34] And I saw, and bare record that this is y the Son of God.

Acts 1:4-5
And, being assembled together with them, commanded them that they should not depart from Jerusalem, but wait for the promise of the Father, which, saith he, ye have heard of me. [5] For John truly baptized with water; but ye shall be baptized with the Holy Ghost not many days hence.

This has NOTHING to do with the New Birth by the Spirit. It is the enduement of POWER for service AFTER one is born again. When one reads this, it is easy to see that a person can be saved by the blood of Jesus and believe for salvation, YET be in ignorance of the baptism of the Holy Spirit. It is clearly stated that such was the case here, and millions of others are in the same condition today. They have been saved by the blood of Jesus, yet they know LITTLE or nothing about the baptism in the Holy Ghost.

> **John 14:17**
> **Even the Spirit of truth; whom the world cannot receive, because it seeth him not, neither knoweth him: but ye know him; for he dwelleth with you, and shall be in you.**

Jesus states plainly in John's gospel that a SINNER could not and cannot receive the baptism in the Holy Spirit. It is IMPOSSIBLE! The vessel must be first CLEANSED (through the born-again experience) and only THEN will the Spirit of Truth (whom the world cannot receive) enter in in fullness. He does come in at salvation as one would pour water into a well; when Jesus baptizes us in the Holy Ghost that well turns into a RIVER that is flowing with living water.

> **John 7:37-39**
> **In the last day, that great day of the feast, Jesus stood and cried, saying, If any man thirst, let him come unto me, and drink. [38] He that believeth on me, as the scripture hath said, out of his belly shall flow rivers of living water. [39] (But this spake he of the Spirit, which they that believe on him should receive: for the Holy Ghost was not yet given; because that Jesus was not yet glorified.)**

John 4:14
But whosoever drinketh of the water that I shall give him shall never thirst; but the water that I shall give him shall be in him a well of water springing up into everlasting life.

The well of John 4 springs up into everlasting life; the "RIVERS" of living water FLOW out of the Lord Jesus into the believer when one is baptized in the Holy Ghost. John defined this experience at the end when he clearly says: "THIS SPAKE HE OF THE SPIRIT because He was not yet given because Jesus was not yet glorified."

Let the reader never forget this important fact about the Spirit of God: before the Cross men could not be filled with the Spirit as they are today under the New Covenant. There were many times under the Old Covenant when the Spirit temporarily came upon people and for a specific service. He may even have briefly dwelled within men, but He could not stay as He did on the Day of Pentecost and beyond because man's sin debt had not been paid in the throne room of heaven.

Praise God, however. Two thousand years ago on a hill far far away, on an old rugged cross, the price for man's redemption and freedom was paid through the blood of Christ. It broke down the wall of partition between man and God and made man fit to be a habitation for the Spirit of God.

Ephesians 2:22
In whom ye also are builded together for an habitation of God through the Spirit.

Individuals who insist that a person automatically receives everything at salvation and that he does not have to seek anything further from the Lord are not correctly interpreting the Word of God.

There IS an experience after salvation and it is called the baptism IN the Holy Ghost. It must follow AFTER, and take place subsequent to salvation, not before. There are times when I have seen people saved and filled with the Spirit almost immediately but the infilling came IMMEDIATELY AFTER being born again as it happened in the house of Cornelius.

Regardless of the timing, one must ASK to receive this second grace experience; it is not an automatic gift from our Heavenly Father, yet this infilling of the Spirit is something EVERY SINGLE CHILD OF GOD who has been saved should seek after they are born again.

> **Luke 11:13**
> **If ye then, being evil, know how to give good gifts unto your children: how much more shall your heavenly Father give the Holy Spirit to them that ask him?**

To state it again, Salvation is the greatest gift of God to the sinner. The baptism in the Holy Ghost is the greatest gift to the believer! God has winked at man's igorance in the past, but now He is commanding His church to REPENT and turn to Him in these last days!

> **Acts 17:30**
> **And the times of this ignorance God winked at; but now commandeth all men every where to repent:**

The church needs to REPENT of its ignorance concerning the things of God. We have a great deal of knowledge of things that do not matter to a hill of beans but we have very little knowledge of Christ.

The fact is that even those baptized in the Holy Ghost NEVER have all that God has to offer. When one is filled with the Spirit, that is but a door to a deeper walk with the Lord that never ends for those who are truly maturing in Christ.

The more mature one gets, the more one sees their utter helplessness in this Christian walk without the grace and power of the Holy Ghost. This is what the Spirit termed the "access into this Grace whereby which we all STAND." For us to inherit eternal life we must learn the simple childlike means of standing and believing!

> **Romans 5:1-2**
> **Therefore being justified by faith, we have peace with God through our Lord Jesus Christ: [2] By whom also we have access by faith into this grace wherein we stand, and rejoice in hope of the glory of God.**
>
> **2 Peter 3:18**
> **But grow in grace, and in the knowledge of our Lord and Saviour Jesus Christ. To him be glory both now and for ever. Amen.**

The very second friend, that you and I stop thinking we need to grow in grace and know more of JESUS through the power of His Spirit is the day we have committed spiritual suicide!

The baptism in the Holy Ghost is a door to a greater revelation and love for Jesus Christ than you will ever receive. Only the Holy Ghost can produce this in the heart and life of the believer!

We cannot divorce Christ from the Holy Spirit and we cannot divorce the gifts and ministries of the Holy Ghost from the Holy Ghost Himself. He will not allow us to do that. Some churches proclaim smugly that they believe in "all the Bible," yet the minute something happens out of the ordinary as a result of the Spirit's work, they seek to shut down what God is doing to make sure there is nothing done outside the realm of what they can control.

This is the work of the Spirit for the believer after they are saved! We so need Him today!

Chapter 9

THE HOLY SPIRIT AND THE GENTILES

TEXT: Acts 10:44–While Peter yet spoke these words, the Holy Ghost fell on all them that heard the word. And they of the circumcision that believed were astonished, as many as came with Peter, because that on the Gentiles also was poured out the gift of the Holy Ghost. For they heard them speak with tongues and magnify God. Then answered Peter, Can any man forbid water, that these should not be baptized, which have received the Holy Ghost as well as we? And he commanded them to be baptized in the name of the Lord. Then prayed they him to tarry certain days.

The message of the Baptism in the Holy Spirit with the evidence of speaking with other tongues has become one of the most attacked doctrines in the Bible other than the Atonement, the Rapture of the Church, and issues relating to eternity.

This attack has come not so much from the world, but from within the ranks of the "evangelical" community that has refused or rejected this great experience from God. This resistance is not new. It goes back to the days when the Holy Spirit first fell on the Day of Pentecost.

Except for Luke, some 120 Jewish disciples and maybe a few others who were Gentiles, gloriously received this great enduement of power from on high that has remained part of the true gospel message ever since. This has come at a great price!

Since the outpouring of the Holy Ghost in the early 1900s in a little tiny home on Azusa Street in Los Angeles, California, millions have been filled with the Spirit and spoke with other tongues as the Spirit of God gives them the utterance. Most Bible scholars believe that this event in this tiny little cottage ushered in the "latter" rain spoken about in James 5:7. There are some who believe the "former rain" spoken of in James 5:7, began on the Day of Pentecost and we are living in the last days before the return of Christ and we are witnessing firsthand Joel's prophecy concerning a great outpouring of the Spirit of God!

Regardless of the terminology or semantics, we are living in the Day of Pentecost NOW; literally waiting on the Feast of Trumpets! Pentecost is on the Jewish feast calendar and it acknowledged the barley harvest where Israel would gather in grain before the coming fall rains. Jesus is gathering in a final harvest before the wheat harvest and rains of judgment fall after the Rapture of the Church. The Apostle John saw an Angel during the Great Tribulation drive a sickle into the earth that represented a harvest of judgement that is to occur at the great Battle of Armageddon.

There was a period of waiting in between the barley harvest of the spring and the wheat harvest of the fall that signaled the physical Jewish New Year (Rosh Hashanah). We are in that waiting period from the day the Holy Spirit fell at Pentecost to the time the Lord Himself shall descend from heaven with a shout and the voice of the Archangel, as the dead in Christ will rise first and we which are alive and remain shall be caught up together to be with Christ in the air forever and forever!

It has been during this waiting period that the Lord Jesus has baptized millions into His Spirit and fulfilled that which was spoken of by Joel. (Joel 2:28-31)

Sadly, instead of this being embraced by the church, it has been mocked.

Most people who speak in tongues today are labeled as fanatics, unlearned and ignorant, while others are even accused of being of Satan. Interestingly enough, this was said of Peter and John when they stood before the religious hierarchy of their day who were questioning the power in which they had caused a man lame from birth to walk.

We may brag about our "education" and "knowledge of the scriptures," but I would rather be accused of "being with Jesus." The bondages we are fighting today will not go away with a three-point sermon, a cute prayer, and an offertory hymn. We are engaged in a spiritual battle beyond comprehension. It is a battle that will only be won on a spiritual plane. The power we are fighting is the power that will set men free! The power the church is fighting will deliver the alcoholic from alcohol. It will deliver the drug addict from drugs. It will deliver the one bound by pornography from pornography and perversion. It will cause the thief to stop stealing. It will cause the liar to stop lying. It will cause the religious to know Jesus more intimately and in truth and grace. It will put life in our dead Sunday school classes on Sunday and church programs. Jesus, through the Holy Spirit will set us free!!

While we are trying to cultivate the minds of our people, the world slips off into hell bound by the powers of darkness. It is time the church of the Lord Jesus stop trying to cultivate the minds of our people to the point our education keeps us from BEING WITH JESUS. Holy boldness from a fire-breathed revival is needed to confront and love a sinful society that mocks and laughs at God and lampoons everything that is holy and just. God is not looking for angry preachers. He is looking for someone whose heart is so ablaze with His love and power that not an ounce of judgment falls from their lips, but the demonic powers of darkness flee in their presence.

The greatest threat to the power of God that will change society is not society. It is backslidden, mossy-back, pharisaic, religion. It is religion and churchism that stands in the way of God and what He wants to do in this last hour. Most of the church is like this council in Acts 4. They could not argue over the miracle that had taken place; the man lame from birth stood healed in front of them. Instead of praising God, they had to "confer among themselves" about it. It was the same during the times of the Apostles.

> **Acts 4:13-20**
> **Now when they saw the boldness of Peter and John, and perceived that they were unlearned and ignorant men, they marveled; and they took knowledge of them, that they had been with Jesus. And beholding the man that was healed standing with them, they could say nothing against it. But when they had commanded them to go aside out of the council, they conferred among themselves, Saying, What shall we do to these men? For that indeed a notable miracle hath been done by them is manifest to all them that dwell in Jerusalem; and we cannot deny it. But that it spread no further among the people, let us let us straightly threaten them, that they speak henceforth to no man in this name. And they called them, and commanded them not to speak at all nor teach in the name of Jesus. But Peter and John answered and said unto them, Whether it be right in the sight of God to hearken unto you more than unto God, judge ye. For we cannot but speak the things which we have seen and heard**

Peter and John say, "whether it be right in the sight of God to hearken unto you more unto God, you be the judge." Then they say something that is very key to that which I hope to minister to you in this article; "WE CANNOT BUT SPEAK THE THINGS WHICH WE HAVE SEEN AND HEARD." The church has a hard time arguing away the fact that millions of people have received this glorious experience of speaking in tongues as those that gathered on the day of Pentecost did in the Bible. (Acts 2:4) Luke also mentions this experience throughout the book of Acts. Paul also gives great attention to it in his epistle to the Corinthians.

Speaking in Tongues is Scriptural, Of God, And for Today

Despite this, the modern church system continues to proclaim that this glorious enduement of power is not scriptural or valid today. There are some who even say it is of Satan.

I was at a church not too long ago in Central Tennessee whose doctrinal pamphlets stated "we cannot believe this (the baptism in the Holy Spirit) is real just because so many people have experienced it. We do not believe in an experience; we believe in the Bible."

Well, if we do not believe in experiences, then we do not believe in salvation. Salvation is an experience. If we do not believe in experience, then we do not believe in people rededicating their lives to the Lord. Rededication is an experience. If we do not believe in experience, then we do not believe in healing (many do not).

What would many evangelicals tell the lame man who got healed in Acts 3 if he were here today? "Your experience is not valid because we believe that went away 2,000 years ago with the apostles." Do you think he would really care what you believed? HE WAS HEALED!

That is the fallacy of the modern gospel today. It denies the very power OF THE GOSPEL when it denies the power of the Holy Ghost!

In Acts 10, 40 years after Pentecost, we are told about the outpouring of the Spirit that took place for the first time on Gentiles at the house of Cornelius. Forty in the Bible is a very prophetic number and the outpouring of the Spirit 40 years after Pentecost was very prophetic as well! This event gives us a blueprint of the plan of God for every single human being on the planet.

The Home of Cornelius: Hunger and Thirst for God–The First Step in One's Quest for More of God

> **Acts 10:1-5**
> **There was a certain man in Caesarea called Cornelius, a centurion of the band called the Italian band, A devout man, and one that feared God with all his house, which gave much alms to the people, and prayed to God always. He saw in a vision evidently about the ninth hour of the day an angel of God coming in to him, and saying unto him, Cornelius. And when he looked on him, he was afraid, and said, What is it, Lord? And he said unto him, Thy prayers and thine alms are come up for a memorial before God. And now send men to Joppa, and call for one Simon, whose surname is Peter:**

The hungry and thirsty heart is the only heart that will receive more of God and the Holy Spirit. It all begins with spiritual thirst!

We can only guess what was going on with Cornelius in his house that day when something in him caused him to seek after God.

Hunger and thirst for God is something you cannot teach. One must remember that when the entire scenario occurred here that Cornelius was LOST without God. He was a deeply religious man, but he had not known Jesus!

All that happened to Cornelius started with hunger in his heart for God. That is how all things must start with us today! This hunger must start in the heart of man and be borne by the Holy Ghost. It must start in our innermost being.

I want to interject this thought right now. God is going to hold America so accountable for our lack of hunger and desire for him. In a country where we have been given so much and God is reverenced so little, it will be more tolerable for Sodom and Gomorra than for us in the Day of Judgment. Think about this.

Cornelius was not even saved, yet he was seeing visions, doing alms before God and was so sensitive to God that he asked the Lord what he was supposed to do when he saw the vision. That is hunger for God. He was so dedicated to serving God without even knowing God Himself through Christ. Neighbor never forget this. One cannot know God except He know Christ! Men today want to know about God without knowing His Son. Those who know about God are lost. Those who know God THROUGH the Son Jesus Christ are saved! There are no exceptions to that. One cannot get to God except they come through Christ and one cannot come to Christ except they come through the CROSS!

How sad it is that many who know the truth about God have little desire to serve God. We are going to be held SO accountable for this attitude in this country. But it is only this type of hunger that God rewards. He is a rewarder of those who DILIGENTLY seek him. The casual seeker of God will never find God! It is when we seek Him with ALL our heart and all our soul that He is so willingly and excited to REVEAL HIMSELF TO US.

> **Heb 11:6**
> **But without faith it is impossible to please him: for he that cometh to God must believe that he is, and that he is a rewarder of them that diligently seek him.**

> **Jeremiah 29:13-14**
> **And ye shall seek me, and find me, when ye shall search for me with all your heart. And I will be found of you, saith the LORD: and I will turn away your captivity, and I will gather you from all the nations, and from all the places whither I have driven you, saith the LORD; and I will bring you again into the place whence I caused you to be carried away captive**

He Shall Tell Thee What You Ought to Do

> **Acts 10:6**
> **He lodges with one Simon a tanner, whose house is by the sea side: he shall tell thee what thou oughtest to do.**

When God saw Cornelius' hunger, he told him to go seek after Simon a tanner and the apostle Peter would tell him what he ought to do. The job of the Church is to tell men what they ought to do as it relates to finding Jesus. If the church does not fulfill this call, who will? The lost will sure not hear it from Hollywood, the school system, the business world, or any other outlet. The CHURCH has been ordained to be the voice to the world about Christ. Peter was the one God ordained to tell Cornelius about the Risen Christ.

Yet instead of leading those seeking into a fuller relationship with the Lord Jesus, many preachers and church leaders hinder the Spirit of God through the prism of their own unbelief and they become great stumbling blocks to world evangelism more so than any other institution on the face of this earth.

The Apostle Peter himself, was very hesitant to go witness to Cornelius because of the animosity Jews had with the Gentiles and vice versa at the time. It has always been intriguing to me that both Peter and Jonah were both from Joppa and both had to be persuaded through supernatural and divine means to get them to witness to Gentiles. It took a whale to get the prophet Jonah's attention while it took a dream in which God told Peter to eat unclean things for the Apostle's to not resist the Gentiles. This same resistance sadly remains today in the modern church, but for different reasons.

The effort of the early church in the book of Acts was simple. Get the people saved and get them filled with the Holy Spirit. I want to say that again. The entire thrust and focus of the gospel in the book of Acts was to get people saved and then get them filled with the Holy Spirit. When you do that, all other things take care of themselves. Preach Jesus to them. Preach the Cross! Preach the Holy Ghost. Preach deliverance to the captives. Preach the Word!

Why do we do that you may ask? It is simple. Because when you get the Holy Spirit operating in people's lives, healing takes care of itself. Prosperity takes care of itself. Spiritual warfare takes care of itself. Gospel truth takes care of itself. All things center on the Cross and when the Cross is preached, the Holy Ghost shows up. When the Holy Ghost shows up neighbor, then heaven shows up!

The problem is that the hierarchy of the church wants something called CONTROL over people's lives! Either the Holy Spirit will control people or something else will control people!

The Holy Spirit does not share ownership with people or churches. That is why most man-made organizations, even though they may have their place in God's scheme of things, usually degenerate into control mechanisms that do more to hinder true ministry than facilitate it.

Peter's greatest resistance to preaching the gospel to Cornelius came from his own brethren. Had Peter listened to them about Cornelius, the Holy Spirit being poured out on Gentiles may have been delayed for years!

Why does the church fight the Holy Spirit? Why are we so quick to label things that are of God as being of Satan and label things that are of Satan as things of God? It is because when we reject the Holy Spirit who is called the Spirit of Truth, we wind up in delusion. Churches may have thousands attending their services but without the moving of the Holy Spirit, nothing will be done for God. Souls will not be saved, people will not be healed, and people will not be delivered. What it takes men years to do, the Holy Spirit can do in seconds!

Peter Became the Key Voice in This Great Event

Acts 10:9-17
On the morrow, as they went on their journey, and drew nigh unto the city, Peter went up upon the housetop to pray about the sixth hour: And he became very hungry, and would have eaten: but while they made ready, he fell into a trance, And saw heaven opened, and a certain vessel descending unto him, as it had been a great sheet knit at the four corners, and let down to the earth: Wherein were all manner of four footed beasts of the earth, and wild beasts, and creeping things, and fowls of the air. And there came a voice to him, Rise, Peter; kill, and eat. But Peter said, Not so, Lord; for I have never eaten anything that is common or unclean. And the voice spake unto him again the second time, What God hath cleansed, that call not thou common. This was done thrice: and the vessel was received up again into heaven. Now while Peter doubted in himself what this vision which he had seen should mean, behold, the men which were sent from Cornelius had made inquiry for Simon's house, and stood before the gate,

God sends Peter a vision to get his attention about Cornelius. The vision given to Peter consisted of unclean creeping things that God commanded Peter to eat. These were not just any certain things, but things thought unclean and against the ceremony by Jews. When Peter objected to this, God did not pause but instead He declared, "**what I have cleansed, call not thou common**." God's message to Peter is His message to the church today.

We are not the judge of who is worthy or unworthy to receive the precious gift of the Holy Spirit. This is mainly directed at Pentecostals. We are not qualified to tell God who can and cannot receive the baptism in the Holy Spirit with the evidence of speaking with other tongues.

The only prerequisite to receive the Holy Spirit is SALVATION and a hungry heart for God. When God saves you, He cleanses you. The blood of Jesus is sufficient to cleanse us from ALL unrighteousness. The blood of Jesus does not need anything added to it nor taken away from it to make us fit vessels for the Holy Spirit. No, you do not have to speak with other tongues to be saved, but you have to be saved or cleansed to receive the baptism or infilling of the Holy Spirit. Once you are cleansed by the blood at Salvation, there is no other requirement to receive this glorious infilling!

God was telling Peter, "your tradition and law has blinded you to My purpose." The same is so true of the church today. Our tradition and legalistic approach to God has blinded us to His higher purposes on this earth. The Gentile church would not be here today empowered as it is had Peter not gone to Cornelius and preached the gospel to him. How much of God's plan and purposes have been missed in our churches and in our lives because of our tradition?

Peter's Message to Cornelius – God Has Anointed Jesus

> **Acts 10:34-38**
> **Then Peter opened his mouth, and said, Of a truth I perceive that God is no respecter of persons: But in every nation he that feareth him, and worketh righteousness, is accepted with him. The word which God sent unto the children of Israel, preaching peace by Jesus Christ: (he is Lord of all:) That word, I say, ye know, which was published throughout all Judea, and began from Galilee, after the baptism which John preached;**

How God anointed Jesus of Nazareth with the Holy Ghost and with power: who went about doing good, and healing all that were oppressed of the devil; for God was with him.

Peter's message to Cornelius was simple. God anointed Jesus of Nazareth with the Holy Ghost and He went about doing good, and healing ALL that were oppressed of the devil, for God was with him. Interestingly enough, the religious men of Israel called the power that Jesus did His miracles with to be the power of Satan. Jesus was a man, anointed by the Holy Spirit. He did not do his miracles as God. He did them as the Second Adam, and He set an example of what we, the church should be doing today!

There are many in the evangelical world that deny the baptism in the Holy Spirit on this very argument. They teach that Jesus himself never spoke in tongues and did not do the things He did as a man. They deny His humanity while not realizing that when they do, they are denying His Deity at the same time! Jesus Christ was always both fully man and fully God in His life! All that He did, including His death, burial, and resurrection, was done as God IN THE FLESH. He did them as a man!

Let us explain this a bit further because it is especially important to grasp. The Bible for the most part, is basically silent about the Lord's life before He was 30. There are some peeks into His early life here or there, but for the most part little is known about His growing up in Nazareth as a carpenter's son with His earthly father Joseph and earthly mother Mary.

Would it be fair to say that the things that took place in Jesus' early life before his ministry were not as important for the Holy Spirit to reveal to us as the events that took place AFTER he was baptized by John in the river Jordan and the Holy Spirit descended upon Him in the form of a dove? Jesus' life before He was 30 is a great example of how someone can be indwelt by the Holy Spirit, but not have the Holy Spirit UPON them.

The facts about the virgin birth and the humanity of Jesus that were recorded in scripture are tied directly into this one fact; The Holy Ghost was IN HIM from birth but did not come "UPON HIM" until He was baptized in the Jordan river by John the Baptist.

> **Matt 1:20**
> **But while he thought on these things, behold, the angel of the Lord appeared unto him in a dream, saying, Joseph, thou son of David, fear not to take unto thee Mary thy wife: for that which is conceived in her is of the Holy Ghost.**

> **Luke 1:35**
> **And the angel answered and said unto her, The Holy Ghost shall come upon thee, and the power of the Highest shall overshadow thee: therefore also that holy thing which shall be born of thee shall be called the Son of God.**

The four Gospel writers; Matthew, Mark, Luke, John are the world's basic authoritative sources on the life of Christ. They relate details about his birth and some of the events in His early life, but the bulk of their account centers on the last three year of his life; THE YEARS OF HIS MINISTRY. The greatest attention is focused on the last WEEK of His life.

It is well to remember that while studying the gospels, the disciples were under the Old Covenant. They received an introduction to the New Covenant, but this was at the very beginning of this period. The New Covenant really begins to be seen operating in the epistles and the other writings that follow the gospels in the New Testament. God made two covenants with Israel called the "Old Covenant" and the "New Covenant." The NEW Covenant relates to redemption through Christ. Instead of being under the law to merit salvation, we now live in the day of Grace. Jesus Christ ushered in the New Covenant with his blood that he shed on Calvary.

Next, He sent the Holy Ghost to fill our hearts and live and to baptize us in the Holy Spirit. There is baptism into the body at conversion as the Holy Spirit baptizes us into the Body of Christ. But there is also a work of God when the Lord Jesus who baptizes those who believe in the Holy Spirit. When this happens, the Holy Spirit has now fully come into one's life, taking up residence and bringing the gifts and the fruits of the Spirit. This is a whole new dimension in Christian living.

Even though we see the writers of the first four books of the NEW Testament as living in the days of the New Testament, we must realize they were reacting based upon their wisdom of the Old Covenant. They would later receive greater wisdom under the New Covenant after the Lord Jesus died and arose again the third day and ascended into heaven.

Both Mary, the mother of Jesus, and her cousin Elizabeth, the mother of John the Baptist, experienced the presence and the power of the Holy Spirit in marvelous ways.

> **Luke 1:35-41**
> **And the angel answered and said unto her, The Holy Ghost shall come upon thee, and the power of the Highest shall overshadow thee: therefore also that holy thing which shall be**

> born of thee shall be called the Son of God. And, behold, thy cousin Elisabeth, she hath also conceived a son in her old age: and this is the sixth month with her, who was called barren. For with God nothing shall be impossible. And Mary said, Behold the handmaid of the Lord; be it unto me according to thy word. And the angel departed from her. And Mary arose in those days, and went into the hill country with haste, into a city of Juda; And entered into the house of Zacharias, and saluted Elisabeth. And it came to pass, that, when Elisabeth heard the salutation of Mary, the babe leaped in her womb; and Elisabeth was filled with the Holy Ghost:

The Holy Ghost set the initial stages of the divine incarnation forth. Jesus was conceived by the Holy Ghost and born of the virgin Mary in a stable. God's highest priority in bringing mankind's redemption to this planet was through the Holy Ghost. So, it is today. Those willing to humble themselves and see the Lord Jesus as a lowly, suffering servant in a stable are the ones most likely to receive the endowment of power from on high.

Many people question the virgin birth and even many church leaders deny this virgin birth. But if we have a real concept of the power of the Holy Spirit, it is no problem to accept the virgin birth of Jesus. As we accept all scripture by faith, we can certainly accept His virgin birth in the same way. But in addition to this, if one chooses to approach it from the point of logic, an understanding of the power and the potential of the Holy Spirit rapidly eliminates any questions. The Holy Spirit, not man, was responsible for Mary's conception.

When Jesus was born into human form, He had to grow in wisdom and knowledge as other children do. He did, of course, develop tremendously because He never yielded to sin or darkness. His mind and spirit were totally open to God the Father. Consequently, He learned very rapidly, and at the age of twelve years, He was able to discuss the Law with the high priests and doctors of the Law. The Spirit anointed him even as a young man, but he was not endued with power from on high for ministry until He was 30.

The Moment of Truth – At the Baptism of Jesus The Holy Ghost Descends

The Holy Spirit was involved in the life of Jesus from before His birth. At the time of His baptism by John the Baptist, the Spirit of God descended upon him in the form of a dove, and a voice from heaven spoke and said, "This is my beloved Son, in whom I am well pleased." The Spirit came "as" or "like a dove." He came gently. This was a witness of the Trinity; God the Father, Jesus the Son, and the Holy Spirit being present at this very moment in time. Jesus was baptized, the Holy Spirit descended, and God the Father spoke.

The Holy Spirit was present to ANOINT Jesus for ministry and to demonstrate His deity. Jesus did not operate on this earth as deity even though we know He WAS deity. He was the Son of God, yet He was also the Son of Man. It was as the Son of Man that He died so that we of the same nature He took upon Himself, might be saved.

If he had operated as a deity, then His death would have meant nothing. When Adam fell, it meant another "Adam" had to come and redeem man from his sin. Under the economy of God, only blood sacrifice would pay or atone for Israel's sin under the Old Covenant. Under the New Covenant, nothing changed. The difference, however, was that for man's sins to be removed, the blood was to be of the like nature of the offending party. It had to be human blood, not the blood of lambs, bullocks, bulls, or the blood of deity.

> Hebrews 10:4-10
> **For it is not possible that the blood of bulls and of goats should take away sins. Wherefore when he cometh into the world, he saith, Sacrifice and offering thou wouldest not, but a body has thou prepared me: In burnt offerings and sacrifices for sin thou hast had no pleasure. Then said I, Lo, I come (in the volume of the book it is written of me,) to do thy will, O God. Above when he said, Sacrifice and offering and burnt offerings and offering for sin thou wouldest not, neither hadst pleasure therein; which are offered by the law; Then said he, Lo, I come to do thy will, O God. He taketh away the first, that he may establish the second. By the which will we are sanctified through the offering of the body of Jesus Christ once for all.**

This was confirmed or witnessed BY THE HOLY SPIRIT:

> Hebrews 10:14-18
> **For by one offering he hath perfected forever them that are sanctified. Whereof the Holy Ghost also is a witness to us: for after that he had said before, This is the covenant that I will make with them after those days, saith the Lord, I will put my laws into their hearts, and in their minds will I write them; And their sins and iniquities will I remember no more. Now where remission of these is, there is no more offering for sin.**

It was through this process of identifying with the humanity of Adam, that the Second Adam delivered us from sin, sickness, fear, bondage, disease, and eternal damnation.

Hebrews 2:14-18

Forasmuch then as the children are partakers of flesh and blood, he also himself likewise took part of the same; that through death he might destroy him that had the power of death, that is, the devil; And deliver them who through fear of death were all their lifetime subject to bondage. For verily he took not on him the nature of angels; but he took on him the seed of Abraham. Wherefore in all things it behooved him to be made like unto his brethren, that he might be a merciful and faithful high priest in things pertaining to God, to make reconciliation for the sins of the people. For in that he himself hath suffered being tempted, he is able to succour them that are tempted

Jesus lived for 30 years with sinless character because of the indwelling of the Holy Spirit, but His ministry of power, which did not start until He was 30, was done by the ANOINTING and in infilling of the Holy Spirit. His life is an example of how you can have Christ-like character and have Christ-like power and anointing. They are two separate things, yet they are related. Discipleship is based upon the development of character through the fruit of the Spirit. Deliverance and setting people free are based upon power and the gifts of the Spirit. The church needs BOTH.

Some camps, such as the Southern Baptists, Evangelicals, Methodists, Presbyterians, etc. major only in character without power. They preach a gospel that embraces the character of Jesus and that is not wrong, but their gospel denies His power today, which is not right. By the same token, other camps, such as most Charismatic and Pentecostal circles only embrace our Lord's power without seeking to become more LIKE HIM. That is also wrong.

Power without character will destroy both us and the people we minister to. It will develop Jezebels!

We need both to have a New Testament church. Speaking in tongues does not make you perfect. There are many that are filled with the Spirit of God and speak in tongues, but they have tremendous difficulties in their lives. There are no experiences out there that make you perfect. Speaking in tongues is a tremendous blessing and a particularly important part of our walk as a believer, but the experience in and of itself does not guarantee you victory. Jesus did not walk in victory because He was anointed with power. He walked in victory because He had a daily relationship with the Father THROUGH the Holy Spirit from the day of His birth to the day he ascended to heaven.

After the anointing of the Holy Spirit, Jesus began to heal, cast out devils and demonstrate the Kingdom of God in a manner of power that was not seen by Israel since the days of Elijah and Elisha the prophets.

First, Jesus was BORN OF THE SPIRIT; then He was Baptized IN THE SPIRIT; and finally, He went forth to work out His life and ministry in the POWER OF THE SPIRIT. We too need to be born of the spirit, baptized in the SPIRIT, and then go forth to live HIS life and reproduce HIS WORKS.

We Are Witnesses of These Things

> **Acts 10:39-43**
> **And we are witnesses of all things which he did both in the land of the Jews, and in Jerusalem; whom they slew and hanged on a tree: Him God raised up the third day, and**

> **showed him openly; Not to all the people, but unto witnesses chosen before of God, even to us, who did eat and drink with him after he rose from the dead. And he commanded us to preach unto the people, and to testify that it is he that was ordained of God to be the Judge of quick and dead. To him give all the prophets witness, that through his name whosoever believeth in him shall receive remission of sins.**

Peter said that the apostles were witnesses of the things Jesus did both in the land of the Jews and in Jerusalem. He testified that God had raised Jesus up and had showed him openly not to all the people, but unto witnesses CHOSEN before God, and even to Peter, who did eat and drink with him after Jesus rose from the dead. He said that Jesus commanded the apostles to preach unto the people. However, before Jesus commanded them to preach, He also commanded them to tarry in Jerusalem for an endowment of power from on high.

The lesson is clear. Before you preach, before you teach, before you sing, before you write books, before you lead children's church, before you take up offerings, you need to be endued with POWER FROM ON HIGH. The power on high the apostles were endued with was the Holy Ghost and the INITIAL evidence of the endowment of power was speaking with other tongues.

The Promise of the Father

As Jesus was approaching death after His fruitful ministry, Jesus encouraged His disciples to see and understand some of the truths relative to the Holy Spirit and His work. In John 16, Jesus told them it was expedient for Him to leave, because if He did not leave, the Comforter would not come. The Comforter is the Holy Spirit.

Jesus said that if He departed, He would send the Holy Spirit to His followers (which we are as believers). The Spirit of God would guide them (and us) into all truths, for He is the Spirit of Truth. Jesus then told the disciples to wait until they were endued with power and strength. As John the Baptist had prophesied, "I indeed have baptized you with water: but he shall baptize you with the Holy Ghost." (Mark 1:18)

Jesus paid the price at Calvary for our redemption, and He rose from the dead. He spoke at great lengths on the Holy Spirit. He commanded the disciples to tarry and to wait, before beginning their ministries, until they had received the promise of the Father. This is a totally new dimension in spiritual life, experienced first by the disciples and today by believers. Jesus in Luke and in the first chapter of Acts promised the precious Holy Spirit would come.

> **Acts 1:8**
> **But ye shall receive power, after that the Holy Ghost is come upon you: and ye shall be witnesses unto me both in Jerusalem, and in all Judaea, and in Samaria, and unto the uttermost part of the earth.**
>
> **Luke 24:48-49– And ye are witnesses of these things. And, behold, I send the promise of my Father upon you: but tarry ye in the city of Jerusalem, until ye be endued with power from on high.**

Peter repeated Jesus' words in his writings when he said, "we are witnesses of these things." Jesus told the disciples the same thing. They would witness the very plan of God through the Master's death, burial, resurrection, ascension, and exaltation.

The outpouring of the Holy Spirit would be the sign that Jesus had made it to the right hand of God and that he had received the promise of the Holy Ghost from God the Father. This promise is paramount to the plan of God for the church. Prophets did not see this time we are living in.

This is a special time for humanity. God is calling out a people to be filled with His Spirit and set captives free in bringing many into the Kingdom of God. This same power is available to believers, without measure, to work in and through Christians as it did in the life of Christ. IN fact, Jesus went on to say that His followers would do the things He did, and even greater things.

> **John 14:12**
> **Verily, verily, I say unto you, He that believeth on me, the works that I do shall he do also; and greater works than these shall he do; because I go unto my Father.**

Peter preached on the Day of Pentecost that what the people were HEARING was what Jesus shed forth when He ascended back to Glory to sit at the right hand of God. By the Pentecostal outpouring, Peter was saying, "God's redemptive plan for man has been completed." Greater works would now be accomplished because the Holy Ghost that would be much more far-reaching than even the localized ministry of Jesus while He was here on earth. That is why Jesus spoke more about the Holy Ghost in the days prior to His death than He did the entire three years He was with the disciples.

> **Acts 2:31-33**
> **He seeing this before spoke of the resurrection of Christ, that his soul was not left in hell, neither his flesh did see corruption. This Jesus hath God raised up, whereof we all are**

The Holy Spirit and The Gentiles

witnesses. Therefore being by the right hand of God exalted, and having received of the Father the promise of the Holy Ghost, he hath shed forth this, <u>which ye now see and hear.</u>

Peter made it as clear he humanly could in relating to the Church what took place with Jesus and the Holy Ghost in relation to Pentecost.

Jesus died on the Cross. He was then exalted to the right hand of God the Father at which time He received of the Father the PROMISE OF THE HOLY GHOST. When He received the promise of the Father, He shed forth the gift upon the disciples and others gathered on the day of Pentecost, during which Peter said, the people outside the temple, SAW AND HEARD. What did they hear? They heard people speaking with other tongues.

> **Acts 2:1-16**
> And when the day of Pentecost was fully come, they were all with one accord in one place. And suddenly there came a sound from heaven as of a rushing mighty wind, and it filled all the house where they were sitting. And there appeared unto them cloven tongues like as of fire, and it sat upon each of them. And they were all filled with the Holy Ghost, and began to speak with other tongues, as the Spirit gave them utterance. And there were dwelling at Jerusalem Jews, devout men, out of every nation under heaven. Now when this was noised abroad, the multitude came together, and were confounded, because that every man heard them speak in his own language. And they were all amazed and marveled, saying one to another, Behold, are not all these which speak Galileans? And how hear we every man in our own tongue, wherein we were born? Parthians, and Medes, and Elamites, and the

> dwellers in Mesopotamia, and in Judaea, and Cappadocia, in Pontus, and Asia, Phrygia, and Pamphylia, in Egypt, and in the parts of Libya about Cyrene, and strangers of Rome, Jews and proselytes, Cretes and Arabians, we do hear them speak in our tongues the wonderful works of God. And they were all amazed, and were in doubt, saying one to another, What meaneth this? Others mocking said, These men are full of new wine. But Peter, standing up with the eleven, lifted up his voice, and said unto them, Ye men of Judaea, and all ye that dwell at Jerusalem, be this known unto you, and hearken to my words: For these are not drunken, as ye suppose, seeing it is but the third hour of the day. But this is that which was spoken by the prophet Joel;

Some 50 days after Jesus ascended into heaven the power of the Holy Ghost fell! Jesus had instructed them to be witnesses to His resurrection, to wait or tarry in Jerusalem and by doing so, they would be endued with power as they experienced the mighty baptism of the Holy Spirit. They were "in one accord," as they waited expectantly for the promise the Lord had given them. A total of 120 people, including the disciples (but without Judas, who was now dead) and MARY, the mother of Jesus, waited together, "in one place." The lessons learned from this passage are especially important to point out.

One, they were willing to WAIT upon the Lord. All too often people tend to be impatient and refuse to wait for the Lord's timetable of events. Often, failure to be still before God results in missing some of His greatest blessings. There are, to be sure, pressing demands and great needs everywhere, but one can more adequately respond to those challenges and needs AFTER waiting on God for His direction and power.

Two, they were all IN ONE ACCORD; IN ONE SPIRIT, as they sought the Lord. There is great strength in unity. Strength lies not in numbers, but in unity of spirit.

The Day of Pentecost

Why did the Holy Spirit outpouring take place on the Day of Pentecost? Why was it simultaneous with the old Hebrew Festival of Harvest? Why not just any day? We know from scripture that the Feast of Passover, which typified the death of the Lord Jesus, had taken place 50 days earlier.

The reason we know this is that the DAY OF PENTECOST is, by definition, the "50th" day after Passover. Passover commemorated the killing of the Paschal Lamb, with the placing of the blood on the doorposts of Egypt. This caused the death angel to pass over the children of Israel during the 10th plague. Blood was applied to the doorpost and life was spared. Primarily, a Passover celebration renews the thought of lives saved by the sacrifice of the Lamb.

It was only a symbolic of Jesus, who offered Himself for us, as OUR PASCHAL LAMB on the commemorating of the Passover. The killing of the Paschal Lamb was the type, the prophetic foreshadowing of Jesus' later role as the Paschal Lamb for the world. The Jews today still celebrate the Passover as a historic occasion, not realizing its prophetic significance regarding Jesus Christ.

Like the Feast of Passover, the Feast of Pentecost had special significance as well. It was the Feast of the Firstfruits as described in Exodus 23:16. It was the "thanksgiving" of Israel's economy and religious festivals. It was a time set aside by God for His children to think about 'Harvest." This Pentecost Day manifestations of the

Holy Spirit baptism was the introduction to the "last days" outpouring foretold in Joel 2:28-29, which Peter referred to in Acts 2:16-21. It represented the "Firstfruits," or "ingathering" of the abundant harvest of souls that was to follow. It was the establishment and endowment of power of the early Church. As a result, there was a tremendous harvest of souls; 3,000 on the day of Pentecost and a few days later, nearly 5,000 more.

> **Acts 2:16-21**
> **But this is that which was spoken by the prophet Joel; And it shall come to pass in the last days, saith God, I will pour out of my Spirit upon all flesh: and your sons and your daughters shall prophesy, and your young men shall see visions, and your old men shall dream dreams: And on my servants and on my handmaidens I will pour out in those days of my Spirit; and they shall prophesy: And I will shew wonders in heaven above, and signs in the earth beneath; blood, and fire, and vapour of smoke: The sun shall be turned into darkness, and the moon into blood, before that great and notable day of the Lord come: And it shall come to pass, that whosoever shall call on the name of the Lord shall be saved.**

> **Joel 2:28-29**
> **And it shall come to pass afterward, that I will pour out my spirit upon all flesh; and your sons and your daughters shall prophesy, your old men shall dream dreams, your young men shall see visions: And also upon the servants and upon the handmaids in those days will I pour out my spirit.**

> **Acts 2:41**
> Then they that gladly received his word were baptized: and the same day there were added unto them about three thousand souls.

> **Acts 4:2-4**–Being grieved that they taught the people, and preached through Jesus the resurrection from the dead. And they laid hands on them, and put them in hold unto the next day: for it was now eventide. Howbeit many of them which heard the word believed; and the number of the men was about five thousand.

The significance of God's choice of the Day of Pentecost as the time of this initial Holy Spirit outpouring is obvious. The celebration of Pentecost took place 50 days after Passover.

> **Lev 23:15-16**
> And ye shall count unto you from the morrow after the sabbath, from the day that ye brought the sheaf of the wave offering; seven sabbaths shall be complete: Even unto the morrow after the seventh sabbath shall ye number fifty days; and ye shall offer a new meat offering unto the LORD.

> **Exodus 23:16-17**
> And the feast of harvest, the Firstfruits of thy labors, which thou hast sown in the field: and the feast of ingathering, which is in the end of the year, when thou hast gathered in thy labors out of the field. Three times in the year all thy males shall appear before the Lord GOD.

This scripture in Leviticus refers to "a new meat offering" unto the Lord. Just as the heavenly fires fell on the sacrifice presented on the altar of Elijah in 1 Kings 18, so the cloven tongues of flame came down on each person on the Day of Pentecost. This manifestation of fire from heaven fell upon those who YIELDED. These were submitted believers, offering themselves up as a living sacrifice, bound in love and obedience.

Which Have Received the Holy Ghost as We

> Acts 10:44-46
> **While Peter yet spake these words, the Holy Ghost fell on all them which heard the word. And they of the circumcision which believed were astonished, as many as came with Peter, because that on the Gentiles also was poured out the gift of the Holy Ghost. <u>For they heard them speak with tongues and magnify God</u>. Then answered Peter, Can any man forbid water, that these should not be baptized, which have received the Holy Ghost as well as we? And he commanded them to be baptized in the name of the Lord. Then prayed they him to tarry certain days.**

The Bible clearly tells us that as Peter spoke these words, the HOLY GHOST FELL ON ALL THEM THAT HEARD THE WORD. This was the scene at Cornelius' house some 40 years after Pentecost and that initial outpouring of the Spirit. HOW did they know they had received the gift of the Holy Ghost? They heard them speak with tongues and magnify God!

The initial physical evidence of one being baptized in the Holy Ghost is that they speak with other tongues as the Spirit of God gives the utterance.

When the Hebrews (they of the circumcision) saw this) they were astonished that the Gentiles had received the same gift that those gathered on the day of Pentecost had received 40 years earlier. The gift of the Holy Spirit first came to JEWS, then to the GENTILES.

To be frank, this is how all the covenants of God have worked from the beginning. The gospel was given to the JEW FIRST, then to the GREEK. Since the Jews rejected these covenants sadly, at least for now, the Gentiles have been mightily blessed!! They have been mightily blessed!

The events at the house of Cornelius echo into the time that you are reading this book! The same Holy Ghost who fell THEN is ready to fall NOW upon You and YOUR household! Praise God!

I ask you again. How did they know the Holy Ghost was poured out on the Gentiles? It clearly says in verse 46 of this passage, "They heard them SPEAK WITH TONGUES AND MAGNIFY GOD." How does one know they are baptized in the Holy Ghost today? They will SPEAK WITH TONGUES as the Spirit of God gives the utterance!

Peter then stands up and says, "Can we forbid these that have been saved AND filled with the Holy Ghost to be baptized in water, WHICH HAVE RECEIVED THE HOLY GHOST AS WE.

We have received the Holy Ghost as "we," meaning all those who were present on the Day of Pentecost! When Peter returned to Jerusalem to tell what had happened, he said they received "this like gift!"

Neighbor, some 2000 years later the Holy Ghost is being poured out upon all flesh and the initial physical evidence of what is taking place is confirmed BY THIS LIKE GIFT! The message has not changed. The power has not changed. The gift of tongues has not changed. God the Holy Ghost has not changed. Jesus is still baptizing folks in the Holy Ghost and with Fire!!!

> **Acts 11:14-17**
> **Who shall tell thee words, whereby thou and thy entire house shall be saved. And as I began to speak, the Holy Ghost fell on them, as on us at the beginning. Then remembered I the word of the Lord, how that he said, John indeed baptized with water; but ye shall be baptized with the Holy Ghost. Forasmuch then as God gave them the like gift as he did unto <u>us</u>, who believed on the Lord Jesus Christ; what was I, that I could withstand God?**

The "us" Peter is referring to is those who were gathered in the temple room on the day of Pentecost some 40 years earlier and who had received the Holy Spirit the same way that Peter witnessed in the house of Cornelius.

Notice he says "us, who BELIEVED on the Lord Jesus Christ." This is for believers! This for those born of the Spirit! This is for those who KNOW the baptizer in the Holy Ghost, the Lord Jesus Christ!

Neighbor, this is not complicated. What has complicated things is a church that has lost its way with God and has been taken away from the Cross of Christ by false teachers and men filled with unbelief and rank heresy in their bones.

We NEED the power of the Holy Ghost today!

What Was I, That I Could Withstand God?

Acts 11:17
Forasmuch then as God gave them the like gift as he did unto <u>us</u>, who believed on the Lord Jesus Christ; what was I, that I could withstand God?

Peter saw the uselessness of withstanding this outpouring on the Gentiles. What was happening was beyond his control. Despite this story and Biblical account, many still try to withstand what God is doing in these last days before Jesus comes. The like gift of Salvation and the Holy Spirit are the two greatest gifts people can receive today!

The word "like," means "equal," and or "identical." In addition to this, the word "gift," comes from the Greek word "dorea," which means a "gratuity." It means a gift or offering made possible by a Sacrifice.

Jesus Christ paid the price with His Blood so that we may be saved and FILLED with the Holy Ghost! This cannot be earned even though the price was not free. It was a price man was unable to pay thus Jesus paid it for us by His blood!

The same Holy Spirit then is the same Holy Spirit NOW. The same "Gift" the Gentiles received was the same "Gift" received by the Jews! And neighbor, there is no other requirement for one to receive this glorious outpouring UPON their lives than SALVATION through faith in the BLOOD OF JESUS CHRIST! If one is saved, they are qualified to receive the mighty Baptism of the Holy Ghost! To deny such is to deny the Word of God.

The fact that Peter never mentioned the Law to his "brethren" was huge. The Jews were very legalistic in their approach to God at times. In this case, Peter realized that these Gentiles had not kept the Law of Moses and they had not even made any attempt to do so. In effect as we have stated, these were basically heathen that the Lord Jesus Christ saved, and He filled most of them at the same time!

To resist what God was doing would have been futile and neighbor NONE of us want to be in that position today! God had gone beyond the "rules" of the Church to fill heathen Gentiles with the Holy Ghost and He has been doing it ever since neighbor! Praise God.

We can sit behind our modern pulpits and flippantly say, "this isn't for today," or "this is of the devil," or "this has no place in our church." We do it to our own destruction.

This has always been the New Testament pattern of ministry. We can call it old fashioned; we can call it out of date, and we can call it vanished from history. BUT IT WORKED THEN AND IT WILL WORK NOW!

The early church did not have the gadgets and the technology we have today, but it had the power and anointing of the Holy Spirit and it set the world ablaze with the gospel of Jesus Christ. It is not the ABNORMAL to see people saved and filled with the Holy Spirit. It is abnormal for Christianity to be lukewarm complacent, unbelieving, cowardly, unforgiving, and ignorant of God's ways. Paul said it in 1 Corinthians, "Let him who wants to be ignorant, be ignorant."

The church cannot say, "We believe the Bible from cover to cover," and then totally deny the power of the Book of Acts. To be frank, the Book of Acts has more relevance for the church today than in any time in the church's history. **We are the harvest generation and with as much as we have been given, we are going to be held more accountable than any generation before us or after us**.

Neighbor, ignorance is one thing, but outright denial of something you know is true or what the Bible says is right is another. Many literally blaspheme the Holy Ghost behind their pulpits and do not even realize it!

Saying the manifestations of the Holy Spirit are of the devil is DANGEROUS and frankly Demonic. Some of you reading this are so hardened by religion and demonic tradition that even if Jesus sent someone back from the dead to tell you differently, it would not matter.

There are those who have settled to believe what they want to believe even if it is leading millions astray, and sadly, in some cases to hell itself.

To the believer I plead with you today!

No matter what man teaches or says, you as a believer NEED to be filled with the Holy Ghost with the evidence of speaking with other tongues. You who are hungry for God will pursue what you have read. The Lord wants to give you the "like gift" He gave Cornelius and his house that day as recorded in the book of Acts Chapter 10. They received the Holy Ghost just as Peter, John, Mark, Bartholomew, Thomas and Mary, the mother of Jesus did on the day of Pentecost.

They "which have received the Holy Ghost as we" and were never the same again. Neither will your life be the same again either.

Pursue spiritual gifts today and seek the Lord to fill you with the Holy Ghost He has never turned away a seeking heart. He longs to satisfy your thirst for him!

> *Are you longing for the fullness*
> *Of the blessing of the Lord*
> *In your heart and life today?*
> *Claim the promise of your Father;*
> *Come according to His Word,*
> *In the blessed, old-time way.*
> *He will fill your heart today to overflowing;*
> *As the Lord commandeth you,*
> *"Bring your vessels, not a few."*
> *He will fill your heart today to overflowing*
> *With the Holy Ghost and pow'r.*
> *Bring your empty earthen vessels,*
> *Clean through Jesus' precious blood.*
> *Come, ye needy, one and all;*
> *And in human consecration*
> *Wait before the throne of God*
> *Till the Holy Ghost shall fall.*
> *Like the cruse of oil unfailing*
> *Is His grace forevermore,*
> *And His love unchanging still;*
> *And according to His promise,*
> *With the Holy Ghost and pow'r*
> *He will every vessel fill.*

Chapter 10

QUESTIONS, ANSWERS ABOUT THE HOLY GHOST

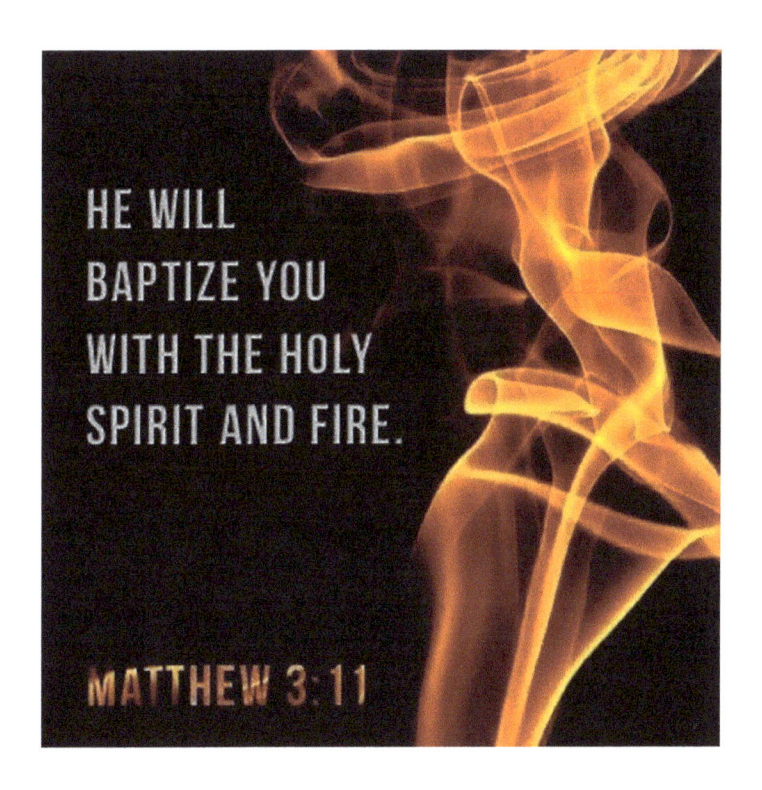

TEXT: 1 Corinthians 14:1-3–Follow after charity, and desire spiritual gifts, but rather that ye may prophesy. [2] For he that speaketh in an unknown tongue speaketh not unto men, but unto God: for no man understands him; howbeit in the spirit he speaketh mysteries. [3] But he that prophesies speaketh unto men to edification, and exhortation, and comfort.

As we conclude, we want to discuss a few questions that constantly come up regarding the Baptism in the Holy Ghost and speaking with other tongues. Some of this may sound redundant but as we close out this book, I do not want there to be any questions as to how we feel and believe regarding this all-important subject!

One of the main dividing lines in the church today is over the issue of speaking in tongues.

Friend, our Lord did not send back the Holy Ghost to divide the church!

John 16:7-13
Nevertheless I tell you the truth; It is expedient for you that I go away: for if I go not away, the Comforter will not come unto you; but if I depart, I will send him unto you. And when he is come, he will reprove the world of sin, and of righteousness, and of judgment: Of sin, because they believe not on me; 10 Of righteousness, because I go to my Father, and ye see me no more; 11 Of judgment, because the prince of this world is judged. 12 I have yet many things to say unto you, but ye cannot bear them now. Howbeit when he, the Spirit of truth, is come, he will guide you into all truth: for he shall not speak

of himself; but whatsoever he shall hear, *that* shall he speak: and he will shew you things to come.

He sent the Holy Ghost to uplift the Son of God and convict men of their sin and to declare the righteousness of Christ. The utter judgment of Satan that was achieved at the Cross by our Lord! He is here to lead the Church into all TRUTH. In addition, He brings with Him diversities in manifestations and ministries for the Church and for the believer!

One of these manifestations given to the New Testament believer is speaking with other tongues as the Spirit of God gives the utterance. This is not an experience for the faithless but for those who believe. Those who do not believe will not miss heaven, but they will miss out on a tremendous blessing and experience that the Lord paid for through His death just as He paid for divine healing to those who will receive.

If we chose not to believe, we best not fight against it or we will happily find ourselves fighting against GOD. One does NOT have to speak in tongues to be saved, but it is a refreshing and rest that the believer needs in this intense warfare that is ahead of the Church in these last days. Many think the war over America is political; it is not. It is spiritual and it is in the SPIRIT that we fight and war against the powers of darkness.

When one is baptized in the Holy Ghost, he is ready to war!

These Signs Shall Follow THOSE WHO BELIEVE, Not Those Who Do not

> Mark 16:17-20
> **And these signs shall follow them that believe; In my name shall they cast out devils; they shall speak with new tongues; They shall take up serpents; and if they drink any deadly thing, it shall not hurt them; they shall lay hands on the sick, and they shall recover. So then after the Lord had spoken unto them, he was received up into heaven, and sat on the right hand of God. And they went forth, and preached every where, the Lord working with them, and confirming the word with signs following. Amen.**

One sign that follows believers is "they speak with other tongues."

The flip side of this is simple. If one does not believe nor desire this, they will NOT speak in tongues. This does NOT mean that one must speak in tongues to be saved but it means that if the believer remains in unbelief, they will not receive from God that which He has ordained them to receive.

Scripture was never designed for people who have made up their mind. Scripture is given as an inspiration to those who seek the truth. Many are hindered by other's opinions on this subject. We can listen to man and miss out on God or we can become like Cornelius and seek after the Lord with all our heart. When we do, he will fill our thirst.

One sign that follows believers is that "they speak with other tongues." As stated, this message is one of many that are under constant attack by the unbelieving evangelical community in these modern times. There are many common objections that I want to take a look at individually in the closing chapter of this study on the Baptism in the Holy Ghost with the evidence of speaking in tongues as the Spirit of God gives the utterance!

Some of these have their roots in men's twisting of scripture while others have no biblical basis whatsoever.

Objection No. 1.–Tongues Are of The Devil and Those Who Speak in Tongues Are Listening to Demon Spirits.

Some people claim those who are baptized in the Holy Ghost are not even speaking tongues but are uttering "demonic gibberish." Or they say, "You are demon possessed," or, "Tongues are strictly from the devil."

First, man's opinion that tongues are of the devil is completely false and without Biblical merit. However, the Bible does ANSWER this objection!

Some people who want to be filled with the Holy Ghost with the evidence of speaking with other tongues use the excuse that they are fearful they will get a demon or maybe the devil will take advantage of them. Jesus spoke of this in Luke.

> **Luke 11:9-13**
> **And I say unto you, Ask, and it shall be given you; seek, and ye shall find; knock, and it shall be opened unto you. For every one that asketh, receiveth; and he that seeketh findeth; and to him that knocketh it shall be opened. If a son shall ask bread of any of you that is a father, will he give him a stone? or if he ask a fish, will he for a fish give him a serpent? Or if he shall**

> ask an egg, will he offer him a scorpion? If ye then, being evil, know how to give good gifts unto your children: how much more shall your heavenly Father give the Holy Spirit to them that ask him?

Jesus is the one baptizing one in the Holy Ghost and He says clearly that you cannot ask for the Holy Spirit and get a demon. A child can understand that. Yet, Bible teachers and scholars with degrees from some of the leading theological seminaries in America, will argue that people speaking in tongues are receiving this gift from Satan. It borders on blaspheming the Spirit!

> Luke 11:14-23
> And he was casting out a devil, and it was dumb. And it came to pass, when the devil was gone out, the dumb spoke; and the people wondered. But some of them said, He casteth out devils through Beelzebub the chief of the devils. And others, tempting him, sought of him a sign from heaven. But he, knowing their thoughts, said unto them, Every kingdom divided against itself is brought to desolation; and a house divided against a house falleth. If Satan also be divided against himself, how shall his kingdom stand? because ye say that I cast out devils through Beelzebub. And if I by Beelzebub cast out devils, by whom do your sons cast them out? therefore shall they be your judges. But if I with the finger of God cast out devils, no doubt the kingdom of God is come upon you. When a strong man armed keepeth his palace, his goods are in peace: But when a stronger than he shall come upon him, and overcome him, he takes from him all his armor wherein he trusted, and divides his spoils. He that is not with me is against me: and he that gathereth not with me scattereth.

Matthew 12:24-32

But when the Pharisees heard it, they said, "this fellow doth not cast out devils, but by Beelzebub the prince of the devils." And Jesus knew their thoughts, and said unto them, Every kingdom divided against itself is brought to desolation; and every city or house divided against itself shall not stand: And if Satan cast out Satan, he is divided against himself; how shall then his kingdom stand? And if I by Beelzebub cast out devils, by whom do your children cast them out? therefore they shall be your judges. But if I cast out devils by the Spirit of God, then the kingdom of God is come unto you. Or else how can one enter into a strong man's house, and spoil his goods, except he first bind the strong man? and then he will spoil his house. He that is not with me is against me; and he that gathereth not with me scattereth abroad. Wherefore I say unto you, All manner of sin and blasphemy shall be forgiven unto men: but the blasphemy against the Holy Ghost shall not be forgiven unto men. And whosoever speaketh a word against the Son of man, it shall be forgiven him: but whosoever speaketh against the Holy Ghost, it shall not be forgiven him, neither in this world, neither in the world to come.

Religious people who were teachers began to get jealous of Jesus. They did not like the fact that the spotlight was on Jesus and not on them. These same religious leaders tried to deceive Jesus' followers by saying the power that He was using to cast out demons was from Satan. Jesus answered this claim with a serious warning to all who would attribute the works of Satan to the works of the Holy Spirit. He told the religious, "If I cast out devils BY THE SPIRIT OF GOD, then the kingdom of God is come unto you." Then Jesus says that everything we do, be it word or deed, and shall be forgiven, but not blasphemy against the Holy Ghost. Then He makes it even clearer. We can speak against Jesus and be forgiven but when we speak against the Holy Ghost, it is a sin that has no forgiveness neither in this world nor in the world to come.

It is one thing to speak out of ignorance. Many of us do and I believe God is very patient and merciful to us. However, if a Christian KNOWS better (and most times this stance is taken by PREACHERS BEHIND PULPITS WITH DEGREES WHO ARE SUPPOSED TO KNOW THE WORD OF GOD), and if he takes something that is of God and says it is of Satan, that individual is in serious standing with God Almighty. If you believe speaking in tongues is not for you, so be it, but I would strongly suggest that you not equate this experience with being demon possessed or of the devil.

> **1 Corinthians 14:37-39**
> **If any man think himself to be a prophet, or spiritual, let him acknowledge that the things that I write unto you are the commandments of the Lord. But if any man be ignorant, let him be ignorant. Wherefore, brethren, covet to prophesy, and forbid not to speak with tongues.**

> **Isaiah 5:20-21 – Woe unto them that call evil good, and good evil; that put darkness for light, and light for darkness; that put bitter for sweet, and sweet for bitter! Woe unto them that are wise in their own eyes, and prudent in their own sight!**

Paul said that if you think you are spiritual, then acknowledge what he wrote as being the COMMANDMENTS OF THE LORD.

If you want to be ignorant of these things, be ignorant but covet to prophecy and forbid NOT TO SPEAK IN TONGUES.

Isaiah gives a deeper warning when he says "Woe" to them who call darkness light and light darkness, evil good and good evil. Speaking in tongues is not of the devil. While blaspheming the Holy Spirit goes a little further than just stating this, I would not want to be in the camp that says such things.

Any type statement (which comes from the heart), shows gross ignorance at best and something more sinister at worse. We need to search our hearts and watch our words about the Holy Spirit!

Objection No. 2 – Tongues Passed Away With The Apostles And Are No Longer Valid For Today

Many believe that tongues, and prophecy too for that matter, passed away after the Bible was completed and the apostles died. Those who believe this objection acknowledge that believers once spoke in tongues as a sign of supernatural occurrence in the Church while the Bible was being written. Then, once the Scriptures were completed, tongues were supposedly no longer needed.

Again, not to sound redundant, but if tongues passed away then, what are we going to do with the millions over the centuries since the day of Pentecost who have spoken in tongues and are speaking in tongues even today? Are we going to say we do not believe people are really speaking in tongues because we believe it all ended with the apostles?

Peter's message on Pentecost was a declaration that what was happening was a fulfillment of Joel's prophecy of the last days. He said that what the people were seeing AND HEARING was the promise that Jesus spoke of before He left this earth. The Holy Ghost cannot be seen, but the INITIAL, not total, result of one being filled with the Spirit is speaking with other tongues.

> **Acts 2:39**
> **For the promise is unto you, and to your children, and to all that are afar off, even as many as the Lord our God shall call.**

What promise? The promise of the Holy Ghost, which was shed forth so that the people who were present on the day of Pentecost could see and hear. He said this promise was unto them, their children AND TO ALL THAT ARE AFAR OFF. The "all that is a far off" is us! That promise is just as valid today as any promise in the Bible. The promise never died out.

Objection No. 3 – Tongues Are Not for Everyone

Some believe that tongues are not for everyone, but are for a special, select few. A few scriptures are generally used to validate this objection:

> **1 Corinthians 12:10**
> **To another the working of miracles; to another prophecy; to another discerning of spirits; to another divers kinds of tongues; to another the interpretation of tongues:**

When people read this verse, they are always quick to point out that the Bible says to certain ones this gift is given to, and to others it is not. This leads them to believe some speak in tongues while others do not. First, being filled with the Holy Ghost is NOT THE TOPIC OF DISCUSSION in these verses. The topic being discussed is spiritual gifts, or gifts of the Spirit used in the corporate, public gatherings of the church.

Only two of the nine gifts of the Spirit are unique to the New Testament: divers kinds of tongues and the interpretation of tongues. The other seven existed in the Old Testament. But all nine gifts, which are in manifestation in the Church Age, are taught in this chapter.

These are gifts that are for use in public settings and corporate gatherings. Not everyone is equipped to minister in tongues in public gatherings. It is not that they are any less special than other members of the Body of Christ. It just means that the Spirit has elected not to use them in this area. It does not mean that everyone should not speak in tongues. Paul said, I wish you ALL SPAKE IN TONGUES.

There is a difference between devotional tongues (prayer language) and the gift of tongues and the interpretation of tongues that are used in public gatherings. One is for private devotion and one is to speak to the church and Body of Christ in a supernatural language.

Objection No. 4 – Tongues Shall Cease

The basis for this objection is hung on one verse.

> **1 Corinthians 13:8**
> **Charity never fails: but whether there be prophecies, they shall fail; whether there be tongues, they shall cease; whether there be knowledge, it shall vanish away.**

> **1 Corinthians 13:9-10**
> **For we know in part, and we prophesy in part. But when that which is perfect is come, then that which is in part shall be done away.**

This verse that Paul is writing about is in context to spiritual gifts. Yes, the day is going to come when tongues shall cease, but neighbor, let me assure you that day is not today!

Some people think that the "perfect" is the Word of God. They believe that upon completion of the written scriptures, tongues were no longer needed because the perfect had come but Paul did not stop there.

> 1 Corinthians 13:11-13;1 4:1-5
> When I was a child, I spoke as a child, I understood as a child, I thought as a child: but when I became a man, I put away childish things. For now we see through a glass, darkly; but then face-to-face: now I know in part; but then shall I know even as also I am known. And now abides faith, hope, charity, these three; but the greatest of these is charity.

> 1 Corinthians 14:1
> Follow after charity, and desire spiritual gifts, but rather that ye may prophesy. For he that speaketh in an unknown tongue speaketh not unto men, but unto God: for no man understandeth him; howbeit in the spirit he speaketh mysteries. But he that prophesieth speaketh unto men to edification, and exhortation, and comfort. He that speaketh in an unknown tongue edifieth himself; but he that prophesieth edifieth the church. I would that ye all spoke with tongues, but rather that ye prophesied: for greater is he that prophesies than he that speaketh with tongues, except he interpret, that the church may receive edifying.

Paul is not making an argument in this discussion for tongues to cease. If anything, he is admonishing the church at Corinth to PURSUE SPIRITUAL GIFTS, including prophecy AND TONGUES. In the very NEXT CHAPTER after this, he spends nearly 40 verses discussing this very statement. His statements are merely saying that when the church is perfected, we will no longer need the Holy Spirit to speak to us and through us any longer.

Even with the Bible, the Church of the Lord Jesus is FAR FROM BEING PERFECT. OUR HEAD, THE LORD JESUS, is perfect but we are **BEING** perfected!

Do we know all the things that need to be answered yet? NO! Do we even yet know EVERYTHING there is to know about God? NO! Those questions, along with a ton of others, will be answered when Jesus comes and raptures the church to heaven. It will be at that time that the Lord Jesus will complete us as His Body, and we will no longer need perfecting. He will make all things known to us.

Paul said, "we see through a glass darkly" but one day we will see Jesus "FACE TO FACE." It will be at that time and that time alone that spiritual gifts will cease. In other words, we have not reached a point where we do not have to depend totally on the power of the Holy Spirit to build the church and keep the church out of darkness and delusion.

If we are going to take this verse by itself and say this is a valid argument for not pursuing the baptism in the Holy Spirit, then we need to eliminate our Sunday school programs because it says knowledge and prophecies will cease too. Have we stopped learning? Has the Lord stopped speaking to us today? Has knowledge ceased? NO! If anything, knowledge is increasing, and the Lord's voice is growing clearer each and every day that we exist on this planet.

Dreams and visions are on the increase like never before. Joel's prophecy of our young men seeing visions and our older men dreaming dreams is coming to pass right before our eyes. But to argue against tongues with this verse, you must argue against knowledge and the prophetic. The truth is, people who say such things are clearly people who have been convinced in their hearts that this is not for them. Even if someone from the dead came back to tell them otherwise, they would not believe.

The time when the "perfect" is come is the Resurrection or the Rapture of the Church. When that takes place, we will no longer need tongues and interpretation of tongues because we will have received glorified bodies at the calling home of the saints! Until then however, we need the spiritual gifts to operate in the Church.

Objection No. 5 – There Is Only One Experience Of Salvation And Not A Second Work Of Grace Afterwards; We Get All Of The Holy Spirit We Need When We Are Born-Again

Some people teach that you receive the Holy Spirit when you are saved and there is no need to seek the Lord for any further infilling of His power. The common statement is "you got it all when you got saved, you do not need anything else." I think Scripture would disagree to some degree with that. If your desire is to just die and go to heaven, then I guess you are set. If your desire is to work for the Kingdom of God, it is not so set.

> **Acts 19:1-3**
> **And it came to pass, that, while Apollos was at Corinth, Paul having passed through the upper coasts came to Ephesus: and finding certain disciples, He said unto them, Have ye received**

> the Holy Ghost since ye believed? And they said unto him, We have not so much as heard whether there be any Holy Ghost. And he said unto them, Unto what then were ye baptized? And they said, Unto John's baptism.

When the Apostle Paul came to Ephesus, he asked some new disciples a significant question; "Have you received the Holy Ghost SINCE you believed?"

These were believers who had been baptized by John the Baptist (the baptism of water unto repentance), but who were completely unaware of the Holy Spirit. Paul told them fully of the redemptive work of Christ, and they were then baptized in water unto repentance. Following this, Paul laid his hands on them and they were instantly baptized in the Holy Ghost, speaking in tongues and prophesying. As in other recorded cases in Acts, the baptism in the Holy Spirit was experienced SUBSEQUENT to salvation by accepting Jesus as their Lord and Savior. There is a great controversy surrounding this question. The proper answer to it is "yes" and "no!"

The Holy Ghost is highly active in bringing the sinner to conviction, repentance, and salvation. So, when a person truly accepts Jesus into his heart, that person does "receive" the Holy Spirit, but there is great difference in being BORN of the Spirit and being BAPTIZED IN the Spirit. The Holy Ghost IS A FACTOR IN SALVATION. He is a major factor and he must be present for a person to be convicted and accept salvation.

> **John 6:44**
> **No man can come to me, except the Father who hath sent me draw him: and I will raise him up at the last day.**

> 1 Corinthians 12:3
> **Wherefore I give you to understand, that no man speaking by the Spirit of God calleth Jesus accursed: and that no man can say that Jesus is the Lord, but by the Holy Ghost.**

So the answer to this objection is "Yes, at salvation the individual does "receive" the Holy Spirit, because it is the Holy Spirit who convicts and draws that person to Jesus," but, the answer is also "no," because the person does not receive the gift of the Holy Spirit at salvation because the deeper, more permanent relationship of the baptism comes only AFTER salvation.

The Spirit of God baptizes one into the Body of Christ at salvation. After salvation, Jesus then baptizes the believer into the Holy Spirit! These are two distinct and separate experiences.

The Well and the River

> John 7:37-39
> **In the last day, that great day of the feast, Jesus stood and cried, saying, If any man thirst, let him come unto me, and drink. He that believeth on me, as the scripture hath said, out of his belly shall flow rivers of living water. (But this spoke he of the Spirit, which they that believe on him should receive: for the Holy Ghost was not yet given; because that Jesus was not yet glorified.)**

> John 4:14
> **But whosoever drinketh of the water that I shall give him shall never thirst; but the water that I shall give him shall be in him a well of water springing up into everlasting life.**

John gives us two great examples of the difference between Salvation and the Baptism in the Holy Ghost.

Salvation is likened to a well experience. Isaiah said it was out the "wells of salvation," that we would draw waters of life. Jesus told the woman at the well that if she drank these waters, she would never thirst again. He was speaking of eternal life. The Holy Ghost is continually active and important in this event in the life of an individual.

The other example is where the Holy Spirit is typified as "rivers" of living water flowing of the innermost being. This experience was NOT available to the disciples until AFTER Jesus was glorified. The temple of man had to be made fit for God's presence. The only way that would be possible would be through the blood of the Lord Jesus Christ.

Some 50 days after Jesus was glorified, He sent back the Holy Ghost upon the believers gathered at Pentecost, who were not there to get saved but to receive POWER! Their lives would never be the same again and the world would not be either. It was the same Holy Spirit, but two different experiences here. When John said, "the Holy Ghost was not yet given," he did not mean the Holy Ghost was not around.

The Holy Spirit has been active in the world since before creation. He is the third person of the God Head. What he meant was that the fullness of the Holy Ghost had not yet been passed on to the disciples because they were not fit vessels before Calvary.

The night Jesus saw them after He had risen, He breathed on them, "Receive ye the Holy Ghost," and from that moment on they were "regenerated." On the Day of Pentecost, the Holy Spirit was just not "in" them, He had come "upon them." Praise the Lord, and "upon them" He came.

Great numbers of people are currently experiencing the baptism in the Holy Spirit all over the world despite their denominations and ignorant pastors. God is pouring out His Spirit upon ALL FLESH in this last hour. Many are dissatisfied with cold, formal, dead religion. Their prayers are now being answered. The Holy Ghost is more than just a vague symbol or a title to put on our doctrinal statements to make sure we line up with the Bible. He is a Person. He is God. He is bigger than the devil. He is the living dynamic power of Christ who lives in our hearts. The baptism of the Holy Spirit is valid for today and speaking in tongues has not passed away.

It is not all over at salvation; it is just beginning; just as it is not over when you speak in tongues. Speaking in tongues is just a door that unlocks a greater walk and revelation of the Spirit that you need to be the type of Christian God is pleased with.

Objection #6 – I am Spirit-Filled Even Though I Have Not Spoke in Tongues

Some believers argue, "I am filled with the Spirit and I do not speak in other tongues. I do not care what anybody says but I am still filled with the Spirit." This is another one of those statements that usually draws a line in the sand between truth and error.

Speaking in tongues is not the only evidence, but we believe and teach that tongues are the INITIAL evidence that one has received the baptism in the Holy Spirit after conversion.

Most Christian churches and denominations believe (to one degree or another) in the Holy Spirit. Sadly, most of this belief is a recognition that He exists, without yielding themselves to His power or allowing Him to move in their midst and lives.

This does not create any major problem. The controversy erupts when you say, "to be filled with the Spirit, you will have the initial physical evidence of speaking with other tongues." When talking about the initial evidence of the Holy Spirit's infilling there then draws the line in the sand that most people do not want to cross over and believe.

Most evangelicals will give in and say, "OK, tongues are in the Bible." Some will even say, "Well, there are really no scriptures in the Bible that say, "tongues went away with the apostles."

You will not find many that will say, "everyone who is saved does not need to be filled with the Spirit," as Paul encouraged the church at Ephesus to do. But you will not find ANY to say, "the initial physical evidence of being filled with the Spirit is speaking with other tongues."

And anyone, be it church, minister, or organization who teaches that, automatically draws fire because that statement is opposed by MUCH OF THE PROFESSING CHURCH.

Let the reader be clear! Everywhere that this same experience is mentioned in the Book of Acts, the participants and those involved always spoke with tongues. Are tongues the only evidence a person is walking in the fullness of the Spirit? Absolutely not. That does not negate the fact that the INITIAL physical evidence that one has been baptized in the Spirit is that they have spoken with tongues as the Spirit of God gave the utterance.

The first occurrence of the Holy Spirit's outpouring happened on Pentecost when THEY SPOKE WITH TONGUES.

Acts 2:4
And they were all filled with the Holy Ghost, and began to speak with other tongues, as the Spirit gave them utterance.

This needs no further explanation. It is concise and clear. They were all filled with the Holy Ghost and began to speak with other tongues.

The second occurrence of believers who are filled with the Spirit speaking with tongues happens in Acts 8, when Peter and John went down to Samaria and prayed for the Samaritans to receive the Holy Spirit. After miracles took place during a revival under the ministry of Phillip, a sorcerer by the name of Simon was saved. Peter and John immediately went to Samaria to pray for the new believers to be filled or to receive the Holy Ghost. Were these people saved when Peter and John arrived? Yes, they were already saved. "For as yet he was fallen UPON NONE of them: only they were baptized in the name of the Lord Jesus." Now, it does not say verbatim that anyone Peter and John laid hands on spoke in tongues. However, when Simon saw what was happening, he offered money to Peter and John so he could lay hands on them so that they might receive the Holy Spirit. If nothing external was happening (TONGUES), then why would Simon offer money and jeopardize his soul to buy it?

Acts 8:16-23
(For as yet he was fallen upon none of them: only they were baptized in the name of the Lord Jesus.) Then laid they their hands on them, and they received the Holy Ghost. And when Simon saw that through laying on of the apostles' hands the Holy Ghost was given, he offered them money, Saying, Give me also this power, that on whomsoever I lay hands, he may receive the Holy Ghost. But Peter said unto him, Thy money perish with thee, because thou hast thought that the gift of God may be purchased with money. Thou hast neither part nor lot in this matter: for thy heart is not right in the sight of God. Repent therefore of this thy wickedness, and pray God, if perhaps the thought of thine heart may be forgiven thee. For I perceive that thou art in the gall of bitterness, and in the bond of iniquity.

The third occurrence of The Holy Spirit happens in the life of the apostle Paul. Walking on the road to Damascus he was struck blind by the light of the Lord Jesus Christ. Looking up, he in confronted by Jesus Himself who asks Paul why he was persecuting the Church. The minute Paul said, "LORD," that signified that Paul had become a believer.

Paul was blind for three days until the Lord led him to Ananias who prayed for Paul that he might receive his sight and be "filled with the Holy Spirit." Paul received his sight in Acts 9. Again, it never says in Acts 9 he spoke in tongues. However, in writing three chapters in his epistles to the Corinthians, Paul clearly says, I SPEAK IN TONGUES MORE THAN YE ALL. Paul received this gift the day Ananias laid his hands on him. Ananias was not laying his hands on Paul to be saved, he was laying his hands on Paul that he might be" filled with the Holy Ghost."

> Acts 9:17-18
> **And Ananias went his way, and entered into the house; and putting his hands on him said, Brother Saul, the Lord, even Jesus, that appeared unto thee in the way as thou camest, hath sent me, that thou mightest receive thy sight, and be filled with the Holy Ghost. And immediately there fell from his eyes as it had been scales: and he received sight forthwith, and arose, and was baptized.**

The fourth occurrence happened 40 years after Pentecost at the house of Cornelius. (Acts 10:44) We have already discussed that in detail in the text that we have been studying.

The fifth occurrence happens nearly 60 years after Pentecost when Paul is walking up the Ephesus coasts and encounters believers who were baptized by John the Baptist but "who had never even heard that there was a Holy Ghost." Paul laid his hands on them and they began to speak with other tongues.

> Acts 19:1-7
> **And it came to pass, that, while Apollos was at Corinth, Paul having passed through the upper coasts came to Ephesus: and finding certain disciples, He said unto them, Have ye received the Holy Ghost since ye believed? And they said unto him, We have not so much as heard whether there be any Holy Ghost. And he said unto them, Unto what then were ye baptized? And they said, Unto John's baptism. Then said Paul, John verily baptized with the baptism of repentance, saying unto the people, that they should believe on him which should come after him, that is, on Christ Jesus. When they heard this, they were baptized in the name of the Lord Jesus. And when Paul had laid his hands upon them, the Holy Ghost came on**

> them; and they spake with tongues, and prophesied. And all the men were about twelve.

The passage says, "They spoke with tongues and prophesied." Now, in three of the five occurrences, the Bible states verbatim, "they spoke with other tongues." The other two occurrences do not take a rocket science to figure out that speaking in tongues occurred because the Bible clarified itself in a later passage. Any honest seeker of truth and one who is hungry for more of God can see that SOMETHING happened to these individuals when they received the Holy Spirit. That something as they spoke with other tongues

Objection No. 7 – Jesus Never Spoke with Tongues

Some people rationalize, "Since Jesus did not speak in tongues, why should we?" Well, there are two answers to this objection. Jack Deere, a former Old Testament Professor at the Dallas Theological Seminary in Dallas, Texas, states in his book **Surprised by the Spirit of God**, "that saying Jesus never spoke in tongues is what is termed in theological circles as an *argument from silence*."

He said even though the Bible never says Jesus never spoke in tongues, we cannot automatically say He did not. There are many things that the scriptures did not record about the life of Jesus simply because, as John said, if it had, there would not have been enough books in the world to record them.

> **John 21:24-25**
> This is the disciple that testifies of these things, and wrote these things: and we know that his testimony is true. And there are also many other things which Jesus did, the which, if they should be written every one, I suppose that even

> the world itself could not contain the books that should be written. Amen.

Just as the gospels did not record everything Jesus did, neither did Acts record everything the apostles did. There are spans of years where the Bible is silent on activity in the lives of Peter, Paul, Barnabas, and the other disciples. Does that mean then that if we do not see an experience in the Bible, then we rule it invalid? For most people, that answer is an emphatic yes. However, you cannot argue that something is not valid scripturally because of that reason because, quite honestly, there are a LOT of things the Bible is silent on. That is why we have the HOLY SPIRIT; to LEAD us into all truth.

> **John 16:13-14**
> **Howbeit when he, the Spirit of truth, is come, he will guide you into all truth: for he shall not speak of himself; but whatsoever he shall hear, that shall he speak: and he will shew you things to come. He shall glorify me: for he shall receive of mine and shall shew it unto you.**

The second part of the answer to this objection is more theological. Jesus ministered under the Old Covenant. Speaking in tongues was not available under the Old Covenant, even though Isaiah had prophesied there would come a day when God would speak to man through "stammering lips and an unknown tongue."

> **Isa 28:11-13**
> **For with stammering lips and another tongue will he speak to this people. To whom he said, This is the rest wherewith ye may cause the weary to rest; and this is the refreshing: yet they would not hear. But the word of the LORD was unto them**

> **precept upon precept, precept upon precept; line upon line, line upon line; here a little, and there a little; that they might go, and fall backward, and be broken, and snared, and taken.**

The New Testament brought with it tongues and the interpretation of tongues. By the time the Holy Ghost came, and tongues were manifested, Jesus was with the Father in heaven. He had done all that was necessary to save us and give us both the indwelling presence of the Spirit and the endowment of power upon us by the Spirit. To be frank, He did not need to speak in tongues as we do today. That is why He sent back the HOLY GHOST TO THE CHURCH!

Neighbor, we as mortal believers need the Baptism in the Holy Ghost. Speaking in tongues is a valid experience for the believer today. I just shake my head, sigh, and wonder how Satan has blinded so many theologically trained men who stand behind pulpits and demean, deny, and resist something more powerful than any terrorist bomb or nuclear explosion.

I pray something you are read has opened your heart to desire more of God. The way He will fill that thirst is through the ministry of the Holy Spirit. Tongues are the door, not the whole ministry. Walk through that door today in Jesus Name.